SECOND
LIFE

An Atheist's Journey
to Spirituality

Anne C. Cooper

To Jason, Dane, and Todd.
You will always be with me,
And I with you.

Mary,

You and Todd have a
special connection — even
on the other side — and
he and I love you for it.

Always,

Anne

CHAPTER ONE

The End

The phone rang before dawn. It startled me awake and I knew instantly that something was wrong. No one calls that early unless something's wrong. My husband Jonathan answered it. Then I heard him hang up.

We weren't sleeping together by then, so he came to my bedroom door. "That was your father. He said, 'Come and get your son.' He was angry."

Jonathan was angry, too—no surprise, since he wasn't speaking to either of my parents, not since my father had told him to get a job three years before. Jonathan was a self-employed industrial designer, had been for nearly sixteen years. But he'd been more out of work than working for the last five. We would have been divorced already if we could have afforded it.

"What's wrong?" I asked.

"He didn't say. Just to get over there now."

I had left our youngest son Todd with my parents the night before, so I could attend the monthly board of education meeting and then drive to the airport.

Jonathan had flown to Miami to meet with a prospective client. I was against him traveling. It had been less than four weeks since his quintuple bypass. But he was desperate for work, and I didn't fight him very hard.

Todd was sixteen and a half, but I couldn't leave him alone. Neither Jason nor Dane, his two older brothers, would stay with him, and he was having an episode. He'd left school after lunch, run crazily across a busy street, oblivious to cars, and gone straight to his therapist's office a block away. But his therapist hadn't been there and the receptionist called the house for someone to come get him. I was at a board committee meeting so his brothers picked him up, brought him home, and kept him calm until I could get there.

It was the second time in five months that Todd had run from school, straight to his therapist. He had admitted to smoking pot, but I knew there was more to it than that. He was so depressed. And he wouldn't tell me what was wrong. Well, I was determined to find out. That same afternoon, I made an eight a.m. appointment with his therapist for the next morning. Things were going to be different. We would not leave the therapist's office without an understanding and a plan. If it meant home schooling, so be it. I would be at his elbow all day, every day, until we got him turned around.

For his stay at his grandparents' I packed him an overnight bag, a toothbrush, clean jeans, and the shirt I'd given him for his birthday seven months before. He had never worn it, refused to wear it, even though it was a perfectly fine shirt. It was from JC Penney, their "cool"

Arizona Company brand. *He'll wear it to our appointment in the morning, like it or not*, I remember thinking.

When Todd got into the car to go to his grandparents', I angrily asked him, "How do you think you can be an Air Force pilot or even a mechanic, for that matter, if you smoke pot? Trust a multi-million-dollar machine to someone who smokes grass? I don't think so."

He looked at me, then said, "I forgot something. I'll be right back." He jumped out of the car and went inside the house. Two minutes later he was back, empty-handed.

"What was it?" I asked.

"Nothing, I just had to do something." He locked his seatbelt and I backed out of the driveway.

I took him to my parents' house, my refuge. He would be safe there and, I prayed, on his best behavior. As I was leaving, he was sitting on the floor in their family room in front of the television. We locked eyes. I silently implored him to be good. It was one of those moments— we connected, heart to heart, soul to soul. Mentally, I embraced him. Then I left for my board meeting.

And now, Dad's call. Pushing down the dread, I sprang up and went to the bathroom, washed my face and brushed my teeth. Automatically I reached for makeup, then looked at myself. *Your son's in trouble. Get your clothes on and go.* I pulled on jeans and a T-shirt and glanced at the clock. It read six forty. It felt like Jonathan and I had just gotten home from the airport.

Jonathan was waiting in his studio. "I'll drive," I said. He didn't argue. The incisions in his legs, from where the surgeons had taken healthy veins for his heart surgery, had been bleeding the night before. It was a fifteen-minute drive to Woodlake, the gated community in Athens, Georgia where my mom and dad had built a home for their retirement.

Waiting for a red light to change, I pushed down the dread again.

"Just go," Jonathan said before the light turned green.

As I turned into Woodlake, the sun hinted at the beautiful day to come. My parents' place was the last house at the end of a cul-de-sac. I parked next to their car, in front of the house. As we entered, Dad met us in the front hallway. His nose was red, with a small cut on the tip.

"Todd had us up all night," he said, his voice hard. "He ran out. We don't know where he went."

"What happened? Where did he go?"

"He woke us up around two," Mom told me. "He couldn't sleep. He tried to call somebody, I don't know who, but he couldn't get a dial tone. Then he wanted to go across the street to use Peggy's phone. I told him he couldn't wake the neighbors in the middle of the night. We tried to get him to go back to bed, but he couldn't stay still. Then he wanted to use our car, and started arguing with your father. I hid the keys. Dad tried to make him go back to bed and Todd knocked him down and began punching him. I tried to pull him off. Then he jumped up and said he was leaving. I told him 'Get out.'"

I was horrified; Todd had never been violent with his grandparents. "We're going to look for him," I told them.

As we turned to leave, Jonathan took the keys from me. "I'll drive and you can get out and look." I didn't argue.

We checked each street and cul-de-sac in Woodlake, but saw no one. *This is a waste of time*, I thought. *Todd must have left a half-hour ago.* It made sense to rule out all the options in his path, but I was frantic to get out to the main road. My mind raced to where he might have gone. A friend of his lived off Timothy Road—did he head that way?

We were back at the gate; it opened automatically to let us out. Jonathan headed toward Timothy Road. The sound of sirens came from the left—the way to his friend's house. We turned right. I leaned out the open window, calling Todd's name, desperately scanning front stoops and yards for a tall, blond-headed figure. Nothing, no sign of him, block after block. As we approached the elementary school, Jonathan slowly turned the car around, back toward the sirens. Silently, numbly, I agreed.

The road was blocked off by police cars. I could see a fire truck farther down the block. Jonathan parked the car at a cut-in on the left side of the tree-lined street. "Stay here," he said, "I'll find out what's going on." He disappeared behind a police car.

I waited, terror seeping into every bone, every cell, until I couldn't stand it anymore. Why wasn't he back? I got out and walked toward the pavement and the first police car. Jonathan appeared in front of me and said quietly, "There's been an accident. Someone's been killed."

I stood there, repeating to myself "no, no, no, no, no, no, no, no," until interrupted by a fireman. He was standing in front of me, a small piece of paper in his hand.

"Ma'am, your husband says you're looking for your son."

"Yes."

"Someone's been hit by a car. The victim was a young male, with no identification. He was wearing," he looked at his note, "Adidas tennis shoes."

He looked up at me; I said nothing. He went on. "Blue jeans." Still I said nothing. It could be anyone. "And a shirt with the label, Arizona Company."

That's when I screamed.

FIRST LIFE

The Beginning

I loved being a mother to three boys. I loved my sons' energy, their curiosity, and their quickness. They never, ever bored me, so becoming a mother at twenty-three and delaying a professional career never felt like a sacrifice. It was always fun.

Todd was my last—another boy, not a girl, as his parents had gingerly, warily hoped—but perhaps that was another reason I always felt so connected to him, because he had spared his father the pain of having a daughter again. Married once before, Jonathan had lost his first child, a little girl.

Unlike my husband, I was oblivious to the perils of parenthood beyond the normal bumps and bruises. As the oldest in a family of eight, I had seen the occasional run to the emergency room for stitches, concussions, even a fractured skull, but nothing life-threatening, which could explain why, on our second date, Jonathan told me my family was a fairy tale. The characterization surprised me, but I had to admit it was true. Looking back, I think he fell in love with my family as much as he did with me.

I loved Jonathan when I married him, but I wasn't "in love" with him the way I knew he was with me. That was my first mistake. However, I truly believed we could make a good life together, one that would give him the family life he craved and me the chance to discover what I wanted to be and do when I grew up. He was a man who had reinvented himself, and I was eager to learn from him.

The two of us met in May 1975 at Gulliver's, a little jazz bar in West Paterson, New Jersey. I was twenty years old, a junior at William Paterson College, now a state university. I was sitting at the bar with a girlfriend, enjoying the music on a Friday night. A week earlier, we had each broken up with the guy we'd been dating, so we were open to whatever the evening had to offer.

Jonathan and his friend Mike happened to be sitting at the bar, too. Mike and I were seated on the outside, my girlfriend Debbie and Jonathan on the inside, and there was a stool between them on which Deb and I had laid our jackets.

Jonathan's opening line was, "Can I buy your friend a drink?" He smiled and pointed to our coats on the stool next to Debbie. "He's looking kind of flat."

Debbie looked over, grinned, and said, "Sure." She and Jonathan talked a lot, with Mike and I adding to the conversation as we could, given the music, the noise, and the seating arrangements. Typical bar conversation: we established that Deb and I were both college students and that Jonathan and Mike were both industrial designers, former roommates in college. They had graduated from Pratt Institute, a design school in Brooklyn we'd never heard of, which shocked them. They spoke of it with such reverence I had to smile.

Since Deb and I both worked part-time on Saturdays, we rose to leave just after eleven. The guys walked us to my car and Jonathan asked me for my number. I was surprised because I thought he was more interested in Debbie. I wasn't particularly attracted to him, but decided to get to know him better before coming to any conclusions.

He called the following week. My mother answered the phone. She gave me a questioning look as I took the phone from her. I could tell she was impressed just from the sound of his voice, and wanted more information. And she always said she knew he was the man I'd marry from that first call.

We made a date for brunch on Sunday and I gave him directions to my home in New Milford, a northern New Jersey town close to New York City. When he arrived, I was chagrined. It wasn't that he didn't have a great car. I didn't care about the bright red-orange Chevy Vega. But he was dressed horribly. He wore a white-and-brown-pinstriped dress shirt buttoned all the way to the top except for the collar, and brown, orange, and white plaid polyester pants nearly a half-inch above his ankles—at a time when jeans were too short if they weren't dragging on the ground!

The patterned pants accentuated the disproportions of Jonathan's body, his long torso, broad shoulders, and short legs, even though he stood five-eleven, a good six inches taller than I. He wore his brown hair in a late-fifties style, slicked back, with no part. His skin was fair; he looked like someone who sunburned easily. And he smoked Camel cigarettes. I didn't smoke. Why I had agreed to a date with him suddenly seemed a mystery.

The sentiment might have been mutual. "Hi, good to see you again," I said as I met him at the front door. I saw him do a double take. The night we met, my hair was long, below my shoulders, but I had gotten it cut. Now it was short, short, short.

"What did you do to your hair?" he asked, smiling. "I wouldn't have recognized you." He was disappointed, he later told me. He liked long hair on women.

"Like it? It's my summer cut."

"What's not to like?" He stepped inside the door and I led him up the stairs to the living room, where my parents waited.

"Mom, Dad, this is Jonathan. Jonathan, my parents, Ed and Barbara Capone."

"Pleasure to meet you." Jonathan shook their hands and glanced around the room. Two younger brothers, eight and ten, giggled as they peeked out from the kitchen.

"We're going," I told Mom and Dad, to spare Jonathan the small talk and to escape the awkwardness I was feeling. "I'll be back before dinner."

We ate brunch outdoors at a small café on the edge of Central Park. I was thrilled. I loved New York, but was intimidated by it, and rarely went there. My dream was to work in the city and one day know it like a native, but what would I be doing? And how would I find a job there? I'd never worked for anyone but my father, in his dry-cleaning business two towns away from our home.

"So you still live with your parents?" Jonathan asked.

"Yes, I'm the oldest of eight. All good Italian Catholics—except for me." I grinned.

"Eight! I have a brother and two sisters. They all live in St. Petersburg where I grew up. My brother's studying to become a pilot like my dad."

"A pilot! Does your dad still fly?"

"No. He started out as a carrier pilot and after the war, he flew for the king of Saudi Arabia. We lived in Cairo, Egypt for a few years. Came back to St. Pete when I was twelve. Dad owned a coffee business there."

Egypt—so exotic! I was beguiled and Jonathan regaled me with stories of his father, who'd grown up on a large ranch in South Dakota, the youngest in a family of seven. The two oldest Cooper brothers had been world-champion rodeo riders who even performed for the queen of England before becoming stuntmen in the early cowboy movies. Another uncle, Conrad, had retired as executive vice president of US Steel, and knew every president from Franklin Roosevelt to Gerald Ford. I loved history and had never met anyone who had rubbed elbows with it. I was fascinated.

"Tell me more about you," Jonathan said. "What's your major?" He smiled in acknowledgement of the classic pick-up line.

"English lit. Don't ask me what I'm going to do with it. I don't know. I thought I was going to be a business major, but my first management class was so boring I couldn't stand it."

"Do you want to teach?"

"I don't think so. But I love to read. And I love my classes. I'm avoiding thinking too far ahead."

After brunch we decided to take a walk in Central Park. The weather was glorious. As we walked, we came upon a stage and a huge crowd of cheering people. Joan Baez was speaking. Without realizing, we'd walked into "The War is Over" rally, celebrating the end of the Vietnam War. Thrilled, I said, "Let's stay. There's going to be music."

A rally of hippies and antiwar demonstrators, however, was Jonathan's cue to leave. "I nearly got caught in a demonstration at Pratt once. Mike and I were getting out of class and policemen were beating students up with billy clubs. Mike was just like you—he wanted to stay and watch. I grabbed him and we got the hell out of there." It was clear he expected me to do the same. Reluctant and disappointed, I agreed to leave.

When we got back to my house, my family was already seated for Sunday dinner. They were just beyond the foyer, in the playroom, the room large enough to fit a table for a family of ten. Glancing curiously at them as he stood at the door, Jonathan said, "Can I call you? I'd like to see you again."

"Sure," I told him, because I didn't know how to say no. He promised to call and left.

We started dating steadily. Why was I going out with him? I hardly knew. He could drink three Scotch-on-the-rocks to my one glass of wine, and that bothered me, though I didn't know why. He could certainly hold his liquor, and never seemed to be affected by it. Other little things bothered me, too. The first time we went out to dinner, I was startled by how fast he ate. I had barely eaten three mouthfuls and although he was doing most of the talking, he'd already finished his meal.

Our conversations often led to me talking about my favorite classes, or the ones that made the greatest impact on me, like Philosophy 101. Examining my belief system, exploring concepts of morality, beauty, mind, and the existence of God exposed the myriad assumptions I was making, without knowing it, about what was real and what was true. I wanted to know what was real, if that were possible. I wanted to be in control of my destiny and thought that if I were logical, if my actions and decisions were based on reality and not simply on feelings, I would discover what was best for myself.

My parents had made religion an integral part of family life, but I was through with Catholicism. It was so mindless. By high school, I was so bored by the repetition, the same rituals, the same gospels, the same endless drone of the same old men, I questioned the meaning of it all.

Q. How shall we know the things which we are to believe?

A. We shall know the things which we are to believe from the Catholic Church, through which God speaks to us.[1]

Matters of the soul were simple. The Catholic Church would tell us all we needed to know, and whatever didn't make sense was to be taken on faith. But my faith had been worn down to nothing. The first time I didn't go to mass with the family, my dad ordered me to a later one. I walked around the neighborhood instead. When I returned, he asked, "Did you go to church?"

I wouldn't lie to him. "No." Dad slapped me across the face, the first and only time. But the message was clear to both of us: he couldn't make me go and he couldn't make me believe.

I believed science, not religion, was the true path to understanding myself and life's mysteries. Science might not ever give me the ultimate answers, but it would lead me to ask better questions. I put my faith in the scientific process and the laws of nature. Newton, Descartes, Darwin, and Einstein were my saints, and although life in their universe was "solitary, poor, nasty, brutish, and short,"[2] it was mine. I was free to create the life of my choosing. The starkness of existentialism appealed to me. No one could dictate to someone who was free in her own mind.

Jonathan had lost his religion too, but in a unique way. His parents, nonpracticing Episcopalians, required him to pick a church and attend services there for fifty-two consecutive weeks. After that he could do whatever he pleased. Gradually I discovered that Jonathan and I had important values in common: not only atheism, but personal integrity, a love of beauty, and a desire to treat others the way we ourselves would want to be treated. If secular humanism were a religion, that would have been ours.

Our childhoods could not have been more different. Mine was idyllic, with two parents deeply in love and seven brothers and sisters whom I count among my most cherished friends. Jonathan had grown up with two alcoholic parents. His earliest memory, he told me, was of running away from home when he was three years old, while his parents were having a party in their backyard. His mother had chased drunkenly after him and, to his horror, peed her pants when she got him back in the house.

Jonathan was full of stories about growing up in Florida, moving to Brooklyn to go to Pratt, and earning his living as a bartender to put himself through school. He said when he first arrived in New York, he handed out rubber bands to guys with long hair. I thought it an odd thing to be proud of. He seemed more like a truck driver with a chip on his shoulder than a designer. But he really was one, and had worked on Madison Avenue for Walter Dorwin Teague before becoming art director for a small semiconductor manufacturer in New Jersey.

We'd been dating little more than a month when he invited me up to his apartment, code for an invitation for sex. I had already decided that I wasn't saving myself for marriage. I'd had a huge crush on a guy at school and crossed that Rubicon already. Besides, I was curious to see how he lived, so I accepted his invitation.

He'd left candles burning while we were at dinner, risky but romantic. We made out on his couch and then he led me to the bedroom. Jonathan was always a terrific lover, until a lifetime of drinking weakened his heart. After the lovemaking, while we were lying in bed together, Jonathan confessed he'd been married before. I was surprised, but then, he was more than eight years older than I. He'd gotten a girl pregnant when he was eighteen. When he asked his father for advice, his dad said only, "A stiff prick has no conscience." Jonathan decided to do the right thing and married the girl, who was from a well-to-do family. The baby was a girl, named Ryder, and Jonathan was determined to settle down and be a good husband and father.

"When Ryder was about eighteen months old, she got the flu, or so everyone thought," Jonathan told me. "She was running a fever and throwing up. She just couldn't shake it. One morning before leaving for work, I went to her room, like I always did, and leaned over the crib to give her a kiss goodbye. Her right eye was turned in toward her nose. I blocked it out and went on to work." His voice cracked. I waited and heard him take a deep breath. "When my wife saw it, she took Ryder to the doctor right away. He ran some tests. Ryder had a brain tumor, malignant, and as it turned out, inoperable. She died a year later."

My head was on Jonathan's chest, so I couldn't see his face, but I could feel my own tears running down my cheeks and onto his skin. I thought that would be the end of the story, but he continued. "At the hospital," he said, "after Ryder was pronounced dead, I began washing her. A nurse told me, 'You don't have to do that, Mr. Cooper, we'll do all that.'

"And I told her, 'No, you don't understand. Now I do *everything*.'" And as he told me how he gently washed and dressed his little girl for the last time, I stifled a sob.

The two weeks that followed, he said, were a blank. I thought then that his terrible grief had blocked all memory of that time from his mind. Years later, I better understood: he'd been drinking so much he was in a blackout for two solid weeks. Better to be numb than to feel the grief and heartache of losing his beloved baby girl.

"After Ryder died," he continued, "my wife had a nervous breakdown and then my mother-in-law killed herself."

He'd spoken matter-of-factly, but I was horrified. I couldn't imagine the pain of those tragedies, one on top of another. But one thing I did know, and I told him, "If something so terrible ever happened to me and my husband, I hope we would turn to each other in love and comfort each other." It suddenly occurred to me that I was destined to marry this man. I wasn't thrilled by the idea, but at that moment it felt like a door had closed, like I had no choice. It felt like a promise.

Todd's birth as the third of three sons felt like a promise, too, the promise that Jonathan would never have to face the fear of being father to another daughter. He was free. And as his partner and the mother of three beautiful boys, I was free too, free to create a fairy-tale family of my own.

CHAPTER THREE

The Marriage Test

In conversations leading up to our wedding in June 1976, Jonathan said he wanted to start a family soon after we married. I agreed. I was only twenty-one, but he was thirty. I wanted our kids to know a dad who was young, full of energy and playfulness, so I was willing to put off my dreams of a professional career. I would be a stay-at-home mom who worked occasionally as a freelance copywriter, and our children would be shaped by Jonathan and me, not by their daycare teachers, babysitters, or anyone else. Two provisos we agreed to up front: I would change the dirty baby diapers and he would change the cat litter. I was allergic to cats, and he became physically ill at the sight of baby poop.

Jonathan had been looking for a new job even before we were married when, after returning from our honeymoon, his uncle Conrad told him about an opportunity in Royston, Georgia, a product development position for a steel products manufacturer. Jonathan interviewed, then accepted the job offer. Rather than live in Royston, a small town in rural north Georgia, we would settle in nearby Athens, home of the University of Georgia, with a more diverse population and urban culture.

Everyone but Jonathan was teary-eyed as we said goodbye on the day after Christmas. Excited though I was, I'd never been separated from my family for more than a week and always envisioned raising my children surrounded by grandparents, aunts, uncles, and cousins, just as I had been. Instead our children would know only long-distance relationships with the people I most cared about. Sure, they'd only be a phone call away, as Jonathan pointed out, but that wasn't the same.

When we arrived at our Athens apartment, the furniture was in place, but not a single box had been unpacked. Jonathan, I discovered, was helpless when it came to creating order in a space. His version of cleaning a room was to put everything in a big pile in the middle of it. Then it took him days to figure out what to do with the pile. And try as I might, I was never able to get him to put things away as he used them.

As I watched him work over the years, I came to realize that Jonathan really didn't understand the value of order or routine. Nothing mattered to him but his final product. If tools were scattered, a surface damaged, or clothing stained in pursuit of an immaculate rendering or pristine model, then they were sacrificed without thinking. I gave up on trying to teach him. If there was to be order in our home, I'd have to create it, and I did.

Taking classes at the University of Georgia to finish my degree wasn't much of a cure for the homesickness and loneliness I felt. Jonathan had become distant, too, in ways that kept me mystified. We had dinner together every night, but then he retreated to his studio, the apartment's second bedroom. He emerged only to eat or to go to bed and sleep. We went without sex for months, so I felt rejected that way, too, more so when he pushed me away. I was too young to realize that remarrying— and the likelihood of becoming a father again—stirred up emotions he'd long kept buried. Nor did I notice how much he was drinking to keep them buried.

Jonathan kept so much of his past, and the emotions that went along with it, buried. As I learned more about his childhood, I was amazed he survived it at all. I couldn't imagine the anger and pain an eight-year-old boy must have felt, placed in the county orphanage, fiercely guarding his younger brother and sister until their parents were sober enough to leave the sanatorium where they'd admitted themselves. Or the revulsion the teenaged Jonathan must have felt when he got into a fistfight with his drunken father to protect his drunken mother. No wonder his mother Jean adored him—he'd always chosen her.

Jean called us almost every night. I'd chat with her for a few minutes, but it was Jonathan she wanted. Invariably, she cried. She cried because she missed her husband, who died a year earlier. She cried too because she had no one to help her. She said that Lina and Taylor, Jonathan's younger sister and brother, told her to take a cab to the emergency room when she was in the throes of a bronchial attack, which made Jonathan furious. He didn't believe their denials or that Jean would lie to him. And she cried because the son who was the apple of her eye lived hundreds of miles away. She had even signed over her St. Petersburg house to him in a quitclaim deed, a bid to get him to move back to Florida, but Jonathan hadn't taken the bait.

Still, he was distraught over his mother's calls. Nothing Sharon, Lina, or Taylor said convinced him that they weren't ignoring her or that she really had all the help she needed. He soon concluded that, although he couldn't move back to St. Pete, Jean could move to Athens. When he first broached the subject with me, I didn't hesitate. Of course she could live with us. She was his mother, and she was sick. To me, she was like another grandmother. I would have done the same for either of mine.

Jean was thrilled. "Isn't this the perfect solution?" she exclaimed, hearing our offer. The three of us were on the phone together, Jonathan in his studio, I in the kitchen. "Now Jonathan will own *two* houses." She was going to give us enough for a down payment, the house would be in Jonathan's and my names, and we'd pay the mortgage and household expenses. Jean would move in with whatever things she wanted from the house in St. Pete, and Jonathan could relax, knowing that she was being properly cared for.

Jonathan's family was appalled. They all reminded Jonathan about how devious his mother could be and tried to talk us out of it. Even his uncle Conrad called and begged him not to go through with it. Jonathan dismissed Conrad's pleas. And I agreed. Jean was old now, and an invalid. How long would she have the strength to fight her emphysema and whatever else was ailing her, never mind stir up trouble? And why would she want to?

It took a month to find the perfect house, a brick ranch, all one level with hardwood floors, so Jean wouldn't have to deal with stairs she couldn't climb or carpeting that triggered her allergies. It had three bedrooms and two full baths, plus a small office that Jonathan could use for a studio. All it needed was a fresh coat of paint inside and a gardener's touch outside.

Jonathan and I were as thrilled as Jean, since neither of us dreamed we'd own a house of our own so soon. When I finished painting Jean's bedroom and bath, Jonathan's sister helped her make the trip to Athens.

Fortunately, I had met Jean before the wedding. When she arrived, I'd be prepared to hide the revulsion I felt since first laying eyes on her. She reminded me of the hag the evil queen had turned herself into in Disney's *Snow White*. Jean had a humpback from osteoporosis, short salt-and-pepper hair, large brown eyes with deep circles, no teeth, and dentures that she wore only occasionally. Her words were a mush of tongue and gums, formed with great effort from the lack of teeth and breath.

There was a honeymoon period. Jonathan left for work by seven each morning and Jean and I kept each other company until he returned, always after six each night. Jean spent much of her time in her room, in bed and on the phone, her gateway to the world. I chuckled when I heard her maneuverings and manipulations of pharmacists and doctors, preachers and handymen, master in her little world. How she would have loved the internet!

Three months later, we learned I was pregnant. My due date was mid-May 1978. After some morning sickness in the first trimester, I felt like my old self and began painting the guest bedroom, which would be the baby's room,

Jean began inviting people over to the house. At first it was just members of the Unitarian congregation she'd become acquainted with over the phone. Then a social worker from the Council on Aging began showing up once a week. I ascribed her visitors to boredom and wanting to see other people besides me. *Perfectly normal*, I thought.

At the same time, Jonathan spent most evenings in Jean's bedroom, and it became clear that I wasn't to be privy to their conversations. I later learned he was simply trying to protect me from the hurtful things Jean was saying about me, the stupid Italian peasant with thick ankles. At one point Jonathan did mention that he'd signed the St. Petersburg house back over to her. Jean wanted it back, so he gave it back. I felt out of place in my own home, a fifth wheel.

Unspoken but palpable was the power struggle between Jean and Jonathan. The true focus of their evening discussions: Who was going to be the head of our household? And who was going to be first with him—Jean or me?

Gradually, I noticed Jean's visitors giving me weird looks and making remarks that didn't make sense. They seemed to imply she was being neglected. Soon after, one of Jean's favorite Unitarians, who no doubt thought of himself as her protector, called Jonathan at home to let him know just what he thought of our treatment of her. While they talked, I could see Jonathan becoming more and more angry, because he became more and more calm and logical as he spoke.

That night after dinner, he asked me to join him in Jean's bedroom. Though just the two of us, we must have looked like a delegation. I could see Jean's defenses going up and she eyed us warily.

"Mother, Cliff called me today," Jonathan said. "He was pretty upset. He thinks we're abusing you." He paused for a response, but she didn't say anything, though her breath became more labored. She hooked the tube attached to her oxygen tank over her ears and inserted the nosepiece into her nostrils, armed for battle.

"Did you tell Cliff we weren't feeding you? That you had to cook your own meals? And that we won't let you out of your room?" Jonathan asked. "Why would you tell him that?"

"I'll talk to anyone I want," Jean answered, dodging.

"That's not the question," Jonathan said.

"*You* are not going to tell me what I can and can't do," she lashed out. "No one tells me what to do." Her voice vibrated from rage and the phlegm in her chest. She was unprepared for the reckoning that came from playing two ends against the middle and furious at being cornered.

"Mother, I'm not telling you what to do. I'm asking what you did," Jonathan replied.

"You think I'm helpless. You'll see. One night I'll go get my cast-iron frying pan and bash your brains in." She inhaled noisily, like someone drowning and surfacing for the last time, then turned on her breathing machine and sucked on the mouthpiece.

We walked out of the room to let her calm down. A sane conversation seemed impossible. I never dreamed that living with Jean would devolve into war. Shock reverberated through me—and astonishment at her threat. Jonathan and I laughed at the image of her lugging a heavy frying pan anywhere, but we also began locking our bedroom door at night.

There was a two-week respite before the social worker was back, as was Cliff. I showed them back to her room and Jean's look at me was a dare to tell Jonathan. But I wasn't about to let her play us against each other; that night I told him about her guests. Jonathan went to Jean's room. I stayed out of it.

Ten minutes later, he returned to the family room. The upshot, he told me, was that he forbade Jean to have Cliff and the social worker in his house and I was not to allow them in.

His house. Those were fighting words. I feared Jean wouldn't let them pass without a struggle and unfortunately, I was right. Hearing her come up the hallway, I braced myself for the verbal assault. Instead she opened the front door and ran down the steps. We heard her screaming "Help! Help!" at a volume that impressed me even in my shock.

She could run, too! By the time we reached the front door, Jean was across the street and pounding on a neighbor's door. Of course they let her in. Jonathan walked over to bring her back, but they wouldn't let him inside. He came back to the house.

I wondered what stunt Jean would pull next. I never dreamed she would call the police. But an officer soon knocked on our front door, and asked Jonathan to step outside.

"Your mother says you assaulted her," the officer said. "Are you aware of the wounds on her arms?"

"No, I don't know what you're talking about," Jonathan replied.

"Mr. Cooper, I'm going to have to ask you to come down to the station to make a statement. My partner is going to bring your mother back to her room and you are going to stay away from her. You are not to enter her bedroom, understand?" The officer looked for Jonathan's reaction. There was none.

"Whatever you say, Officer. Let me get my wallet." Jonathan went into our bedroom to get his things. I was crying quietly. He kissed me and said, "Don't worry, honey, I'll be back in an hour." Then he walked with the officer to the police car.

I could see the other officer walking Jean back to our house. Gauze had been wrapped around both her forearms. Gasping for air, she gazed at me triumphantly as she came in the door. I said nothing. I waited in the foyer for the officer to come back from her room. He stayed there longer than I expected. As he was leaving, he said, "You shouldn't have any more trouble tonight. I looked at her bedroom and bathroom. They're clean." He looked me in the eye, as if to say, 'I see what's going on here,' and continued. "So are the clothes she's wearing. She's clean, too, must have bathed recently, no signs of neglect."

"What about my husband?" I said. "He would never hurt her. She's sick."

"He'll have to make a statement, then he can leave," the officer replied. "It will be better if he stays away from her for the time being." He left, closing the door behind him.

When Jonathan returned, he had little to say. "The next move is hers. She'll have to decide if she's going to press charges."

"What did they tell you about her arms?" I asked.

"Nothing. They asked me about them. Did you see them when she came back?"

"She had bandages on them. I couldn't see anything." I would try to solve that mystery in the morning.

* * *

Jonathan went to work the next day, as if all were normal. But for Jean insisting on making her own breakfast, it was. I was in no mood to be helpful, and let her do as she pleased. But I did notice her arms. She had taken off the bandages, and there were dark-purple marks on the insides of both arms, from her elbows to her wrists. They looked like the bruises one gets after donating blood. *Of course! She stabbed her own arms with one of her hypodermic needles.* No wonder the neighbors wouldn't let Jonathan in their house—her arms were bloody. I felt sick to my stomach, but marveled at her, willing even to injure herself to manipulate the people around her. What else was she capable of?

Jean stayed in her room and on the phone all morning. Nothing happened, but the suspense kept me on edge. At lunchtime, Jonathan called from work.

"Mom has a lawyer," he said. "There's going to be an emergency hearing this afternoon."

"Is she pressing charges?"

"I don't know. Marshall recommended a lawyer, Tom Strickland. He's going to represent us." Marshall was an engineer who worked with Jonathan. "I'm leaving work early. Meet me at Strickland's office at four. He's in the phone book."

"I'll be there."

As soon as we entered the attorney's office, Strickland rose and shook our hands as we introduced ourselves.

"Well they tried to pull a fast one on us," Strickland announced as we took a seat opposite his desk. "Your mother's lawyer was surprised to see me. He didn't think you'd be represented this afternoon."

"What were the charges?" Jonathan asked.

"No charges," he answered. "Your mother asked for a restraining order that would forbid you to enter your own home. And that would require your wife to stay."

"Can she do that?" I asked, outraged.

"She can try. I pointed out to the judge that it was unreasonable to kick a man out of his own house. If anyone should leave, it's her. She's free to leave if she feels threatened. No one's stopping her." He paused. "And then there's the matter of involuntary servitude. I pointed out to His Honor that slavery had gone out of style a hundred years ago." He grinned my way.

"What was the verdict?" Jonathan said.

"It's going to be awkward," Strickland warned. "The judge granted the restraining order, but you don't have to leave. You're prohibited from crossing the threshold of her bedroom. She's to stay in her room. She can come out for meals, but she's to keep away from you, too."

"How long is this going to go on?" I asked.

"No telling. Her lawyer argued that the house belongs to your mother in all but name. I expect they'll sue for ownership. Can they claim that?"

Jonathan explained how we'd bought the house with Jean's help. Strickland listened, then drew his conclusion. "Your mother made you a gift. The title's in your name. Your name is on the mortgage. They may argue that there was some quid pro quo, some promise made, but there's nothing in writing, correct?"

"Yes," Jonathan replied.

"Then it's her word against yours. I don't think you have anything to worry about."

When we left Strickland's office, neither of us felt reassured. We decided to have a quiet dinner downtown. Jean would have to fend for herself.

The stress of the following weeks was unrelenting. We received official notice from the Department of Family and Children Services that it was investigating a complaint against us. Jonathan took a morning off to go with me to meet with an investigator, an older woman who glared as we entered her office. *Shouldn't she at least try to appear impartial?* I thought. She asked routine questions: name, address, employment, then got to the point. "Have you ever laid a hand on your mother?" she asked Jonathan.

"Of course I have," he said. "I've given her injections and helped her bathe. I've carried her when she wasn't able to walk." I could hear from his voice that he was barely controlling his temper.

"You know what I mean," the woman said.

"I do," he replied testily. "No, I never struck my mother."

She looked at me. "Your mother-in-law says she's afraid you're going to poison her."

I stared at her in disbelief. "Then why did she try to get a court order to make me cook and clean for her?"

Jonathan stood. "We're leaving. If you need anything else, you can ask our lawyer," he said, and we walked out.

At my doctor's appointment a week later, the nurse informed me that I'd lost two pounds. "You're supposed to be gaining weight—not too much—but you shouldn't be losing it," she said.

That little piece of information jolted my priorities back into place. Jean had all the time in the world to wear us down, but Jonathan and I had a deadline. The baby was due in May, only three months away. Jean had become a deadweight, possibly a danger, and we were going to bring a newborn home to that? *No house is worth it,* I decided. And I didn't want her near my baby. I couldn't bear the idea of her even touching it. I called Jonathan at work and told him what I was thinking. "Tell Sharon we'll take her up on her offer to help us move," I said.

"All we really need is the deposit. I'll find a house to rent. Let's get the hell out of here."

"I came to the same conclusion myself," he said. "I was about to call you." I let out a relieved sigh.

That afternoon, I combed the classifieds in the newspaper and found an ad for a house that looked promising. We saw it, liked it, signed the lease that day, and moved in the following weekend. We never saw Jean again. Until the day she died she remained in Athens, to live on her own with hired caregivers—addicted again, we later learned, to alcohol and prescription meds.

We had won our freedom—and Jonathan his release from guilt. No more phone calls or reproaches from his sick, lonely mother. We never talked about her. I never thought about her, and I hoped it was the same for my husband. But he continued drinking. I just didn't see it.

Jonathan gave back the two houses with which Jean had tried to buy him. He could have kept them, but his personal integrity wouldn't allow it. I was so proud of him. Now there would be only the consciousness of giving his mother a chance to live surrounded by those who would love and care for her. As Jean's lawyer said when Jonathan and I signed over the house title and mortgage to her, "All I ever saw was a son trying to do the best for his mother." We could live with that.

CHAPTER FOUR

The Boys

Necessity had made me a pro at moving, so it didn't take long to get settled in. Those three months before Todd's oldest brother was born were restorative, a time of peace and serenity. I discovered I loved being alone.

My nesting hormones were in high gear, too. I scrubbed the house's entire screened-in porch from floor to ceiling and painted its wood framing and porch swing. I would sit there, I knew, to nurse my new baby. I made drapes for the dining room and Jonathan installed the hardware. My parents shipped down the crib I had slept in, and I reassembled it in the baby's room. I bought tiny outfits I couldn't resist. I packed an overnight bag for the inevitable trip to the hospital. I read *Thank You, Dr. Lamaze* and, once our Lamaze classes started, practiced my breathing faithfully. I was determined to go through childbirth without drugs of any kind.

The prospect of parenthood wasn't settling as peacefully over Jonathan as I believed. On the surface, all was well; he was my enthusiastic birth coach. Right before my May 15 due date, we toured St. Mary's Hospital together. The following weekend, we were invited to a party at the home of one of Jonathan's friends from work. It was Bud's birthday, and his wife Sylvia had invited a group of friends to celebrate. Unaware that Jonathan had had too much to drink, I was in the kitchen when Tom, another of Jonathan's colleagues, gently told me he thought Jonathan was sick and needed to go home. I barely had time to react before Jonathan came in behind him. His face was gray. He looked like he was about to vomit as well, and Tom leaned him over the kitchen sink so he could.

Soon, I learned that Jonathan had challenged a guy twice his size to a "Greek finger-wrestling match," that is, two people lock hands and try to capture the other person's thumb under their own. Jonathan lost the first round, and insisted on another. That didn't surprise me; he always seemed to have something to prove. He won the second round, but broke his index finger in the process. That was why he was so gray. He was in excruciating pain.

We left for Athens right away. I wanted to go straight to the emergency room, but Jonathan said no, it was just a bad sprain and he would ice it. By Monday, however, the pain drove him to a doctor, who re-broke his finger without anesthesia in order to set it. Jonathan told me he did pass out that time.

Our first child, Jason Paxton, was born a week later, at ten in the evening on May 30, Memorial Day. I only vaguely recall the "hot and heavies" of eight hours of labor and transition, and when it came time to push, it took a few contractions for my body to learn what to do. And then Jason was born, perfect, crying immediately at the shock of life on his own. I was so grateful that he was a boy, for Jonathan's sake.

Broken finger and all, Jonathan held his newborn son. Then he laid Jason on my belly and I nursed him for the first time. The pain of labor vanished. What I remember most vividly is the rush from whatever endorphin-and-adrenaline mix my body served up, of oneness with the Life Force. Exhausted though I was, I was Woman, the Life-Giver, Invincible and All-Powerful.

Reluctantly, I gave Jason back to the nurses, and Jonathan collected my bag and clothes while my room was readied. He looked exhausted, and I urged him to go home and sleep after he made the obligatory phone calls. All I wanted was a shower and some sleep too.

Two days later we drove Jason home in our new car, a blue 1978 Honda Accord. Jonathan was taking the week off. Our plan was for the three of us to be alone together as a family during the first week, then for my mother to fly down to help me when Jonathan went back to work.

It was a good plan that failed miserably. Instead of having him to help me, I had a husband as well as a baby to care for. Jonathan was in bed with what appeared to be the flu. He ached all over and could hardly walk to the bathroom. His cure for the flu was a bottle of Scotch and a hot bath. It never occurred to me that Jonathan was drinking to quash the fear and sorrow innately connected to becoming a parent again. So deeply buried were those emotions and memories in the amnesiac fog of alcohol, it wasn't possible for him to share them with me. Instead, I felt like he'd let me down. We were both miserable.

Not wanting to catch whatever Jonathan had, I slept on the couch in the living room. I felt alone and sad and sorry for myself. I had no idea what Jonathan was going through. But the situation I found myself in wasn't a coincidence either—I too faced a choice, though I didn't see it that way at the time. I saw myself as the innocent victim. I didn't see that my marriage would be punctuated with invitations to admit that my husband had alcoholism and to step into my own power. Time after time, I stepped away.

When my mother arrived, everything was instantly better. Jonathan recovered and went back to work on Monday as though he'd never been sick. My world was righted: laundry done, groceries purchased, meals cooked. Mom made it all look easy. She stayed for two weeks. In the middle of the second week, Dad drove down for a long weekend with an unannounced traveling companion—Jonathan's friend Mike had helped Dad with the long drive from New Jersey to meet the newest Cooper. The whole weekend was joyous.

After my parents left, life settled into a routine. I'd learned so much from helping my own mother with baby brothers and sisters, becoming a mother myself felt easy and natural. I loved to walk around the house holding Jason, his little head on my shoulder, eyes closed, our cheeks touching.

Jonathan's younger brother and sister, Taylor and Lina, visited during the Christmas holidays. They stayed at Jean's house, but spent a lot of time with us. Through them we learned that Jean had cut Jonathan out of her will. We expected no less. I found it fascinating that inheritances, a subject that was never even thought of in my family, was a competition in Jonathan's. Lina was getting Jean's house in St. Petersburg, and Taylor the Athens house and all its contents. I could see Jonathan was irked that Taylor was getting Jean's two-hundred-year-old Seth Thomas grandfather clock—he did love it so. He believed Taylor would lose it. (And he was right; at some point Taylor lost or sold it. I just hope it's in a museum somewhere, where it belongs.)

* * *

Jason was fourteen months old when I became pregnant again. Jonathan and I had agreed that three children were about right and I wanted them spaced close together, so I might one day have a career.

It was an easy pregnancy, though I tired easily in the last three months. By my ninth month, I was very, very ready for the baby to come. I remember sitting on the front stoop of our house with Jason and crying on the day before my due date. I felt like I would be pregnant forever.

That very night, at four in the morning, my water broke. We waited only for a friend to arrive to stay with Jason before racing to the hospital. Our second son, Dane Pierce, was born about four hours later. Mom flew down right after Dane's birth.

Jason was startled by Dane's arrival. He wasn't jealous, but he felt the loss of being the sole focus of my attention. Jonathan was particularly sensitive to his feelings and went out of his way to make him feel special. From that time forward, he and Jason shared a close bond that, in hindsight, I can see never developed as strongly with Dane, and never happened at all when Todd was born twenty-three months later.

* * *

When Dane was fourteen months old, as if on schedule, I became pregnant for a third time. It seemed a more difficult pregnancy. Having two little ones to look after probably made it so. I had more nausea in my first trimester than in the two previous pregnancies combined and, due to the hypoglycemia I had developed carrying Dane and Dane's high birth weight, I was put on a low-carbohydrate diet immediately.

We celebrated Christmas 1981 with my family in New Jersey. Jason and Dane were the star attractions and their aunts and uncles piled on the gifts, one toy better than the next. We left on New Year's Day, and it was hard to say goodbye and fly back to Georgia.

Perhaps Dane picked up a cold on the flight back to Atlanta, but in less than two weeks it had developed into pneumonia. Dane's illness made me realize just how cold our house was, especially the hardwood floors, with no insulation underneath. Jonathan and I decided to move, and found a ranch-style house we liked. Since I was seven months pregnant, we decided to paint the interior first, and gradually move in over the course of a month. Then a blizzard hit, with over eight inches of snow in a town that shut down when an inch was on the ground. Even worse, our pipes froze. Instead of using all of February to gradually move into our new house, we rushed pell-mell into it at the end of January.

My due date, March 23, was approaching rapidly. Preparing for a third drug-free delivery, I realized that Mom had never been conscious for a single one of her children's births, even though she had nearly delivered my sister Theresa in a police car. It was one of my favorite stories and I told it to Jonathan, who agreed that we should invite Mom to be my "photographer," so she could finally witness a live birth. Since Mom would be going to the hospital with us, our neighbor across the street offered to babysit Jason and Dane when the time came.

The time came at two in the morning on March 27, 1982. As promised, our neighbor came over in her pajamas to stay with the boys while Jonathan, Mom, and I headed to the hospital.

I soon discovered that this third labor would be very different from my previous ones: I was experiencing acute lower back pain. Alice, the nurse-midwife, said that the baby was in a posterior position, with the back of her head against my tailbone. (I never had sonograms to learn the sex of my children ahead of time, so we were hoping our third and last child would be a girl.)

Alice recommended walking. I began walking in earnest and soon shifted to a wide, side-to-side, hip-swinging gait. Where that wisdom came from I have no idea, but before a half-hour passed, I felt my insides spin. The baby had turned around!

No more back labor, but it was another five hours before Todd arrived. When it was time for me to push,

Alice tried to slow me down, as if she weren't ready for him, but my body was in a hurry. In just two pushes, Todd was born. Another boy! I wasn't at all disappointed he wasn't a girl. Boys were easy, I'd found, and much easier for Jonathan.

Alice laid Todd on my tummy and I held him close. He was blond like Jason, with a dusting of peach fuzz on his little head. I looked in his eyes for the first time and was shocked to see that his right eye was turned in toward his nose.

How could my baby be less than perfect? In my alarm and concern for Todd, I never thought what a crossed eye meant for Jonathan. If it brought back memories of his daughter Ryder, he never shared them with me. Instead everyone—Jonathan, my mother, Alice— tried to reassure me. Even our pediatrician downplayed the seriousness of Todd's crossed eye. He said that some- times a baby has a little fold of skin that makes an eye look crossed at first and that we shouldn't jump to con- clusions, just wait and see. Instinctively, however, I knew that Todd's eyes were going to be a problem.

Meanwhile, we racked our brains for a boy's name that would be as beautiful as Jason Paxton and Dane Pierce. I came across the name Todd on the lists I was consulting and liked the single-syllable sound of it. My grandfather's mother's maiden name was Fielding. Jonathan agreed: Todd Fielding Cooper he would be.

When Todd was six months old, his eyes were un- changed. Jonathan and I took him to a pediatric ophthal- mologist at Emory University, who diagnosed congeni- tal esotropia—crossed eyes, a failure of the eye-control mechanisms in the brain to develop properly. The poor little guy then suffered through a year of therapy, a combination of eye patches and glasses, in an attempt to teach the right eye to self-correct. Every morning, as soon as Todd woke up, before I even lifted him out of his crib, I would put an adhesive patch over his left eye, the good one, and then add a pair of tiny eyeglasses. But there was no improvement in his vision or the alignment of his right eye.

His doctor, also a surgeon, then recommended surgery. He would operate on both eyes. However, because Todd's eyes would continue to grow, the doctor warned that his right eye would still be slightly crossed after the surgery. He didn't want to overcorrect the muscles. Todd would still need glasses, and when he turned eighteen, we could take another look to see if further surgery was needed.

Todd underwent eye muscle surgery when he was eighteen months old. The surgery went perfectly, but the after-effects of the anesthesia made him violently ill. To see a baby retching with nothing in his stomach was horrible. I held him and tried to comfort him as he cried and cried. I felt helpless. Jonathan had to leave the room. It never occurred to me that it was not his first time witnessing the aftereffects of anesthesia on a baby. So completely had Jonathan quarantined the emotions and memories of Ryder from our life together that, until Todd and my marriage were both unraveling, I did not make the connection.

* * *

Looking back at our life in the eighties, I would say it was the most carefree time in my marriage. We had no money worries. Jonathan's motto was "Don't save, make more money." Although we weren't able to save money, we lived comfortably.

Jonathan's mother died in 1981. Upon Jean's death, the Cooper Coffee building and land in St. Petersburg went to her four children. That arrangement had been Conrad's doing. When he first purchased the property for his brother, he set it up so that upon Gene's death, his wife would have only a lifetime interest in it. Jean had no say in who would inherit. Thanks to Conrad, we had a down payment for a house.

We bought a house two years later in Westgate Park, a development ahead of its time. The streets were wide, with islands down the center, where all the utilities were buried—no telephone poles or overhead electrical lines. There was a small lake with a picnic area at the front of the subdivision and a pool far from the main road, deep in the woods. Our house sat on three-quarters of an acre of heavily wooded land.

Both the house and property were fixer-uppers. The first thing we did was convert the two-car garage into Jonathan's studio. Instead of twin garage doors, Jonathan had a waist-high brick wall built, on which sat a steel frame for wide sheets of tinted glass that rose to form the remainder of the wall and roof, Jonathan's own clever design. I hung white and gray vinyl wallpaper and Jonathan built floor-to-ceiling display panels, which I upholstered in a gray-blue material that, along with a vinyl slate-tile floor and a wood-veneer ceiling system, pulled the room together and made it the handsomest one in the house.

Neighbors stopped by to welcome us and encouraged us to join the neighborhood homeowners association, which was responsible for the maintenance of the pool, the picnic area around the lake, the subdivision entrance, and all the islands in the streets. Membership was voluntary and the association was always short of funds and heavy on controversy. At the first meeting I attended, arguments broke out over the cost of keeping the pool running. One resident even offered to buy dynamite to blow it up!

Perhaps my childhood memories of the Capone family pool at the center of our neighborhood fun were the motivation behind my adopting the cause of the Westgate pool. I wanted my own kids to have a pool to swim in during the summer, so I became pool chairman, responsible for pool maintenance and improvement. Over the next several years, with the help of some key families, I was able to sell the association on making the needed improvements.

Westgate was going through a generational shift. We were the second family with young children to move in. Within a few years, there were a dozen kids at our end of the neighborhood. Jason was the oldest and led the activities, from building forts in the woods to forming the "Bike Cats" neighborhood bicycle club. Todd, the second youngest in the group, worked extra hard to keep up with his older brothers and their best friend Andy. Determined to the point of stubbornness, Todd vied with Andy for his brothers' approval. They could be hard on him, but Todd held his ground. He would not be excluded.

The neighborhood parents enjoyed each other's company, too, and we took turns hosting three- and four-course dinners, featuring the cuisine of a different country each time. Life seemed a fairy tale.

A vacation in St. Petersburg to visit Jonathan's two sisters when the boys were two, four, and six, is among my happiest memories of their childhood. It was their first time seeing the ocean. Jonathan wasn't very good at vacationing. We'd start out with him in the driver's seat, but he would become sleepy within thirty minutes and give me the wheel. The 80-20 rule reliably predicted how the driving was divided between us. When we arrived at our destination, he would be ill-humored and impatient. At the time I ascribed it to being away from work and destressing. Looking back, I believe not being able to drink was the more likely cause.

Every summer, the boys and I took a trip to New Jersey to visit their grandparents, aunts, uncles, and eventually, cousins. Perhaps it was for the best that Jonathan stayed home to work. Only once in our years of travel did we tangle with disaster.

In the summer of 1986, my sister Edna and I foolishly decided to drive straight through from Georgia to New Jersey, rather than stop overnight. Edna fell asleep at the wheel and I awoke to the sound of our car scraping along the concrete highway divider. Turning immediately back to the boys, I saw that Jason and Dane had managed to grab hold to keep from being thrown about, but Todd hadn't. I threw my arm out like a lifeline and grabbed him at the shoulder to secure him.

The car was totaled, but no one was injured, just badly shaken. From that time forward, we always stopped overnight whenever we drove to New Jersey. The boys quickly forgot about the accident, but I couldn't. The two nightmares it inspired haunted me. In one, I was struck head on by a vehicle, and I felt my head snap back from the impact. My head must have actually jerked backwards in my sleep because I awoke with a start and felt a stinging sensation in my neck. In the second, one of my sons had died and I was walking up the aisle of a church filled with hundreds of people. I looked at no one, but I could feel them all staring at me. That one woke me up too.

I worked hard to give my sons a childhood as good as my own, with magical summers and family times to treasure. The boys and I would spend two days driving up, ten days with the family, and another two days driving back. At my parents', the boys swam in the same backyard pool I did growing up. Dinner each night was a party, with my brothers and sisters and their spouses joining in, or us visiting them in their homes. Occasionally we found time to visit New York City—the Museum of Natural History, with its blue whale and dinosaurs, the Hayden Planetarium, the Bronx Zoo, and the Statue of Liberty.

When Jason was around eight years old, I began having a talk with him as I tucked him into bed at night. We processed whatever happened during the school day and occasionally I told him a story about the universe, evolution, dinosaurs, whatever he wanted to talk about. Dane and Todd soon clamored for their own "talks," so I spent time with each one, sitting on the side of the bed, talking with him alone. Bedtime became a special bonding time, reminiscent of intimate talks with my own mother.

For a long time, Jonathan and I resisted owning a television. The boys didn't miss it, unless the TV was on in a neighbor's house. Then they would be glued to it. At home they read books, drew pictures, and played games. We fended off that particular Christmas present from my family until the year Todd turned eight.

The older the boys grew, the more distinct their personalities became. Jason was the ringleader. Dane and Todd naturally looked up to him. Highly creative, he combined the best talents of his parents, Jonathan's artistic talent and my love of reading and book smarts. Dane, the classic, socially gifted middle child, was the bridge between Jason and Todd, who butted heads more often than not. Easygoing, patient, and slow to anger, Dane took after my father in temperament, with the same sense of independence and self-confidence. I'll never forget his answer when he graduated from UGA, and I invited him to live with me until he found a job: "Mom, if I had to move in with my mother after graduating from college, I'd consider myself a failure." I was disappointed, but proud, too.

Todd was always trying to keep up with his older brothers. He was the annoying little brother who wanted to win their respect, so he often competed with them. Dane had more patience with him than Jason did. Todd and Jason had a way of getting on each other's last nerve. Perhaps at the root of their bickering was the chemistry between Todd and Jonathan: they were also always at odds with each other. Not surprising then that Jason, with his close relationship to his dad, tended to be at odds with Todd, too.

As Todd grew from a toddler into his own independent person, he and Jonathan seemed always to be just slightly annoyed with each other. A root cause, I couldn't name, but that annoyance often flared up without warning into a test of wills. Jonathan would tell Todd to pick up his toys or put his glass in the dishwasher, and wanted Todd to respond instantly. Todd would say "Okay," but finish what he was doing. That was enough to set Jonathan off. Then they would both lose their tempers.

I frequently refereed, saying things like, "C'mon, Todd, put the game on pause and do what your father wants." And Todd would make a couple more moves, just on principle, then do as I asked. Or sometimes, it was, "He'll do it in a minute, Jonathan, just let him finish this level." Then Jonathan would relent, begrudgingly, and walk back to his studio.

Highly sensitive to the feelings of those around him, Todd internalized the family's emotions without realizing it. It must have confused him and made him a mystery to himself. Looking back, I see that, long before I was ready to admit it, Todd sensed my growing anger and frustration with Jonathan. He would ask me in exasperation, "Why don't you divorce him?" He said it because he was angry with his dad. Neither of us realized that I was the angry one.

Todd and I were always close. In part our bond grew out of his struggles with his eyesight. He hated wearing glasses, but needed them. The happiest moment of his life came in the eighth grade, the first time he wore contact lenses to school. It was like the classic movie scene, when the girl takes off her glasses and is discovered to be a beauty. All his friends, especially the girls, then saw him as he truly was, handsome, blue-eyed, and golden.

All his life, Todd had a way of wrapping me around him, as if to recharge and feel safe. Signature moments would arise between us that made the hairs on the back of my neck stand on end. They called my attention to a special connection between us—electric, beyond time. I was keenly aware of those moments and can still call them to mind, like the time the boys, three, five, and seven, were flying kites with their Uncle Jim in the field at the entrance to Westgate. I was watching, sitting Indian-style on the ground. Todd suddenly withdrew and fit himself into the space between my crossed legs and my chest to draw me around him. Or at my sister's wedding reception, when he was five, and, with great solemnity, reminded me that we hadn't yet danced together, and led me to the floor. Or the night he graduated from middle school, when we lay side-by-side on our backs on the family room floor at midnight to watch heat lightning illuminate the entire backyard, our heads barely touching. Or two years later, when Jonathan's friend Mike came for a visit and took the family photograph—and caught the moment when Todd reached up for my arm, wrapped it around his neck, and drew me close. The memories still make me shiver.

I was proud of the life Jonathan and I were making. Jonathan may have been the sole breadwinner, but I did everything else. I gave and gave, as I had seen my parents do in their own marriage, without keeping score or expecting a return. If not for Jonathan's drinking, I could have done that forever. So when our marriage began to fall apart, no one suspected, least of all Jason, Dane, and Todd.

CHAPTER FIVE

The Jonathan Company

When his friend Mike went into business for himself, it lit a fire in Jonathan. Mike had resigned from the New York graphic design firm where he was working to start his own company. His experience in developing signage systems for large architectural spaces, such as office centers and hospitals, and his location in the New York metropolitan area, where design was valued by developers and their clients, enabled him to rapidly make the transition to a successful self-employed designer.

Jonathan was itching to do the same. He felt limited by working for a steel products manufacturer, and saw that steel furniture would never be an economical choice for the convenience store industry, the rapidly growing market into which his company had chosen to expand. At thirty-six, he reasoned that if he didn't make his move soon, it would be too late.

"It's now or never, Anne," he said a few months after Todd was born. "We're not going to have any more children, and we have no major expenses. We've paid off my school loans and the car. I'm healthy, you're healthy. Now's the time, if we're going to do this."

Would I deny him his dream? I was apprehensive. We were in Athens, Georgia, not New York City. There was no market for industrial design where we lived. We had three children and no savings. How would we pay the bills? Jonathan, however, was full of confidence.

"Anne, I will sweep floors, I will do anything to provide for my family. Poverty is a state of mind. We will never be poor," he assured me.

I knew Jonathan was a maverick, definitely not the corporate type. All his self-esteem was invested in his identity as an industrial designer and artist. Succeeding as an independent designer would confirm his self-worth. Rising from the ashes of death and divorce, he had transformed his life once already, so I took a leap of faith, in him and with him, and agreed to his going out on his own. Jonathan gave a month's notice to the company he worked for and prepared to launch "The Jonathan Company." At the end of the month, it was official. He had received his last paycheck.

The first hurdle we had to clear was the noncompete clause in Jonathan's contract. He negotiated an agreement with his former employer, and began providing design services to one of its biggest customers. Income! We were still living hand-to-mouth, but we were launched.

He also contacted a consultant he'd met who provided marketing and merchandising plans to the convenience store industry. Jonathan and Bill soon began working together. In Bill, Jonathan found a way to market his design services to a burgeoning industry; in

Jonathan, Bill found a way to diversify his business and implement his merchandising recommendations in a client's physical space. And Bill would be able to mark up Jonathan's design fees.

In 1983, the "c-store" industry was growing rapidly. Mom-and-pop stores were highly profitable, and needed to develop their brand identity as they acquired more locations. Through Bill's consulting business, The Jonathan Company designed graphic systems, store layouts, and eventually, full plans for building conversions and the construction of new stores.

New chains were popping up in every state that allowed the purchase of gasoline and food at the same location. When the big oil companies began moving into the c-store business several years later, gas stations that offered car repairs and maintenance needed to be converted. Bill had the contacts to acquire those clients as well. As competition in the industry increased, the most successful independent chains began acquiring the smaller ones. That consolidation also meant new business for Bill and Jonathan.

Business was good and I was grateful. We still had no savings, but we were paying our bills and living comfortably. Jonathan ran the design side of the business and I ran everything else. The business side of The Jonathan Company became my responsibility. I kept the books, wrote the project proposals, drew up the invoices, and did the taxes. I ran the Cooper household, too, cooking, cleaning, doing laundry, cutting grass, painting, hanging wallpaper, paying the bills, whatever kept life comfortable and orderly. I ran the boys to T-ball games, soccer practice, and piano lessons. At first, Jonathan volunteered as a T-ball or soccer coach, but as the boys got older he gradually withdrew from those activities.

Having Jonathan at home all the time was pleasant. There was only one source of conflict between us: his drinking. The first time we fought over the amount of liquor he consumed was after we'd had some friends to dinner right after Todd was born. We had never kept a "liquor cabinet" in the way my parents did when I was growing up, and I wanted to stock one so we didn't have to buy alcohol every time we entertained.

For that particular dinner, I bought a quart of several varieties of hard liquor and after-dinner liqueurs. The following weekend, with another couple coming to dinner, I went to the liquor cabinet to see what mixers we'd need. Every liquor bottle was empty! I was astonished that Jonathan could consume so much in a single week and very, very angry. I confronted him and he blew up.

"You're going to tell me I can't have a drink in my own house? I'm working my ass off. Go out and buy some more. What's the big deal?"

"It is a big deal," I answered. "It's not healthy to drink that much in a single week. Do I need to keep it under lock and key? Do I have to hide it if I want to keep liquor in the house?"

"Just try it. If I want a drink, I'll have one. You're not going tell me what to do. I'm not your father." He lit a cigarette and walked back to his drawing board.

I ignored Jonathan's snide insinuation that my mother dictated to my father. And I was in too much denial to push harder. Deep inside, I knew there was no resolution to our quarrel and that I couldn't force him to stop. Instead, I gave up on keeping liquor in the house and only bought what we needed when we entertained. For his part, Jonathan began hiding his drinking from me. After that fight, I never saw him drink during the day.

Subconsciously, I realized that it was the one battle I could never win. Blindness to my husband's addiction was far easier than confrontation. Confrontation meant risking failure and loss of control. I'd have no guarantee of the outcome, and with three small children, the breakup of my marriage and becoming a single mom was an inconceivable risk. I made an existential choice, a choice to avoid conflict. From that time forward, I suffered from low back pain; the lower back, I now know, is where rage settles and expresses itself in the body.

After our non-fight, Jonathan's behavior lulled me into a false sense of security. He worked all the time, it seemed. How could I reproach him when he was working so hard? What made it even more difficult was that he never appeared to be drunk. He seemed to be completely unaffected, however much he was drinking.

Several years later, I learned what it meant to be able to drink and seemingly be unaffected by it—that is, to have a high tolerance to alcohol. Jonathan and I attended a program offered by the local school system called "Talking With Your Kids About Alcohol."[1] Jason was in the fifth grade and I wanted to be prepared for the middle school years, when peer pressure to try alcohol or drugs became real issues for kids. Secretly I hoped it would make Jonathan confront his drinking problem.

We attended the sessions together and learned that, while high tolerance may appear to be a good thing, it actually means that the body is adapting to greater and greater amounts of alcohol. When the body has so adapted to alcohol that its presence in the body is normal and its absence abnormal, alcoholism has been triggered.[2]

Jonathan and I talked about his high tolerance and whether he had alcoholism. He wouldn't say that he did, and I didn't push him, although I suspected that was the case. He did agree that he needed to cut back, but I doubt he ever made a serious effort. When we bought a six-pack of beer on a Friday night or opened a bottle of wine on Saturday, it would be gone by morning, even though I had one or two drinks at most. Being unable to stop drinking once you start, or stopping only when forced to—when the alcohol is all gone or you've run out of money—is another symptom of alcoholism, another signal we both ignored.[3]

Running his own business was a liberation for Jonathan, but it was years before I realized that it mostly liberated him from restrictions on his drinking. Working at home, he could drink whenever he wanted, which was all day long. He needed a certain amount of alcohol in his system to function normally, but that realization came to me much later, when he literally ran out of money and had no alcohol to drink.

According to Jonathan, The Jonathan Company meant that he could set his own hours, take time off during the week, but rarely did it work in favor of his spending more time with us. He had to be available when clients wanted to reach him, which was during the typical workday. Nonetheless, the lines that separated the weekdays from the weekends did disappear—Jonathan worked all the time.

Jonathan's work schedule never interfered with the fun the boys and I had together, from getting ready for Christmas to celebrating birthdays, Easter, the Fourth of July, or Halloween. Springtime meant birthdays, one a month from March to May. Typically, a birthday kicked off with the arrival of a large box from New Jersey, filled with presents from my parents for the birthday boy, but always with a little something for the other two. There was always a party, too, for about a dozen kids from the neighborhood and school.

Most memorable was a Saturday-night sleepover party for Dane's eighth birthday. Todd was six, Jason, ten. The three of them helped me set up two large tents in the backyard for a dozen boys and their sleeping bags. That evening, with dinner eaten and presents opened, Todd, Jason, Dane, and friends played touch football while I cleared away the debris. The big plan for the night was a game of "German Spotlight," played after dark with flashlights, a form of hide-and-seek with teams capturing opposing team members. Dane promised me that everyone would stay in the yard and go no farther than the wooded lot next door, so I wasn't monitoring the game too closely when it began. Curfew was at eleven.

As darkness fell, beams of light flashed across the backyard. Occasionally a cheer went up. At nine thirty, Todd came in the back door. His face, arms, and legs were black and green. "What is that all over you?" I asked, mystified.

"Camouflage," he answered, excited. "Andy brought it for the game." He ran to the kitchen sink, gulped down a glass of water, and ran to the door. "I gotta get back."

"Wait!" I cried. "Is *everybody* in camouflage?"

"Yeah, we had enough." He disappeared. I groaned.

I walked into Jonathan's studio. He was leaning back in his chair, feet up on the desk, smoking a cigar. He had switched from cigarettes in an attempt to quit smoking. "Jonathan, we've got a problem," I said.

"What's up?" he said as he lowered his feet.

"Every single kid out there is covered in black-and-green makeup. I promised their mothers they'd be ready for church when they come tomorrow." Then I started laughing; I couldn't help it. "What are we going to do?"

"Clean 'em up, I guess," he answered. "Let's go see."

We walked to the back door. "Dane, Jason, Todd! *Everybody in!*" I shouted.

A dozen guerrilla fighters, armed with flashlights, bandannas, and a variety of plastic guns, slowly arrived at the door. Todd was right, there had been enough paint to go around. Jonathan ran for his camera and posed them for a group photo.

"Okay, listen up, you savages," I told them, "You have about forty more minutes to play. German spotlight is over at ten thirty. Then we're starting baths."

"But you said eleven," Dane protested.

"That was before the camouflage," I told him.

Jonathan oversaw the bathing, which transformed the boys' white-tile bathroom into a bizarre, black-and-green abstract painting. It was two a.m. before everyone was asleep. The next morning, some very annoyed mothers carted their groggy sons off to church. Though apologetic at the time, I can't help but smile at the memory.

The boys were thriving at home and in school. I taught all three to read before they reached first grade, so they were always in the top ten percent of their class. Without a television, reading and drawing were the ways they spent their evenings. Together, Todd and I read the same books Dane and Jason had enjoyed, like *The Indian in the Cupboard, Tales of a Fourth Grade Nothing,* or *Where the Red Fern Grows,* always just a little above his reading level. He'd read a page to me, then I'd read one to him. Wherever the story led us, we'd laugh or get teary-eyed together.

I was so proud of my sons; they would be my best gift to the world. In my hubris, I pitied those less fortunate, or whose children were a worry or a burden, and envisioned a future where I made life better for scores of children, not just my own.

* * *

Although I had long abandoned Catholicism, I never abandoned the desire to save the world and to make sacrifices for a cause. Those inculcated values dovetailed perfectly with the powerlessness I felt in the face of the greatest challenge to my marriage.

Having Jonathan work at home liberated me from being a strictly stay-at-home mom during the day. As the boys progressed through elementary school, I became more and more involved in school and community affairs. I started as a homeroom mother, then got involved with the school PTO. There was a terrific group of parents committed to supporting and improving the school, and Jonathan and I had fun working with them on different initiatives, fundraisers, and improvement projects. There were spaghetti dinners, a "Koality Kids" branding campaign and school improvement effort, plantings of daffodil bulbs and Bradford pear trees, tutoring kids in reading, and more.

I strove to exert my power outside of my home by adopting the cause of children and education in the Athens community. Thus my role as a homeroom mother, school-fundraiser leader, and president of different school PTOs as the boys moved up from elementary to middle school. By 1988, I was co-president of an annual countywide fundraiser for summer school scholarships. The area's problems of poverty, race, and student achievement were apparent to anyone who chose to see them, and with parents from around Clarke County, I advocated for free summer school for families unable to afford it. As part of promoting the need for summer school in the school system—classes that weren't just remedial, but fun and creative, with the potential to inspire a love of learning—I obtained a grant that provided education and training on issues of race in education by the Southern Regional Council, an illuminating and deeply moving set of experiences stretched over two years of periodic, weekend-long meetings.

I was one of two white women in a group of fifteen activists, men and women from around the South, from Louisiana to Virginia. Yet, could a white woman understand the black experience? Very rarely does a white person find him or herself in the minority, an outsider not automatically accepted prima facie. I learned about institutional racism and white privilege from its victims. The deeply felt injustice, the stifled rage, the great sadness and frustration of seeing another generation of African-American children failing in school—all that had to be put aside by those courageous advocates for me to be accepted into the group. I was so aware of the irony of our situation—that they should have to accept *me* despite *my* race. I didn't feel worthy.

Ultimately, I ran for a position on the Clarke County school board. I lost the first time, but won the second. Running for election, running fundraisers, running the Clarke County School District's Foundation for Excellence as president, running a household and my husband's business—all that running preserved my dearly held illusion of control. I was really running for my life, running scared. And I ran as hard as I could.

CHAPTER SIX

The Breakdown

From 1982 to 1992, The Jonathan Company was a successful business. I thought we had made it. Most small startups go under within five years, but The Jonathan Company was ten years old and had grown to the point that Jonathan hired a draftsman to work with him. Larry was like one of the family. He worked long hours when a project was on deadline, and never seemed to mind the noise and commotion that went with working in an office in someone's home. However, business slowed as we began to feel the effects of the recession of 1990–91, and Jonathan had to let Larry go.

Try as I might, I was always scrambling to keep our checkbook balanced. Jonathan would write checks to "cash" but not enter an amount, and then together we'd try to figure out what the checks were for and what the amounts might be. In hindsight, I see that those omissions were Jonathan's way of hiding how much he was spending on alcohol. I was so frustrated by his behavior. Just fill out the goddamn check stub! And when I tallied our monthly expenses, I couldn't understand how he could be spending so much money. What was he buying? Art supplies? He charged those. Gasoline? He worked at home. Booze was the answer, and neither of us would admit it.

The boom days of the convenience store industry were over and new design projects were scarce. I yearned for the security a corporate position would give. When I learned a large drugstore chain was looking for someone to run its in-house design team, I urged Jonathan to apply. But he didn't want to. Did I want to leave Athens and move to Florida? Uproot the kids? Not really, but I was willing to pay that price for security and peace of mind. I didn't realize that Jonathan was drinking all day long. He could never have gone back to a traditional corporate job.

My parents were another reason it would be hard for us to move. In 1988, Mom surprised the entire family when she announced that she and Dad were going to retire in Athens. They bought property in a new development called Woodlake and built a beautiful one-story home. Athens was ideal for them. Its cost of living was low and they benefited greatly from the swing in real estate prices between New Jersey and Georgia. I loved having my parents close by. They were an escape for me. Although I didn't confide in them, my load felt lighter when I was with them.

The boys were growing so fast, it was hard to keep them in clothes and shoes. Todd and Dane, ten and twelve and deep into baseball, played Little League in the fall and spring, an expense we somehow afforded. Dane was a natural athlete like his grandfather, and I always regretted that he didn't have a father interested in throwing the ball with him every night and helping him get better. Todd had the desire and determination to excel, but handicapped by his eyesight, specifically poor depth perception, he was an average ballplayer. But he was fast. Once on base, he was a daredevil and sure to steal second.

Jason, on the other hand, had tired of sports; our oldest was more interested in drawing and in books—fantasy and science fiction. I introduced him to *The Hobbit* when he was in the fourth grade, and it changed his life. He devoured *The Fellowship of the Ring* trilogy. In middle school, he discovered *Dungeons and Dragons*, which brought all his talents into play; he created elaborate adventures for himself and his brothers, complete with detailed maps and drawings of weapons and characters. They would play for hours.

Despite how well the boys were doing, the Coopers limped through the fall of 1992. Money was tight. After a small check came in, Jonathan splurged on a television for the studio. I was astonished. We were struggling just to pay the mortgage. But it was more than the money spent that so upset me. I knew that Jonathan had crossed a line, that once a TV was ensconced in the studio, he would never come out. And that is exactly what happened: Jonathan came into the house for coffee, for meals, and to sleep. He no longer lived with us. He became a recluse, personally and professionally.

Long reliant on Bill for clients and subsequently on Dick, to whom Bill sold his business, Jonathan no longer had a professional network through which to meet new clients and obtain new business. He waited for the phone to ring. It didn't.

By December, old projects were finished and, with the start of the holidays, no one was launching new ones. We had one invoice outstanding and, according to my calculations, four hundred dollars in checking. It would be tight, but we had just enough to live on until the end of the month, when that invoice would be paid. A small Christmas to be sure, but I knew the boys would scarcely notice. Jonathan's sister Sharon was giving them their first computer as a Christmas present, and I'd bought them a video game, *Secret Weapons of the Luftwaffe*. They would be mesmerized.

On Friday, the week before Christmas, Jonathan went to the post office to pick up the mail and came back with several notices from the bank. We were bouncing checks. Instead of four hundred dollars, we had less than zero, with over two hundred dollars in bank charges. My estimate of the amounts Jonathan was spending, those blank check stubs, was much less than he'd actually spent—four hundred dollars less. I'd always avoided calculating the hit our household budget was taking from tobacco and liquor and now reality forced me to face it. Why did I even bother trying to manage our finances?

I choked down my fury and tried to deal with the issue at hand. Jonathan called Dick and asked if he could expedite payment of his invoice, but Dick couldn't. He would send us a check as soon as he was paid.

"I hate to do it," I told Jonathan, "but we're going to have to go into the boys' savings accounts to get us through." Like my parents, I had put any gifts of money the boys received for birthdays or holidays into saving accounts for them. "We'll pay them back once we get past this," I assured him.

"I already closed their accounts," Jonathan said. He wouldn't look at me.

"You took their money without telling me?" I couldn't believe what I was hearing. "What did you do with it?" I asked. I already knew, but I wanted to make him tell me. Without saying a word, Jonathan walked away. I heard him go up the stairs to our bedroom and close the door behind him.

I was in a panic. The boys had no idea of our difficulties and wouldn't, if I could help it. I had some food in the freezer and some canned goods. I would find a way to stretch those out. It was the weekend, and we'd be having our usual Sunday dinner with my parents, so I could count on the boys having at least one good meal. "Jonathan's not feeling well," I told Mom and Dad when the boys and I arrived for supper without him.

The next day, we were out of milk. I had five dollars in my wallet. A gallon of milk would cost two. Practically in tears, I walked around the grocery store. I didn't know what to do. How was I going to feed three growing boys on three dollars for a week? They were already complaining about how often we were having spaghetti.

"Anne, are you okay?"

I looked up. It was a neighbor. "Yes, thanks, I'm all right." Embarrassed, I managed a smile and got away as quickly as I could. I bought a pound of ground beef. I'd make a Bolognese sauce and could probably get two meals out of it, spaghetti one night and baked ziti the next. On the way home, I stopped at the post office to check The Jonathan Company box—empty. *Please let a check come soon*, I pleaded silently to I don't know whom.

When I arrived home, I could see from the driveway that Jonathan wasn't in his studio, as I'd expected. It was past noon, and he had slept the entire weekend. I went up to our bedroom to check on him. Still asleep. I laid my hand on his forehead. No fever, but he looked terrible. I didn't try to wake him.

Somehow we made it through the week. Dick's check arrived two days before Christmas, but it didn't make Jonathan feel any better. He was seriously depressed, which I thought accounted for all the sleeping. I didn't realize he was actually going through physical withdrawal. Looking back, I believe he also suffered a nervous breakdown. His personal identity was based on his success as a designer; when The Jonathan Company failed, he fell apart.

The boys had a merry Christmas, so enthralled with their new computer they didn't notice their father's terrible condition. I told my parents Jonathan had the flu when he didn't join in the Christmas festivities.

* * *

After Christmas, I persuaded my ailing husband to talk to a neighbor, a psychiatrist. Matter-of-fact and businesslike, he managed to treat Jonathan without wounding his pride. But there was no escaping the diagnosis this time: Jonathan had full-blown alcoholism. The only cure was to stop drinking. Jonathan was given medication to help him get past the withdrawal symptoms and the depression, as well as a pill that would make him sick if he were to take a drink. And he was supposed to get counseling.

As the new year began, I felt hopeful. Jonathan was getting professional help. He loved me, he loved the boys, and he knew we counted on him. I had faith in him to do what he needed for himself and his family. Most of all, I believed he would do it for me.

In the meantime, I had to find a job. With keeping The Jonathan Company's books and volunteer work as my only recent work experience, I wouldn't earn enough to pay the mortgage, but I'd make sure we always had enough to put food on the table. I scoured the local classifieds, applied for an office position with a local builder, interviewed, and was hired.

I was so lucky. Not only did I get a job immediately, but I was hired by the warmest, most understanding and generous employers imaginable. The office atmosphere was businesslike but good-humored; no one took themselves too seriously. I was the resident liberal in an office of Republicans, and the young guys who supervised construction projects loved to engage me in seriocomic debates on topics ranging from welfare to women's rights. Yet over the years I worked for them, the owners supported the educational causes that were so important to me, the summer school fundraising as well as my two campaigns for a position on the school board. They likely had some inkling of the difficulties I was facing at home, too, and I was grateful that they could show they cared discreetly, without making me feel embarrassed or ashamed.

Working in an office with systems and predictability was a respite from the unrelenting disorder of The Jonathan Company. With those of my own household in such disarray, it was therapeutic for me to manage the day-to-day finances and pay the bills of a stable entity.

My world was no longer under my control. I couldn't tell if Jonathan was taking his medication; he took charge of it. He complained that it was making him impotent, but that, I thought, was the least of our problems. While I knew that alcoholism could cause heart disease, I didn't connect it to his impotence, but that turned out to be exactly the case. The strong heart he was so proud of was failing.

I urged him to take the medicine the psychiatrist had prescribed, but he must have stopped taking it after the first month. He also didn't like his therapist, and soon stopped seeing him. We couldn't afford it, he said, and he was right about that. He had no work at all, and was still sleeping the greater part of the day and getting up only after the boys got home from school. He watched TV in the studio the rest of the day. We were managing to keep the phone and lights on, but were months behind on everything else.

When Dick finally landed a design project, Jonathan's outlook and spirits improved but little. He was rarely up and shaved by the time I left for work in the morning, and I worried about what the boys were returning to when they came home from school in the afternoon.

To keep me engaged with The Jonathan Company, Jonathan would occasionally walk me through his designs and thinking on a project. One Saturday morning, as he showed me his latest drawings, I idly picked up his coffee cup to take a sip.

He cried out, "Don't—"

It was laced with vodka. "You're drinking!" I was so surprised that I punched him in the arm. Hard.

"Ow, you struck me!"

"Here I am thinking you're trying to get better and you're drinking?"

"I have never struck you, Anne, and never would. You hurt me," Jonathan replied as he rubbed his bicep.

That he thought he could turn the tables by accusing me of physical abuse ticked me off even more. "Good. I'm glad. Don't even talk to me." I walked back into the house.

* * *

It was a week before I could bring myself to say anything to him. In my frustration and despair, I turned to my sister Edna. In some ways, we were in the same situation: we married the men our mother wanted us to. But it was more than that. Edna recognized Ken, as I had recognized Jonathan, as the man she was destined to marry. There was an inner knowing not to be denied.

Edna and I commiserated as we struggled with the consequences of our decisions. There were long phone calls at night after our kids were in bed.

"A girlfriend gave me this book," Edna told me one night. "It's called *Many Lives, Many Masters*. You gotta read it and tell me what you think."

"Okay," I said. "What's it about?"

"It's by a psychiatrist about one of his patients," she replied. "I don't want to tell you too much. I want your opinion."

So I read it. The author, Brian L. Weiss, MD, was the Chief of Psychiatry at Mount Sinai Medical Center in Miami, Florida. The book is a detailed account of his treatment of an extremely troubled young woman whose nightmares and phobias were ruining her life. Using hypnosis, he uncovered childhood traumas she had suffered, and naturally expected her fears to diminish when those were brought into consciousness and dealt with by her adult mind. But severe phobias continued to plague her. Frustrated but determined to find the root cause, he told her, while she was still under hypnosis, to go back to the event that was causing her fear of water. She did, but she recounted an event that she said occurred in 1863 BC, nearly four thousand years ago. Then her water phobia disappeared.[1]

Each time Dr. Weiss regressed the young woman to a past-life trauma, she improved, until finally they both agreed she'd been cured. In the process, he also discovered that she was a medium, and through her, he conversed with "Masters," advanced spirits who described the death of Weiss's own infant son, the meaning behind it, and more generally, why a soul reincarnates.[2] The book proclaimed there are spiritual lessons to be learned in the physical dimension, and agreements between souls to be fulfilled. If a soul exits a lifetime before fulfilling an agreement, it's sometimes allowed to remain with those in the physical dimension, especially if its life ended abruptly.[3]

As an atheist, I found the book both fascinating and fantastic. Reincarnation was an exotic concept, far outside the bounds of traditional Christianity. Weiss also offered a different perspective on the existence of evil in the world, one of the classic arguments used to disprove the existence of God. Evil arose out of fear, he wrote. Evil was the absence of love.

Edna and I discussed the book and wondered about our relationships with our husbands. Was there a past-life connection? Why had we felt compelled to pick them? Why had I felt fated to marry Jonathan?

We brought our cousin Hannah into the conversation and asked her to read Weiss's book. With a PhD in neuropsychology, she was in a similar field, and she had recently converted from Catholicism to Judaism. What did she think? How did Weiss's book align with Jewish thought? Hannah even went to hear Weiss speak at the 92nd Street YMCA in New York City. I was eager to hear her opinion of him.

"No, Anne, I don't buy it," Hannah told me when I questioned her. She wouldn't explain why, only said she found him unconvincing. With her scientific background I'd hoped she had a rational explanation for Weiss's experiences with his patient. Had her new religion gotten in the way? I was disappointed, but didn't push. Suffering from breast cancer, Hannah was fragile, and I didn't want to risk upsetting her.

Edna and I continued to confide in each other about our marital troubles. Edna went into counseling to explore her resistance to her husband's need to control her and the threat that posed to their marriage. I watched in admiration as she slowly transformed her relationship with him by changing her own self-esteem and self-confidence. I, on the other hand, thought I could do it on my own. I still suffered from the illusion of control, and believed I could make the world right for the people I loved. All they needed to do was listen to me and do as I asked.

* * *

Todd, Dane, and Jason continued to excel in school. To my delight, Todd was named "Best All-Around Student" at the end of sixth grade. In middle school, he found a new set of friends. He became best friends with Ryan and Chip, and was always asking me to drive him to one or the other's house. Thrilled that he had friends his own age, I happily obliged.

In seventh grade, he developed a huge man-crush on his science teacher, Mr. Guy, a former army colonel who had fought in Vietnam. When Mr. Guy assigned a big project on rocks, I knew Todd wanted to impress him with his work, so I wasn't surprised when I overheard him ask Jonathan for help. Jonathan often helped Jason with posters and displays for school, and taught him techniques that gave his projects a professional look. Clearly Todd wanted that for his project for Mr. Guy. At first, I listened with eagerness to their exchange.

"Okay, what's the assignment?" Jonathan asked.

"We have to make a book that teaches first-graders about different kinds of rocks," Todd said. "I have the list of rocks I want to do."

"And when's it due?"

"Monday," Todd answered.

"Monday? This Monday? I've got drawings that have to go out by Monday. When did you get this project?" I could hear the irritation in Jonathan's voice, and I cringed.

"Forget it," Todd blurted out, then slammed the door behind him as he walked out of the studio and came to me. "Mom, I've got a science project that's due Monday."

"What have you done so far?" I asked.

"I have a list of the rocks and some notes." Todd showed me his papers. All the rocks were gems or semiprecious stones. "We have to make a book that has pictures, and an explanation that first-graders can understand."

He needed help, and I wanted to take away some of the sting of Jonathan's refusal. "Let's go to the jewelry stores at the mall," I said. "I bet they have pictures of some of these."

At the mall, Todd raced from store to store to collect brochures and ads. "Look at these!" He ran up to me as I came out of a department store emptyhanded, and showed me his haul. One jeweler's brochures had exquisite photos of gems inset in scenes of animals in their habitats.

"These are perfect, Todd!" I said. "You can cut them out and mount them in your book, with a paragraph about the stone."

When we got back home, Todd and I worked at the spare desk in the studio to put together his book. I showed him how to cut out the part of the photo he'd selected with an X-Acto blade, how to use spray adhesive, and how to use a cover sheet so as not to smear a page as he wrote. He put his whole heart into it and the little book was a gem in itself.

"I got an A+ on my book," he announced proudly a week later. "Mr. Guy asked me if he could keep it. I gave it to him."

"Wow, Todd!" I gave him a squeeze from behind as he poured himself some juice. "He must have really liked it. That's awesome." I was thrilled that Todd felt appreciated by a father-figure he admired, but ached that he didn't get the same from his actual father.

What had happened was still heavy on my mind when, one night after putting the boys to bed, I walked into Jonathan's studio. "We need to talk," I said. I leaned against the four-foot wall that guarded his desk. Jonathan swiveled in his chair to face me. "You say you love me, you love the boys, but you won't stop drinking. You won't do the one thing that's most important for all of us."

"You're right," he admitted.

"What is it going to take?"

"I don't know."

"Go back to seeing Jim." Jim was the therapist he'd started seeing after Christmas.

"No, he can't do anything."

"What about AA?" Jonathan wasn't a joiner, but I was desperate. I had to find some way to make him stop.

"No. I'll handle this my own way."

We struggled on. Occasionally, when I cleaned up the studio, I'd find an empty vodka bottle in a desk drawer or the trash. Sometimes I confronted him with it;

other times I left it on the large worktable in the center of the studio, as an accusation and a reproach.

By January 1996, it was clear to me that I had to become the family's primary breadwinner. I decided to go back to school. The University of Georgia had a reputable MBA program, I could work part-time while putting myself through school, and in two years I'd have a degree that would open doors to a new level of career opportunities. I applied in the spring and was admitted to the fall entering class.

In May, Jason graduated from high school and, through a combination of scholarships, a Pell grant, and Stafford loans, he would attend Emory University in the fall. We'd be college students together. That summer, I ran for the school board and was elected. The win felt like progress, and masked the fear that was stealthily eating away at my peace of mind.

We moved Jason into his dorm at Emory in mid-August. My parents bought him a mini-refrigerator, and we helped him settle into what had to be the smallest room on campus. The used Sentra we'd bought for him the summer before stayed in Athens so that Dane, now a junior, could drive himself and Todd to school. They hated riding to Clarke Central High on the bus, as rowdy and dysfunctional as the school itself. As a school board member, I intended to push for improved leadership there.

* * *

We were driving home one Sunday night in the fall after dinner at my parents' house, when Jonathan announced in a quiet, angry voice, "I'm not going to your parents' ever again. And I don't want them in my house. I'm not some young kid Ed can order around. Who does he think he's talking to?"

"What are you talking about?" I asked.

"Your father took me outside tonight and lectured me. He said I should get a job and take care of my family." Jonathan's voice was harsh, his words clipped.

"But Jonathan, you have to look at it from his side. He sees how we're struggling. He only wants what's best for us."

"What did you say to him?"

"Nothing! I don't have to. He has eyes. He just has to look around our house. Or at the cars we drive." My parents had given us their car the last time they bought a new one.

The following Sunday, and every Sunday thereafter, Dane, Todd, and I had dinner with my parents, and Jonathan stayed home. Dad and Mom said nothing, but generously sent home dinner for him. And he always ate it.

As we fell further into debt, I begged Jonathan to give up The Jonathan Company and find a job. He refused. "What about a part-time job?" I asked. "Any income is better than nothing. Remember when we first talked about starting the company? You said you'd sweep floors if you had to. It's time."

"I can earn ten times as much here as I can working for somebody else. And what do I tell Dick? Turn down the work he gives me? When the phone rings, who's going to answer it?"

I backed off. I couldn't force him to look for a job, and had no idea what he was qualified to do other than what he did. I was desperate to believe that he would find new clients, to pick up at least a few of the bills. What choice did I have but to believe? Todd and Dane were in high school, Jason at Emory. If I left Jonathan, where would we go? If I made him leave, how could he support two separate homes when he couldn't even support one? I didn't see how I could support three boys on my own and stay in school either. Asking my parents for help was out of the question too.

Ironically, my co-worker was dealing with the same issue. Her husband was an alcoholic, her son a toddler, and she thought she couldn't afford to walk away from her marriage. But she had worked many years for the company's owners and with their help, was able to leave her husband and buy a small house. I was happy for her, but her example didn't light the way for me. I would have to find my own way.

In early November, The Jonathan Company phone rang, finally. The owner of a chain of convenience stores in Alabama wanted Jonathan to visit and discuss a redesign of their image. Jonathan updated his portfolio, ran blueprints of drawings that demonstrated his abilities, and prepared for a long day on the road. He would leave early in the morning to get through Atlanta traffic, and arrive for his meeting at the client's Birmingham offices by ten. Depending on how the meeting went, I wasn't to expect him home before midnight.

At ten the next day, seated at a desk at school, I imagined him presenting his portfolio, talking about the work he loved. At last, the chance to turn everything around. A big project would mean a deposit and then months of regular invoices.

When I got home—after classes, Todd's baseball practice, dinner, and homework—I checked the studio phone's answering machine for an update. The message light was blinking and in high spirits, I hit the play button. But it wasn't Jonathan.

It was the client in Alabama, asking for Jonathan, asking where was he? *Atlanta traffic must have been worse than he expected*, I thought, and made him late getting to the appointment. I studied for two hours before finally giving up on hearing from him, and went to bed. I slept fitfully, listening for the sound of a car in the driveway, and awoke the next morning to an empty bed. *Where could he be?* my sleep-heavy mind wondered. *Has he been in an accident? Why hasn't he at least called?*

I saw Dane and Todd off to school and went to work. It was Friday, meaning no MBA classes, and I was scheduled to work all day. I couldn't concentrate. I called the studio every thirty minutes, in hopes that Jonathan would answer. At lunchtime, I went home and called the client's office.

"This is Anne Cooper, Jonathan Cooper's wife," I said. "Can you tell me what time he left there yesterday?"

"He never showed up," said the angry voice at the other end of the line. "And you can tell him not to bother."

"But he left here yesterday at five a.m. He never arrived?"

"That's right," the voice said, a little more softly as the implication settled in. "We haven't seen him."

"I'm very sorry," I replied, "thank you." I hung up. *What could have happened? Is he in a hospital somewhere?* Fear gnawed at my empty stomach.

I called the police department of Winder, the closest city I could think of with jurisdiction over Highway 316, which Jonathan would have taken to Atlanta on the way to Birmingham. I asked if there'd been any accidents involving Jonathan Cooper.

"No, he wasn't in an accident," was the response. There was an edge to the reply, a coyness that told me I wasn't getting the full truth.

I tried again. "Can you tell me his whereabouts?"

"I'm not allowed to give out information over the phone," I was told.

More worried than ever, I went back to work. I racked my brain. Who would Jonathan call if he were in trouble, if not me? Never my parents. I could check with neighbors when they got home from work. Who else? Maybe Larry, who used to work for us? I called him.

"Hi Larry, it's Anne Cooper. By any chance, have you heard from Jonathan? He never came home from his business trip yesterday. I'm so worried. I'm calling everyone I can think of."

"He's okay," Larry answered.

"He called you? Where is he? What happened?"

"Anne, he's okay. That's all I can tell you."

"Larry, you've got to tell me what happened. I've been worried sick. I'm going out of my mind."

"He made me swear not to tell you."

"Please, Larry, nothing's as bad as not knowing. Please!"

There was a long pause. Poor Larry.

"He's in jail. He was arrested for DUI. I'm heading to Winder to bail him out. I had to get the title to my house."

"Oh my God." I felt Jonathan's pain and shame. I winked back the tears. I couldn't cry at work. I couldn't tell anyone.

"Look, he's okay. He'll be home this afternoon."

"Thank you, Larry, you're a good friend. I'm sorry to put you through this."

As I hung up the phone, the full weight of Jonathan's arrest crushed me. Not only was he drinking again, he'd blown the best chance we'd had in a long time for earning serious income. Now he faced legal problems, the loss of his driver's license, and fines. I felt betrayed, yet what was I going to do? Leave him? Make him leave? Mentally I ran through the same arguments. He couldn't support himself, never mind pay child support. I didn't earn enough to keep the house. Sell it? Jonathan would never agree to that. Besides, it would never sell in its current condition, not without a new kitchen floor, new carpeting, and painting all the rooms. And how would I get through school?

There was no one I could turn to. No one could know about Jonathan's drinking, the DUI, or our financial troubles. I interacted with lots of people all the time, family, classmates, constituents, co-workers, but without realizing, I had agreed to a code of silence, one enforced by loyalty, shame, and fear. Undeterred, the Universe kept piling on. Each crisis was an opportunity to change my life and to make different choices. Above all, they were an invitation to take a leap of faith. But I didn't see them as such—they were only terrible problems I was ashamed to admit to and hid as best I could. Asking for help from anyone, even my parents, was out of the question. Praying for help was ludicrous and pathetic. I was truly alone.

CHAPTER SEVEN

The Breakup

Jonathan's DUI case was unusual. When the police officer who stopped him asked him to take a Breathalyzer, Jonathan refused, and the officer slapped him across the face. Jonathan didn't have to tell me why—he never backed down, especially when he was in the wrong. I knew the sneering grimace, the smart mouth, the snide, tough-guy posture that taunted his adversary into throwing the first punch.

Jonathan pled no contest to the DUI charge. He received a six-hundred-dollar fine and had his license suspended for six months. I wasn't present at his court hearing, but he believed that getting the police officer to strike him mitigated his sentence.

"Is that supposed to make me feel better?" I asked. "Where are we going to find six hundred dollars?" I wanted to say it was too bad the guy hadn't beat the shit out of him, that maybe it would have cost us less. But I didn't. Jonathan was depressed and contrite, so I didn't rub it in.

That Christmas the boys and I drove up to New Jersey to spend the holidays with the Capone clan. Mom and Dad were already there, visiting friends and relations and spending time with their grandchildren. For me, spending Christmas with my family was an easy way to turn the threadbare and depressing Christmas we would have had in Athens into a season of family togetherness and fun. We stayed at my sister Mary's house. She and her husband Ron had gradually made their home the center of Capone family celebrations after Mom and Dad moved to Georgia. Ron was a successful businessman who never forgot how to have fun. His mantra was, "Whoever dies with the most toys wins." Jason, Dane, and Todd loved staying at Aunt Mary and Uncle Ron's any time of year, but Christmas was the best.

Christmas morning arrived at eight thirty, a not-uncivilized hour, and we all came together in the family room—Grandma and Grandpa, Mary, Ron, and their two children, and Jason, Dane, Todd, and I—to see what Santa had brought. It was truly breathtaking: a mountain of presents not only surrounded the gorgeous two-story tree, but rose halfway up the wall on one side, between the tree and the fireplace. Todd gasped aloud at the sight and murmured, "I wish we lived here."

I flinched, though Todd echoed my own feelings. My three sisters had married well and I wondered what was wrong with me, that I had been so blind, so oblivious, not only to Jonathan's drinking, but also to more practical issues, like his ability to provide for a family. His clothes, his car, his apartment, they had all been clues, and I had ignored them.

Celebrating Christmas with their New Jersey relations diverted the boys from noticing how bad things were between their parents. Jonathan and I still shared a bedroom and a bed, but after his arrest we were barely speaking to each other. It was sad to realize that the boys had gotten so used to Jonathan spending all his waking hours in the studio, they saw no difference in our relationship. Unspoken but clear was the understanding that neither he nor I would tell the boys about his DUI. For him, it was a matter of pride. For me, it was almost the same. I didn't want my sons to be ashamed of their father.

1997 heralded no great changes. Jonathan had gone back to sleeping the greater part of the day, but he did get some small jobs from Dick to keep funds flowing in. As I started the second semester of the MBA program, I held on to the hope that he would stop drinking and that we'd be able to put our life back together. We were down to the one car that I took to school every day—a blessing, as I saw it, because with the suspension of his driver's license and one car between us, Jonathan had no way to go to a liquor store.

The last day of January was a Friday, meaning no classes for me, but all the first-year MBA students were required to attend a seminar on business etiquette at the Athens Country Club. The presenter would teach us the proper way to do all the things we thought we already knew how to do, from shaking hands to eating with the correct fork. I was looking forward to it. That morning, as I was getting ready to leave, Jonathan informed me he needed the car.

"No," I told him. "You've got another four months before you can drive."

"It won't be a problem. No one's going to stop me," he replied.

"What do you need? I'll pick it up this afternoon."

"I can't wait all day for you. Give me the keys and I'll take you to the country club."

Reluctantly, I allowed him to drive me. "I'll need a ride home this afternoon. I'm not sure of the time. I'll call you," I said as I got out of the car. "It'll be after three."

The seminar ended later in the day than I thought; it was four o'clock when I called the studio. No answer. I left a message and waited. Standing at the large window outside the ballroom where our seminar had been held, I watched for the car. After fifteen minutes, I called again. No answer. Then I called the home phone, still no answer. Getting angrier and more frustrated by the minute, I waited. It was after five thirty when I recognized the two-tone gray Caprice my parents had given us coming up the drive. I walked out the front door and into the car as soon as it pulled up.

"Where the hell were you?" I asked as Jonathan began driving away. "I called you over an hour ago!" It took just a few more seconds in that enclosed space with him for me to know the answer.

"I fell asleep," he started to explain.

"Stop the car!" I shouted at him. "Liar! You bastard. You're drunk. I said stop the car!"

"I can drive," he mumbled, but he stopped in the middle of the parking lot.

I jumped out of the car and wrenched open the driver's side door. "Get out. Get out of the car."

He put the car in park, then stepped out. As I got behind the wheel, he got in on the passenger side. "Whassamatter?" he asked innocently. "I overslept."

"You reek, Jonathan. You've been drinking. I can smell it."

We drove the short distance home in silence. I was coming to a decision. As I turned into the driveway, he said, by way of explanation, "When I got up this morning, I decided I was going to drink. I don't know why. I just knew I was."

I got out of the car and watched as he pulled himself out on the opposite side. He waited for me to go past him into the house. I stopped squarely in front of him. "It's over. I'm through with you. *I am done.*"

He looked back at me and said nothing.

"I want a divorce. If I could afford to move out now, I would, but I can't. And you can't. I don't know how you're going to do it, but I'm going to live here another year and you're going to pay for it. And you're going to put me through school. You owe me that."

I walked through the studio and into the house. Seconds later, I returned with The Jonathan Company checkbook and slammed it onto his desk. "Here. It's all yours. I'm opening a separate account. I'll buy the food." I turned and walked back into the house.

That weekend, as the anger subsided, the pain set in. It was not the pain of a broken heart, but the pain of failure. I had sacrificed my dreams for his and given my all, but I had failed. The hard work, the struggles to make ends meet, the anxiety and worry, had led only to betrayal and defeat. Alcohol was the other woman, and I could not compete.

I had loved Jonathan. I had truly believed he'd do anything for me. It was a shock to realize how wrong I'd been, that he would let us go hungry rather than go without a drink. He had lied and stolen from us and nothing he could say, no promise he could make, would ever lead me to believe in him again, in us again.

That night, he found somewhere else to sleep, probably on the sofa in his studio. I didn't care. *He lives there all the time anyway, he might as well sleep there, too.* The boys never even noticed. That was a relief. I wasn't ready to tell them their parents were breaking up. I wasn't ready to tell anyone, not my children, my parents, anyone. I could not see the way ahead. I would just keep my head down and get through one day at a time.

* * *

In March, spring break coincided for Jason, Dane, Todd, and me. Jason and Dane had plans to go to Daytona Beach with a group of friends and Todd, a freshman in high school, begged to go with them. Both Jonathan and I agreed that, turning fifteen at the end of the month, he was too young to go on spring break with guys two to four years older. Jason and Dane were relieved, but Todd was bitterly disappointed.

"You and I will go to Florida together," I said. "We'll go visit Aunt Dolores. We'll have fun, I promise." My great-aunt Dolores, a widow, lived by herself in a small house in Ft. Lauderdale. I knew she would welcome a visit from us. It would be a relief to get away from Jonathan for a time.

Todd and I left for Florida early on a Friday morning. The nine-and-a-half-hour drive to Ft. Lauderdale from Athens was long but doable in a day. Aunt Dee was gracious and enjoyed the company. In her late eighties, she no longer cared for the beach, but Todd and I visited the beach every day and worked on our tans. We also drove over to the Gulf of Mexico, below Ft. Myers, to swim and look for seashells.

The Gulf was a two-hour drive from Ft. Lauderdale, and I used the time to talk with Todd about school. His grades had gone down and I was concerned.

"You're smarter than your grades, Todd. You need to pull them up." He listened, but didn't answer. "Don't you want to go to college?"

"Yeah. But school's so boring." Todd leaned over to the satchel at his feet, pulled out a plastic bag of carrot sticks, and began munching on them.

"You've just got to get through high school so you can do what you want. You need to do better than C's to get into Georgia."

"I know." He squirmed in his seat.

"You never do homework. Or study."

"I do it at school."

"I never had enough time when I was in high school to get all my homework done at school."

No response. I glanced at him; he was staring out the passenger window.

"Look, I can help you with your geometry. It's logic and a lot of memorization. We can practice together.

And let me look over your assignments before you turn them in."

"I can do it myself." He put the bag of carrots back in the bag on the floor.

"Then I want to see some improvement. You're too old to have me ask your teachers to send me your assignments, but I'll do it if I have to."

"Okay, okay!" In frustration, he pushed back the car seat to its farthest reclining position, released it with a snap to vertical, then adjusted it to his liking.

I bit my lip. I wished rather than believed Todd was going to make more of an effort, but said nothing more. We were on vacation. A lecture from Mom wasn't fun for either of us.

When we arrived, we bought sandwiches, chips, grapes, water, and juice for a picnic on the beach. The sun, bright and warm, coaxed us into the water for a swim before lunch. The turquoise-blue Gulf was calm and quiet, like a big bathtub, and we had to wade far away from shore to reach water higher than our waists. When we realized we were hungry, we swam and hiked back to the old brown quilt I'd brought along. The sand, soft and white as baby powder, squeaked and crunched beneath our feet. The salt and sea air turned my ordinary sandwich into savory mouthfuls. The chips tasted saltier, the grapes sweeter, the water fresher, and I, likewise, felt more truly my essential self.

When we finished, we shook the crumbs and sand off the blanket and stretched out to soak up the sun. I didn't bother with my book, but slipped my bathing suit straps off my shoulders and laid next to my golden son.

His hair had never darkened after he was born, but remained a blond halo loosely curling above a high forehead and sky-blue eyes. Todd had every right to be vain about his looks. At home I would often catch him in the upstairs bathroom, staring into the mirror, as if he could figure out who he truly was if he just looked long and deep enough.

After a nap, we hunted seashells. Fascinated by them, we found lots and, after debating on whether to keep them all, we decided to pick through them and take only the best ones back to Georgia.

Todd's birthday followed the week after our return. He always needed clothes and I gave him a pair of jeans, a shirt with a crazy zigzag pattern from JC Penney, and two T-shirts that I'd bought for him while attending the National School Board Association conference in New Orleans. He loved the T-shirts, especially the one with the old-time lamppost and New Orleans logo on the front. He wore them so often I eventually asked him why he didn't wear the other shirt I had bought, the one from Penney's.

"It's ugly," he said.

"No it's not. It'll look good on you," I told him.

"I'm not wearing it," he said. "I hate it."

"Why didn't you say something sooner?" I asked, exasperated. "Now it's too late to return it." I think because they didn't want to hurt my feelings, my sons would never tell me if they didn't like a birthday gift or Christmas present. They just let it remain at the bottom of a drawer until they outgrew it and could send it to the Salvation Army.

Despite our talk over spring break, Todd's grades went from A's in middle school to B's and C's by the end of his freshman year. Concerned, I met with his guidance counselor to discuss his courses for sophomore year. He had taken Algebra I in eighth grade, but from his poor performance in geometry and my own recollection of his struggles in algebra at the end of his eighth-grade year, I believed he hadn't grasped some foundational concepts. I wanted him to take Algebra I again, rather than advance to Algebra II. However, the counselor said that was impossible. Todd couldn't repeat a course he'd already passed, at least not for credit. Did I want him to fall a year behind in his college requirements? Todd also opposed the idea. He wanted to stay in the same classes as his friends. Reluctant and fearful, but recognizing Todd couldn't take the same course twice, I backed down.

On a brighter note, I interviewed and was offered the position of marketing director with a local consulting group, three independent consultants who'd recently formed a partnership. I would work as a paid intern over the summer, then work part-time until I graduated. It seemed the answer to my hopes for the future—a job in Athens, which meant Todd could finish high school without changing schools, and a salary that meant I could support myself and my sons, independent of Jonathan.

The goal for the summer internship was to create a marketing plan for the new consulting group. I started with a series of questions for the partners about the services they offered, the clients they served, and their vision for the firm. Getting no answers, I struggled to find a core message for the company, and quit at the end of the summer, defeated and frustrated, feeling as if I'd wasted my time and their money.

Frustration and defeat stalked my efforts on the Clarke County School Board as well. The first one-penny local sales tax had been approved by Athens voters that March, which made possible the start of major school construction projects, including a new Cedar Shoals High School and major renovations to Clarke Central High. A local architect and educator showed me his proposal for a renovated Cedar Shoals, a proposal that could save a great deal of money. I argued for exploring his ideas, but found no support among my fellow board members.

Looking back, I can see that there were many social and emotional factors involved that I never considered. The eastside had been predominantly black when Cedar Shoals was originally built, so its construction was second-rate from the very start. As it aged, poor ventilation, insulation, roofing, and heating and cooling systems made many of the classrooms toxic. Since then, white families had moved into new eastside neighborhoods and found the conditions that had historically been considered acceptable for black kids intolerable. They weren't interested in logic, or making the best use of school funds. Emotion was the key factor and I was stuck in my head, thinking instead of feeling.

Another source of frustration was the dishonesty of my life at home. After six months, I was ready to tell everyone, including the boys, that their father and I were going to divorce. Jonathan was opposed, but I insisted that we set a time to sit down and tell the boys. We agreed on mid-August, before Jason went back to Emory.

We got together early on a Saturday afternoon in the family room. Jonathan sat on the long sofa against the windows and I took the shorter one perpendicular to it. The boys stretched out on the carpet at varying angles at our feet. I recall thinking that Todd's legs had gotten as long as his brothers', and could see they had no idea what was coming. A glance at Jonathan told me he wasn't going to start.

"You may not have noticed," I said, "but your father and I haven't been speaking to each other much or sleeping in the same bedroom. We've been pretty unhappy with each other for a long time." I took a deep breath. "We've decided to get a divorce."

Shock spread across the boys' faces. A tear slid down the side of Dane's face to his ear. Todd covered his eyes with his arms, as did Jason. I waited for them to say something.

Jonathan spoke up instead. "Your mother wants a divorce. I don't."

I could scarcely believe my ears. I wanted to scream at him, *Bastard! You're making this my fault? It's your fault!* I kept silent, but fury burned my throat.

Jason got up to his feet. "Come on, Dane, let's go for a ride."

Dane sat up, looked over to his younger brother and said, "Todd, want to come with us?" Todd nodded, and he and Dane silently followed Jason out. I was so grateful that Dane had included Todd—that at this, of all times, the three of them were together. I wiped my eyes. Jonathan went back to his studio.

Over the next few weeks, I found time to be alone with each boy to tell him in greater detail why I wanted a divorce. I gave them the long version about why Jonathan drank, about their father's terrible childhood, his alcoholic parents, his first marriage, and the death of his daughter. Each listened quietly, but when I got to the present, about why I wanted out, each one said he didn't want to hear anymore. In their way, each boy said he didn't want to take sides and didn't want me to put him in the middle. Even Todd, whose feelings toward his father ranged from irritation to anger, wouldn't hear me out.

I told my parents, brothers, and sisters. They were surprised, too, even Mom and Dad. Jonathan hadn't set foot in their house for two years, but they still sent dinner home for him every Sunday night. Everyone believed our marriage to be rock solid, despite our financial woes. Moreover, they had accepted Jonathan as one of the family and didn't want their relationship with him to end. I didn't ask them to choose. There was no loyalty test. I didn't want it to get ugly. He and I still had to live together for another year.

* * *

September and a new school year felt like a fresh start. Jason was back at Emory, Dane was a senior, Todd, a sophomore, and I, a second-year MBA student. I was fortunate enough to receive a graduate assistantship at the end of my first year, which reduced my tuition to fifty dollars and paid a monthly stipend for thirteen hours of work per week. Not only did I keep food on the table but I also made it easier for Jonathan to pay for my schooling and keep a roof over our heads. Doing our 1997 tax return in January, I had to laugh at the irony of my situation—feeling proud that I had earned more that year as a full-time student than he had as a full-time designer.

That fall, in addition to my own studies, I tried to tutor Todd in algebra. Algebra was easy, so long as you followed the logical hierarchy of its laws. They would lead you, step by step, to the answer. But I couldn't get Todd to understand that. He lost patience and became frustrated, especially when I tried to lead him through a problem by asking questions. Gradually, he stopped doing homework at home, and I, too busy to notice, lost track of his progress, confident that my sons were good students and would ask for help when they needed it.

Todd's friendship with two girls in his group of friends had become important to him. I could see his face light up whenever they called. Over the summer, Jenny and Emily would call to invite him to one or the other's house, and I'd drive him there to spend the afternoon. I couldn't tell which one he liked better. Like Jason and Dane, Todd never talked with me about girls, what was happening at school, or what the gossip was. I had to rely on getting that kind of information about Jason and Dane from our neighbor's daughter, but for Todd, I had no one his age to keep me in the loop.

I was curious to find out whom Todd would take to Clarke Central's homecoming dance in November. My heart ached for him when he told me Emily had turned him down. He was disappointed and confused, especially because she urged him to ask a friend of hers, who wasn't Jenny, to the dance instead. Ultimately he did as Emily asked, but his heart wasn't in it.

After chauffeuring Todd and his date, just as I was getting into bed, Jonathan came up to my room.

"Dane just called. He's in the county jail," he informed me. "He's been arrested for underage possession."

"Dane?" I said, aghast.

"I'm going to bail him out. Do you want to come with me?" Jonathan had gotten his license back and was driving again.

I threw on some clothes, raced downstairs, and got in the car. "How did it happen?" I asked as he backed out of the driveway.

"I don't know. I told him not to say or sign anything, to wait for us."

It took twenty minutes to drive across town to the jail. I waited in the car while Jonathan went in to get Dane. Sitting in the dark, I agonized over the plague that alcohol had become for the Coopers. Dane had never been in trouble before. He and his friends, as far as I was aware, didn't drink. He was always home by midnight and had never been intoxicated. While I suspected there'd been some partying involving alcohol on their spring break trip, he had never given me any reason to be concerned. I was so naïve.

Thirty minutes later, he and Jonathan emerged from the jail and got into the car. Dane's eyes were red from crying. I waited for him to speak.

"I'm sorry, Mom. I was so stupid."

"I thought you were going to the dance. What happened?"

"A bunch of us put our money together to rent a room at Howard Johnson's for a party. David and I were in charge of buying the beer. We were carrying the cases to the room when the cops caught us."

"You were the only ones arrested?"

"Everybody else ran, we couldn't. We were loaded down."

"I thought you had better sense than that!"

"I said I was stupid! The cops were laughing at us. They said they catch kids every year."

Dane was humiliated and obviously angry with himself. I said no more to him that night. He felt just enough betrayed by his friends that I suspected being grounded was a relief to him.

His arrest was my introduction to the Athens legal system. It had a specially designed program for underage kids arrested for alcohol possession. This pretrial diversion program kept many hundreds of UGA and local high school students moving through the system without clogging up the courts. It also gave offenders an incentive to never break the underage possession law again. Offenders agreed to six months' probation, underwent random drug and alcohol testing, and paid a fee, and if they stayed out of trouble until they turned twenty-one, their record would be expunged. At the time of Dane's arrest, the program was run through a private probation service. Today it's much improved, run directly by the local government, and requires an alcohol education course and community service.

* * *

As the year neared its end, I was happy to see that Todd had a new friend from school he enjoyed hanging out with. He and Todd frequently spent weekends together, and slept over at one or the other's house on Friday nights. One Friday night stands out. Around eleven that night, the two of them decided to take a walk to the community's lake. It was a beautiful night, and at the time I thought nothing of it. When they came back, they were laughing and silly, enough that I took note. Did they smoke pot on their walk to the lake? They were home safe and in bed soon after. No harm done, I thought, so I didn't ask them about it, an omission for which I will always reproach myself.

CHAPTER EIGHT

The Decline

Work boots. That's all I remember about our Christmas in 1997, that Todd wanted work boots. Everyone was wearing them at school, and he wanted a pair, too. We went shopping together and found a beautiful pair at Charbon's, a sporting goods store in Athens. They were soft, brandy-colored leather, and he loved them. He proudly wore them to school on the first day back after the holiday break. But he came home in his stocking feet.

"Where are your boots?" I asked when he came into the house.

"Somebody stole them out of my gym locker," he said.

"Stole your boots?" I could hardly believe it. "Did you report it? Did you go to the principal?"

"No."

"Then I'm going to call," I said, outraged.

"There's no point. They're not going to do anything."

I did call, and Todd was right. At that time, the high school was so poorly run, teachers locked their doors once the bell rang so that kids roaming the halls couldn't barge in and disrupt class. The new principal, coming from a rural school district, had no idea how to manage an urban high school with demoralized teachers, pot-smoking in the bathrooms, poor race relations, and no discipline. His solution to the morale and discipline problems was having the main hall repainted in the school colors. He really believed that better school spirit was the way to change behavior.

I was so angry. I was a member of the county's board of education, and I couldn't help my own son. If high school had been a haven instead of a zoo, would Todd have made different choices? I avoid the question even today. Blame serves no one. At the time, I was furious with everyone in charge, more so because Todd was so sad and bitter about the theft of his new boots. I offered to buy him a new pair, but he said no, he didn't want them, there was no point.

From that time on, after he got home from school, Todd would lay down on the couch in the family room and go to sleep or play Nintendo. Every day, week after week. I couldn't understand the change in his behavior, why suddenly he had no energy and could find no joy.

"Don't you have homework to do?" I'd ask.

"I don't have any."

Soon I received a note from his history teacher, saying Todd was sleeping through class. Alarmed, I asked him about it as he sat Indian-style in front of the television, playing a video game.

"Todd, your history teacher says you're sleeping in class."

"Yeah, he's so boring. I can't keep my eyes open." He clicked furiously on the controller.

"You can't do that. How do you think you're going to pass?"

He shrugged.

"Pause that thing, will you?" He froze the game and turned around to face me. "Isn't history your first-period class? How can you be so sleepy first thing in the morning?"

"I told you. He just goes on and on. It would put anybody to sleep."

"Maybe the three of us should sit down and talk. To find a way to make it more interesting for you."

"Nooo! That's too embarrassing."

"Then I'll go by myself."

"No, I'll do better. I will." He ran his hands through his hair, then squeezed his temples with the palms of his hands as he looked me in the eye.

"And I want to see you doing homework," I said. "I had homework every night when I was in high school. I don't believe you don't have any."

"Okay."

"I mean it, Todd."

"Okay!" He turned back to the TV and worked the controller ferociously.

Todd had never done poorly in school before high school. When having trouble with a subject, he asked me for help. He knew he had only to ask. I had all the con-

fidence of a mother who had never encountered a problem she couldn't solve for her child.

But when I saw his midterm grades, I learned history wasn't the only problem subject. A "C" in history was
disappointing, but he was failing geometry. It was time
for a showdown, all the more so because he still never
did homework, and was sleeping every afternoon when
he got home. When I questioned him, the answer was
always the same.

"I did it at school."

"Let me see it."

"It's in my locker."

And I believed him. I wanted to believe him. I
trusted him. I'd never had any reason to think he would
lie to me. But something was out of whack. His sleeping reminded me of his father's sleeping. Was Todd depressed? He'd had a tremendous growth spurt—he was
at least five inches taller than he was six months before—
and was obviously going through puberty. His voice had
deepened noticeably. Perhaps hormones and growth had
overtaxed his body. I was worried about him and told
him so.

"Leave me alone. I'm fine," he answered. I was
standing over him—he was lying on his side on the
couch, his face toward the pillows.

"Todd, look at me." He didn't. "We can't go on like
this. You've got to make an effort." No response.

I walked up the three steps from the family room to
the kitchen and watched him as I began preparing dinner, racking my brain to understand what the problem
might be and how I could help him. He still lay with his

back to me on the sofa, and I tried desperately to fathom what was going on in his head.

Suddenly he sat up and shouted, "Get out of my brain!"

I jumped, I was so startled. He'd frightened me. It was if he were reading my mind as I tried to read his. How did he know?

He didn't care about anything, had no drive or interest in anything. The only thing I could think to do was make an appointment with our family doctor, who prescribed the antidepressant Wellbutrin for him.

* * *

Spring semester of 1998 was so different from the previous year. Todd had passed all his classes his freshman year, but the outlook for his sophomore year appeared grim. It looked to me like he was going to have to repeat it. Together, Todd and I planned to catch up with some of his schoolwork during spring break. If he could make some progress, perhaps he'd feel better about himself. His sixteenth birthday, March 27, was at the end of the week, and I'd promised to take him and Ryan to Six Flags if he made progress on his assignments. But he couldn't. It was as if everything he read were in a foreign language; he comprehended none of it.

Despite our efforts, Todd was at the same place at the end of the week as when he started. Yet I couldn't bear to cancel our trip to Six Flags and see him disappointed and sad about one more thing. So on Friday morning, we picked up Ryan from his house, then stopped at Publix to get some discount tickets I'd seen there. Fortunately or unfortunately, we learned from the tickets that Six

Flags wouldn't open for another month. Scrambling to come up with something else to do with two teens, I remembered a rafting company on the Broad River about forty minutes away. My two disappointed companions brightened up. Agreed, we would go rafting!

I had rafted on the Broad once before. A few rapids, nothing serious, just enough to make the trip exciting. We rented three kayaks, donned our life vests, and began paddling downstream.

The river wasn't deep. Once, we had to stand up and carry our kayaks across the rocks. But there were still a few challenging areas. Todd and Ryan both got turned around in a patch of whitewater and struggled to keep their kayaks afloat. I yelled for them to head for shore, paddled to the riverbank, got out of my kayak, and waded into the water to help them. Todd made it out of the churning water and we dragged his boat to shore. Ryan, however, had abandoned ship and was swimming over to us. Three experienced kayakers who saw our distress wrestled Ryan's kayak to the surface, emptied it, and returned it to the cheering and grateful trio of soggy amateurs onshore.

We put our kayaks back in the water downstream from the whitewater. Ten minutes brought us to the spot where we were to go ashore and ride the bus back to our starting point. Towels waited for us in the car. We dried off, wrapped them around ourselves, and headed back to Athens with the car heater blasting. I stopped for a late-afternoon snack of hamburgers and fries before taking Ryan home.

"I wish I stuck with soccer," Todd confided as we drove home. "Ryan and Chip are on the same team with a bunch of kids from school."

"Do you want to get back into it?" I asked.

"I can't. They're so much better than me."

"You can still go to their games and hang out. I'll take you if you like."

"Yeah, I guess."

He never brought it up again, and remained as disengaged and depressed as ever. Searching for a clue, any clue, it occurred to me that he might be smoking pot. I believed he would tell me the truth if I asked him.

"Todd, help me understand what's wrong. What has happened?"

"Nothing. I don't want to talk about it."

"But you have to. Don't you want to feel better?"

"I said I don't want to talk about it. Leave me alone."

"I can't. I'm your mother."

"Do you think I'm gay?"

"No. Do you?" While I'd managed to answer quickly, his question came out of left field. Perhaps something had happened that had him questioning his sexuality? "Your body's going through a lot of changes now. It's normal to feel confused and to have a lot of urges."

"Yeah."

"What's bothering you?"

"Nothing, I'm fine."

"Todd, tell me something. I want the truth. Do you smoke pot? Have you been getting high at school?"

He wouldn't look me in the eye. "Yeah."

"Do you see what it's doing to you? How you're hurting yourself? It's no wonder you can't get ahead in your classes."

No answer.

"Todd, you have to promise me. This has to stop."

"Yeah, okay."

His tepid agreement gave me little confidence. I started calling therapists who worked with young people with substance-abuse issues. When they learned that Todd was under eighteen, many said they couldn't work with him. Others had a full caseload. I was referred by one to a therapist she believed would work with Todd. I called and made an appointment in mid-April.

I picked Todd up from school and took him to the therapist's office, barely a block away from Clarke Central. Of course he didn't want to go. But I felt he needed a man to talk to. Todd and Jonathan didn't get along well enough that I could count on him confiding in his father, and I suspected that Todd wasn't telling me the full story either. Perhaps he'd confide in an outside third party.

Todd began therapy appointments once a week. I participated in many of them, and could see how difficult a client my son was. He didn't want to be there, and didn't want to talk. Perhaps he was different when I wasn't there, but it was obvious that his therapist had a challenge in front of him.

One afternoon toward the end of April, I arrived home from class and walked into the kitchen. There, in place of the old refrigerator, stood a brand-new stainless steel one. Food from the old refrigerator had been left on the kitchen table, and the kitchen was a mess. Cursing Jonathan even as I wondered why he wasn't in his studio, I started cleaning up. I heard a car in the driveway and figured that was him, and primed myself to blast him for wasting money to replace a refrigerator that had been working fine. Of all the things to spend money on!

But it was Jason. At the end of fall semester, my oldest had concluded that Emory wasn't the right school for him and transferred to UGA. He was living at home again.

"Dad asked me to take him to the emergency room," he said. "They're admitting him. They don't know what's wrong. I've got to pack a bag for him."

Surprised, I stopped washing dishes and dried my hands, feeling guilty that I hadn't been home to take Jonathan myself, guilty that I didn't care more about him being sick. "I'll help you," I said, and walked past him to go upstairs. That's when I saw the stairs were strewn with vomit. Rationally, I knew Jonathan must have been too sick to clean up his mess, but at that moment I couldn't be rational. Feeling used, repulsed, and angry, I threw underwear, a robe, his shaving kit, and a toothbrush into a bag and picked my way back down the stairs. "Here." I handed the bag to Jason.

"Are you coming?"

"No."

Without another question, he left to take Jonathan his things.

* * *

When Todd arrived home from school, I explained what had happened. He stood in the kitchen and said nothing. I approached him and said, "Todd, let's get out of here. It's Friday night. We deserve to have some fun." I hugged him, but he didn't hug me back, just stood there, empty and spiritless. He had gotten so tall, I couldn't reach his face to touch my cheek to his, and he didn't bend down. His eyes had a glassy, faraway look. I fought tears and held him closer, as if that were the way to reach him.

"Do you feel like Mexican?" I asked, blinking to absorb the threatening tears. I pressed my cheek against his chest and waited.

"Okay."

"And then we can go to the movies. *Out of Sight* is playing at the campus theatre. I really want to see it. I think you'll like it—cops and robbers, sort of. It got great reviews." I let him go and looked up to his face.

"Okay," he repeated with a shrug.

We had dinner together. I told him about my plans for the two of us to move into an apartment after graduation and I found a job, how things would be better once we were on our own. He said nothing. When it was time for the movie, I paid our check and drove over to UGA's Student Center. As we walked into the theatre, Todd said, "I'm not sitting with you."

"Fine, you can sit wherever you want." *So he doesn't want to sit with his mom on a Friday night with college students all around,* I told myself, but it hurt nonetheless. I took an aisle seat and watched him walk farther down to find a seat in the center, then disappear.

The movie was great fun. While the credits rolled, I sat and waited for him to find me. He looked somewhat shamefaced as he approached and said apologetically, "Good movie."

"Yeah, George Clooney was terrific. Not bad to look at either. You hungry? Want some Dairy Queen?"

"Can I get a Blizzard?"

"Whatever your little heart desires!" I teased in a singsong voice, a rare lightness in my heart. All three sons were then going through their Oreo Blizzard phase. It made me happy that Todd was emulating his big brothers. I hoped he would do more of it.

Back at home, we both went straight to bed. I left the vomit on the stairs, unable to bring myself to clean it up. It felt too demeaning, and I waited to see if Jonathan would clean it up after he came home. He never did. I let it sit there for several weeks, until it dried completely. Eventually I vacuumed it up so I wouldn't have to look at it. If only I could make the rest of my troubles disappear as easily.

CHAPTER NINE

The Last Months

Jonathan remained in the hospital over the week-end. Early Monday morning before class, I went there to visit him. On the walk from the parking deck, I met Dr. Johnson, our family physician. He seemed to understand what I was going through without my even saying. "How are you holding up?" he asked.

"I'm hanging in. Have you figured out what's wrong with him?"

"Not sure," he replied. "It's some form of blood poisoning, maybe a spider bite."

"When will he be able to go home?"

"Later today perhaps, if his bloodwork looks okay."

I thanked him and went on to the hospital. I received dirty looks from the nurses as I entered. Jonathan was deep into playing the role of the charming, long-suffering patient. I had been cast as the wife who couldn't be bothered to visit. I asked him how he felt, without a note of sympathy in my voice.

"Better, thanks. I should be able to get out of here today."

"What time? I've got class until two."

"Jason's coming to take me home."

"Okay. Well, I've got to go or I'll be late."

I escaped. Classes were winding down, exams were looming, and I had a project to finish. Todd had a therapy appointment after school, too, and I wanted to be there. That evening, with Jonathan home, I kept dinner light, soup and toast, a salad.

The next morning, I awoke with a headache so fierce I could barely see. It made me nauseous. I drove to Dr. Johnson's office without an appointment and begged to be squeezed in. I must have looked terrible, because a nurse took me to a room right away, made me lie down, put a cold compress on my head, and turned off all the lights. I was there for a long time, I never knew how long. But when Dr. Johnson came into the room, I was able to sit up.

"How are you doing?"

"Better, I think. I've a bit of a headache left, around the edges."

"That was a migraine. Have you ever had one before?"

"Only once, years ago, and it went away after a few hours."

"Well, this should do the same. Have you been under some stress lately?" He smiled. Neither of us needed to mention Jonathan or Todd to know what we were talking about.

"Oh, just a little." I smiled back wanly. "I've just got to make it through exams."

"I think we can help you with that. I'm going to prescribe an antidepressant, very mild, for thirty days. We'll see how you do, okay?"

"Okay. I don't want to go through this again." I stood up and straightened my clothes. "Thanks for seeing me today."

"Absolutely. Take care of yourself." A great bear of a man himself, Dr. Johnson wrapped his arms around me in a mighty bear hug. Healing energy, strong and caring, flowed into me, and tears came to my eyes. *Yes, somehow I'll get through this*, I told myself.

"Thanks, I needed that." I hoped he could see how much I meant it, and how grateful I was. Later that same week, I stopped to buy a thank-you card and, serendipitously, came across a whimsical little paperback, *The Hug Therapy Book*, complete with illustrations of hugging bears. I dropped it off at his office with a note.

* * *

Graduation cards from my brothers and sisters started arriving at the house, including a present from my sister Edna, a print on wood. It was an abstract painting of a woman with a poem by Jayne Relaford Brown beneath. "Finding Her Here" told of all my soul's hopes for the future, beyond its present sorrows. I read it often that summer.

> I am becoming the woman I've wanted,
> grey at the temples,
> soft body, delighted,
> cracked up by life

with a laugh that's known bitter
but, past it, got better,
knows she's a survivor—
that whatever comes,
she can outlast it.
I am becoming a deep
weathered basket.[1]

Yes, I would survive; I was becoming the woman I wanted, in spite of everything. Two momentous years of investment in myself were coming to a close. It was time for me to launch into a new life and a new career, but I had scarcely given it any thought. One day at a time had landed me at graduation, without a job. I would figure that part out over the summer, I promised myself.

Shannon, a friend I'd made in the MBA program, invited the boys and me to lunch with her mother and cousin before the graduation ceremony. I was proud to accept and show off my handsome sons, touched that Jason and Dane had taken time off from work to attend, and that even Todd was enthusiastic and happy for me. After lunch, the four of us met my parents at the Performing Arts Center, where graduation was held. As my name was called and I walked across the stage, my three boys cheered and waved wildly from the front row of the balcony. I had earned my MBA.

Dane was graduating, too, and two weeks later, I had the pleasure of personally handing him his diploma at Clarke Central's graduation ceremony—a perk of being on the school board. He was thrilled to have been accepted into the University of Georgia and, eager to live on his own, made plans to move into a rental house with two friends before the end of May.

Todd, on the other hand, failed to thrive. He hadn't passed Algebra II and would have to go to summer school if he didn't want to repeat it in the fall. I hesitated to send him. A complete break from school might be more therapeutic, I thought, but he wanted to go. To him, it was better than the embarrassment of repeating the course while his friends moved on. Mom and Dad helped me pay for it, and he started class at the beginning of June.

One night just before summer school started, I was in bed, asleep, when I felt a presence in my room. I opened my eyes to see Todd standing at the foot of the bed.

"Todd? Todd, what's the matter, honey?"

"I'm scared."

I sat up, stood on my knees in front of him, and wrapped my arms around him. He was trembling. "Did you have a bad dream?"

"I think I'm going to die."

Fear crawled through me. I replied to reassure us both. "But think about it, Todd. How is that even possible? You're strong and healthy. Nothing's wrong with you."

"I'm scared. I think I'm going to die," he repeated.

I tried again. "You're not sick … you're strong and healthy. The only way you could die is if you did something to your—" Horrified, I stopped short. "Todd, you wouldn't hurt yourself, would you? … Todd?"

"I'm scared."

I held him tight, rocked him from side to side in my arms. "I'm here, honey. Tell me what's wrong. Please." I kissed his cheek, then pressed mine to his. We stayed there for a long time. He said nothing more.

"Let's go downstairs and talk to Dad." I threw on my robe, drew him to the stairs, and walked down to the studio with him. The lights were still on and Jonathan was seated at his desk. "Jonathan, Todd can't sleep. He's having bad dreams. About dying even."

Jonathan saw my fear, got up from his chair and put his arm around Todd's shoulders. "Want to tell your old man about it?" He nodded to me to leave and I went back into the house, confident that Jonathan would rise to the occasion with the compassion and understanding I knew he was capable of. He and Todd irritated each other on the petty, everyday level, but this, we both knew, was different. He loved his son and would do his best to comfort him.

Sleep was impossible now. I turned off the light and waited in the dark, listening. Finally, I heard the creak of the stairs. I sat up and saw Jonathan and Todd turn down the hall to Todd's room. Moments later, Jonathan stood at my door. "He should be able to sleep now. We ended up going for a walk around the neighborhood. He had a lot of nervous energy. He needed to walk it off."

"What did he say? Did he tell you what's wrong?"

"Not really. Look, I'm tired. Let's talk in the morning." He turned and walked downstairs. But in the morning, he had nothing to add. If Todd had confided in him, he wasn't sharing it with me.

A week later Todd started summer school. I flew to Indiana to a weekend conference on education featuring Eli Goldratt, the business guru and originator of the theory of constraints. Searching for my way forward in a career, I was interested in how the processes he developed intersected with education. On Friday night, Jonathan called me at the hotel.

"It's me. I had to pick Todd up from school today. Actually from the therapist's office."

"But his appointment isn't until Tuesday."

"He ran out of school after lunch, straight to the therapist's. He wasn't there, so they called me to come get him. I was driving home and he physically attacked me. I had to pull into a parking lot. We practically got into a fistfight. I was ready to call the cops."

"He attacked you? For no reason?"

"For no reason. Anne, I'm telling you, if he does it again, I am calling the police."

"Where is he now?"

"He's quiet, watching TV."

"Look, I'll be home sometime after lunch tomorrow. Thank God it's Friday. We'll have to talk about whether he should go back to school on Monday."

When I got home and tried to talk with Todd, he was sullen and defensive. Not even he understood his behavior.

"What made you run away from school?" I said. He shrugged his shoulders. "Did you smoke pot? Is that why you ran to the therapist's?"

"I just had to get out of there."

"And when Dad came to get you? Why did you start hitting him? While he was driving?"

"I don't know."

That weekend, my mind closed around Jonathan and Todd's relationship and wouldn't let go. What was behind their antipathy toward each other? There was no actual cause I'd ever witnessed. It had simply always been there. Mentally, I began taking inventory of their relationship, and recalled Todd's infancy, a baby with an eye patch, wearing glasses, the surgery. Poor little guy, born with a crossed eye.

And then it hit me. A crossed eye! What was a crossed eye to Jonathan? Nothing less than the sign of death, the first sign that his baby daughter Ryder had a brain tumor. Undoubtedly, she'd had surgery as a baby—as had Todd—and he'd been so sick afterward, crying and retching. Poor Todd was a living reminder of all Jonathan's pain and grief. So dangerous to admit to loving him!

And Todd, so sensitive to the feelings of all around him, instinctively felt the rejection. And was angry, so angry.

When I broached the subject with Jonathan, he belittled my theory and refused to discuss it.

Together, however, we did talk with Todd about whether he should go to school again on Monday. Faced with the choice of finishing summer school or repeating algebra class in the fall, Todd chose summer school. He'd try.

On Tuesday, at Todd's appointment, I talked alone with his therapist about my theory of the crossed eye and

Todd and Jonathan's relationship. The therapist thought my insight significant, and that a family session might be helpful for everyone, not just Todd.

I asked Jonathan, Jason, and Dane to go with Todd and me to his next appointment. No one wanted to. Todd was the one with the problem, not them. Why did they have to be there? But I wouldn't let them off the hook and, reluctantly, they agreed to show up.

It was a disaster. Everyone was angry, no one would talk, and I left feeling hopeless, helpless, and alone. Soon after, I was called into school for a meeting with Todd's teacher and the summer school's principal. They described Todd's bizarre classroom behavior, laughing at a student because, he said, she had the head of a chicken, then perching on a desk and crowing like a rooster. Mortified, I agreed that summer school wasn't the place for him and pulled him out.

When I told Todd's therapist of his crazy behavior, he wanted Todd to have tests done—blood and urine— and recommended a doctor, a specialist in substance-abuse treatment. I expected the tests to show THC in his blood. However, the results were negative. There were no drugs in his system, which puzzled me no end. The doctor prescribed Risperdal for him, an antipsychotic. An antipsychotic? I thought, but desperate for something, anything that might help him, I ignored the implications.

Looking back, I'm ashamed that I didn't push for a clear diagnosis of Todd's illness. But he confused me. Whatever he did in front of others, he never did in front of me. With me he was always on his best behavior, rational and in control of himself. And I was desperate to believe that, whatever was wrong, it was temporary and something we could heal together.

Home was not a good place for him. Dane wasn't living there, Jason was gone most of the time, working or in class, and Jonathan and I interacted only when we had to. Knowing that my parents were driving up to New Jersey for the middle school graduation of their oldest granddaughter, I asked them to take Todd with them. He loved visiting all the family in New Jersey. Perhaps being there, he would feel lighter and recapture his capacity to feel happiness again. He would be around my brothers and brothers-in-law, which would only do him good, and he enjoyed his cousins. Mom and Dad agreed without the slightest hesitation, and hearing of their arrival in New Jersey without incident was a relief. Everyone in my family was glad to see him. They knew about his problems and welcomed him even more enthusiastically.

Midway through the visit, my sister Mary called to tell me that Todd had asked her daughter Carla to smoke pot with him.

"Oh Mary, I'm so sorry. I don't know how he's getting it. He doesn't have any money. Somebody must be giving it to him."

Mary answered, "We had a long talk. I told him about how I'm trying to raise my children and asked him to respect that. I don't think he'll do it again."

"I'm so glad Carla told you about it. You should be proud of her."

"Carla and I are close. She tells me everything. She's worried about Todd, too. Anne, he talks as if his life is over. I'm worried about him."

"What do you mean?" I pictured Todd in front of me, standing in the dark at the foot of my bed.

"He talks about things he wished he'd done, as if his life were over. Like playing soccer. He told me a lot of his friends play in an advanced league, and he says he's not good enough. I told him, 'Todd, you're only sixteen, you have your whole life ahead of you,' but he feels like it's too late."

"He's said things like that to me, too," I admitted. "Mary, I don't know how to help him."

"Don't say anything to him that I called you. We had a good talk and I don't want him to think I told on him."

"Of course," I agreed.

Were Todd's problems purely emotional? Psychological? Physical? What was the root cause of his depression? What had made him lose hope? The divorce? Being poor? No matter where I was or what I was doing, my mind was working on that puzzle.

* * *

Todd returned home at the end of July without any noticeable improvement in his spirits. However, he wanted a part-time job. He'd taken it into his head to work at a carwash where some of Jason and Dane's friends worked. He thought he could start by helping dry cars as they rolled off the line, for tips to start, and then get hired. Thrilled to see him take a positive step, I agreed to drive him back and forth. On the third day, he called me early to take him home. He would tell me only that the guys there were jerks and that he quit.

Failure, loneliness, and disappointment stalked him and, through him, me. I didn't know what to do. He started school again this month, August, and I was afraid to send him back to Clarke Central. The school was a zoo, and Todd needed order. And peace, so he could think straight. *Should I homeschool him?* I wondered. *But then how can I find a job and go to work?* I hadn't changed my mind about the divorce. Todd and I both needed a new start. But how could we do that if I weren't working?

I talked with him about going back to Clarke Central and my fears that he would smoke pot again. He told me what I wanted to hear, that he wouldn't smoke, that he would pay attention in class, that he wanted to go back and be with his friends. Seated together at the kitchen table, I had him make a list of goals and he wrote them out on a piece of loose-leaf paper.

1. Graduate in the year 2000.
2. Get a good job.
3. Have fun with friends.
4. Get a car.
5. Get a girlfriend.
6. Move out.
7. Make A's.
8. Make tips.
9. Get laid.
10. Win in *Goldeneye* (a video game).

Then I asked him what things would keep him from reaching his number-one goal, graduating. He thought a minute, then said, "Distractions."

"Like what? I asked.

"Not being able to focus on schoolwork."

"But what are the things that keep you from focusing?"

"Goofing around. Having fun with friends. I miss the starting point in class and then don't understand the rest of the time."

"Okay, then. Let's make a list of the things you need to do instead. What do you need to do to make good grades in your classes?"

He thought for a few moments, then said, "Pay attention."

"Good start. What else?" We ended up with another list.

1. Pay attention.
2. Bring paper and pencil to class.
3. Take notes.
4. Do homework.
5. Ask for help when I need it.
6. Study for tests.

I think he wanted to do these things, but as school began there was a weariness, too, of going through the motions of living, that was too terrifying for me to acknowledge. Instead, I drove him to school every day, feared for him every day, and halfheartedly began looking for a job.

In September, a former professor helped me get an interview with a local Athens manufacturer. I would have taken anything to be able to move out of the house and afford an apartment for Todd and myself, but it wasn't a good fit for me or them. I never heard back from them, but by the time I should have gotten a response, I was too distracted to ever follow up.

The night after my interview, I'd just gone to bed when Jonathan came up to my room.

"Anne, I think I'm having a heart attack. I need to go to emergency."

I quickly dressed and took him to the hospital, where they performed an electrocardiogram. No evidence of a heart attack, but the cardiologist on call wanted him back at six in the morning for a stress test. He told Jonathan not to eat or drink anything in the meantime.

No sooner had they started the stress test than they halted it. More tests showed almost complete blockage of all five arteries. They scheduled Jonathan for an immediate quintuple bypass. Fortunately, he hadn't actually suffered a heart attack; they'd caught him in time, and the cardiologist said his prognosis was excellent.

The surgery would take at least five hours, and both Jonathan and the cardiologist urged me to not wait at the hospital. The surgeon's office would call when the surgery was over to update me, and I could see him in intensive care the next day.

I visited him every day until he was out of intensive care, then alternated visits with the boys. He tired easily, so visits weren't long. It hurt to look at him and I pitied him, but it was hard for me to sympathize and I reproached myself. How could I be so heartless?

While his father was in the hospital recovering, I took Todd to a concert. The University of Georgia Symphony Orchestra was going to perform Beethoven's Fifth Symphony, and I wanted Todd to experience it. On the way to the concert, I explained the Fifth's famous four-note motif and how it appeared in every movement. As we sat in the hall, I told him about Beethoven's unhappy life and how he struggled with deafness and depression even as he tried to write and perform his music. Todd was interested in spite of himself, so I described how the music begins in darkness and gloom and ends in glorious light and joy. I challenged him to listen for it.

At the beginning of the third movement, Todd must have been tapping his foot to the beat against the chair in front of him. The woman seated there abruptly turned around, glared at him, and whispered nastily, "Would you stop?"

Todd turned red and sat up in his seat. I laid my hand on his knee and squeezed it, and whispered, "Just ignore her." I looked daggers at the back of the old woman's head. *Can't my son ever have a moment of pure enjoyment?*

Jonathan was in the hospital for ten days and while he was gone, I moved out of the master bedroom and into Dane's old room so Jonathan would have a real bed for his recovery, rather than the sofa in his studio. His cardiologist prescribed complete bed rest for at least three weeks, and told us that full recovery would take longer, six to eight.

Having surrendered all family and company finances to Jonathan more than a year and a half before, I never attempted to calculate his medical expenses. We had dropped our health insurance years before. I didn't want to know how many months behind we were with mortgage payments. I refused to worry about money.

I had enough to worry about. I picked Todd up from school every afternoon, grateful the two of us had made it through another day. I was living day to day, and all I cared about was Todd.

CHAPTER TEN

The End

Jonathan was out of bed and spending at least half of each day in the studio by the first week of October, so he was at his desk when the phone rang. The caller was the owner of a chain of convenience stores in Miami, in the market for new graphics and store design. Jonathan had been recommended to him. Would he fly down to Miami to see his stores and make a proposal?

Badly in need of work as always, Jonathan agreed. The day of his flight, October 7, he would be out of the hospital barely three weeks, but he never considered postponing. I understood. A project of such magnitude could mean a year's worth of work.

Jason drove him to the Atlanta airport Wednesday afternoon, and I agreed to pick him up the following evening, though my schedule was tight, with several board of education committee meetings that day and the monthly board meeting that same evening. As I drove Todd to school that morning, I felt uneasy about him, but no more than usual. In fact I never stopped worrying about him; it had become as normal as breathing. "Be good, Todd, you can do this," I said, and looked him in the eye to make sure he saw my concern. "I'll see you tonight."

He nodded, said, "Yeah, see ya," got out of the car and walked up the school steps. I watched him go inside.

I didn't get out of my last committee meeting until after four o'clock, and drove home to grab a bite before the board meeting. Dane met me at the studio door. "Where have you been?"

"I had a meeting downtown."

"Todd ran out of school again. His friends said he could've been killed running across Baxter Street. He didn't even look." Dane didn't try to hide his exasperation. "He ran to the therapist's again. He wasn't there, so they called here for someone to come get him. Jason and I went and picked him up."

"Is he okay? Where is he?"

"He's inside, watching Star Wars. We quieted him down."

I walked into the family room and saw Todd seated in his favorite chair, watching TV.

"Todd, what happened today? Are you all right?"

"I'm fine." He stared glassy-eyed at the television.

"Why did you run out of school?"

He didn't answer.

Distraught, all I could think was that I'd sent him to a school that wasn't safe for him, where he was unhappy and lost. And ironically, I had a school board meeting to attend. I couldn't stay with him. I had to go.

I called the therapist's office and made an appointment for eight the next morning. Then I ran up to Todd's room, took a Risperdal capsule from the bottle on his nightstand, got a glass of water from the kitchen, and took both to him.

"Here, take this," I told him.

"I don't want it," he said.

"Take it!" I commanded.

He popped the capsule into his mouth. "Drink," I said and handed him the glass. He drank. I was suspicious. "Open your mouth." He opened: nothing in it. "Lift your tongue." There was the capsule. "Todd, I'm going to stand here until I know you've swallowed it. Now drink!" He drank again, lifted his tongue to show me nothing was there, then stuck it out at me. "Thank you," I said sarcastically.

In the studio, I found Jason and Dane leaning over the computer. "Can one of you stay with Todd until I get back? He can't be alone."

"I can't," said Dane.

"I have to go to work," Jason replied.

And I had a board meeting. I felt the full weight of holding an elected position. You didn't miss the monthly board meeting unless you were on your deathbed. I walked back into the house and called my parents. Mom answered. "Can Todd stay with you tonight?" I said. "I don't know what's wrong with him, but he's acting weird and I don't want him to be alone. Jason and Dane can't stay with him. I've got my board meeting tonight, and then I have to pick Jonathan up from the airport. I don't know what else to do."

Mom readily agreed to help. "We haven't had dinner yet. Bring him over. He can eat with us."

I ran upstairs and packed Todd's toothbrush and a change of clothes in a gym bag, including the shirt I'd given him for his birthday, the one he'd never worn, then hurried back down. I leaned over him with my hands on each arm of the chair he was in, blocking his view of the TV. "We're going to Grandma's," I said. "I've got a board meeting, and then I've got to go pick up your father at the airport. You're going to sleep over at Grandma's house tonight, and then we're going to get to the bottom of this, Todd, once and for all. I'll pick you up tomorrow morning at seven thirty, so be ready. We have an eight o'clock appointment."

Todd frowned, but said nothing. "Let's go," I told him. He got up and followed me to the car. As I fastened my seatbelt, I told him how disappointed I was in him, and assuming he'd smoked pot again, I asked, "What made you do it, Todd? What happened?"

He didn't answer.

"You've got to finish high school. Don't you want to go to UGA? What about being a pilot?" In my frustration I went on, wanting to motivate him to make a change.

That's when he said, "I forgot something. I'll be right back," jumped out of the car, and went inside. He came back almost immediately.

"What was it?" I asked as I backed out of the driveway.

"Nothing, I just had to do something."

When we arrived at my parent's house, I filled them in on what had happened at school—that Todd had nearly gotten himself killed running to his therapist's office. Meanwhile, Todd had propped himself against the coffee table in front of the TV. I gave Mom his prescription.

"Make sure he swallows it. I'll be over first thing in the morning, seven thirty." I wanted to go over to Todd and hug him, but didn't. Our eyes met for one long look. I said a silent, pleading prayer to him, that he be good until I got back in the morning.

There were no surprises at the meeting but one. The superintendent had learned that the next day was my birthday, and at the end of the meeting, asked everyone in the room to sing "Happy Birthday" to me. Embarrassed, I managed to smile and thank all my well-wishers, and escaped as soon as I could.

It was after eleven by the time I reached the Atlanta airport, a half hour after Jonathan's plane landed. When he found me, he looked wan and tired. I noticed he was limping, took his bag from him, and led him to the car.

"Thank God you got here," he said. "They wanted to take me to the hospital."

"Who did?"

"That policeman over there." Jonathan waved to him, to show he was okay and on his way. Then he sank into the front seat and fastened his seatbelt as I closed the door.

When I was behind the wheel I said, "What happened?"

"My leg started bleeding, that's all. Come on, let's go."

As we drove away, I asked, "Well, how did it go?" As he told me about his meeting, it felt like old times, back when I was so heavily invested in The Jonathan Company, when his wins were my wins. It couldn't have gone better, to hear him tell it, and I reveled in the temporary security a large project would provide, and the idea that the future was looking brighter.

Then I told him about Todd, how I wished I knew what had triggered this latest episode. "I have an appointment set up with his therapist first thing in the morning," I said. "Do you want to come with me? We have to get to the bottom of what's going on with him, Jonathan. I think it's important you be there."

"All right, I'll go."

We were passing through Monroe, one of the few four-lane sections of Highway 78, when I glimpsed a possum, gray with its white death mask of a face, dart into the road and freeze in front of the car. All I could do was straddle him with the wheels. As I passed over him, I heard and felt a thump against the chassis. In my rearview mirror, I saw him writhing in the road.

I felt terrible. "Why did he jump?" I asked Jonathan. "If he'd just stayed still, he would've been okay."

"It's instinctual," he answered. "He couldn't help it."

Road kill. From the next day forward, a reminder, a dagger in the eye and a blow to the heart.

It was after one a.m. when we turned onto Athens's Atlanta Highway and approached the turn to Mom and Dad's house. Jonathan asked, "Should we stop and get Todd now?"

Todd was in my place of refuge, my safe haven. "No, they're all asleep. I don't want to wake them. We'll get him tomorrow." I drove past.

Laura Martin

Todd.

Haigwood Studios

My eldest sons, Dane and Jason.

Jonathan with Dane, Jason, and Todd.

SECOND LIFE

CHAPTER ELEVEN

Rebirthday

"Noooo, you can't leave me!"

I screamed the words from the deepest part of me. I imagined Todd's spirit lingering at the scene of his death and I called to him, *How can I go on without you? You can't leave me! This is not happening.* My mind was one long wail. Sobbing, I turned to Jonathan. He wrapped his arms around me and we wept.

Somehow we ended up in the back of a police cruiser, with Jonathan directing the officer back to my parents' house. I was oblivious to all but the pain of knowing that Todd was gone, that I would never hold him, touch him, see him again. My gut told me this was no accident, and I reproached him in my heart. *Todd, why couldn't you give me more time? Why couldn't you trust me to help you?*

The police car pulled into my parents' driveway, and we got out. Jonathan walked through the front door ahead of me, for the second time in a single morning breaking his vow to never cross that threshold. My parents were standing in the living room.

"Todd's dead," Jonathan announced, his tone abrupt and flat. My mother gasped. He might as well have punched her.

I walked past him into her arms; we both collapsed into the sofa. I cried and she held me close to her breast, soft, warm, and comfortless. The pain was so strong, so unrelenting, all I could do was cry out to it as each new wave knocked me down.

Meanwhile, the police brought our car back to the house and spoke to Jonathan and my father. They gave Jonathan their initial report, with the name of the driver that had struck Todd, the manager of a car rental service on his way to work. Todd's body was being taken to St. Mary's Hospital, and someone would need to go there to identify it. Jonathan refused to do it and forbade me as well. Bravely, Dad agreed to.

My mind turned to Jason and Dane. I couldn't bear the thought of them learning about Todd from anyone but me. Mom and Dad had turned on the local radio station; there were already news reports of a fatal accident involving a Clarke Central student. I called our house, but no answer. Jason had already left for his first morning class. Then I called Dane's house. No answer there either. I left a voicemail message to call me at his grandparents', then became frantic to leave and find him.

Jonathan and I were at the front door when the phone rang. Dad answered. "It's Dane," he called out and handed me the receiver.

I told Dane what happened, heard a moan, then a sob. I promised him that Jonathan and I were heading to him right away.

As we turned onto his street and approached the house he was renting with friends, I saw him, in T-shirt and sweatpants, standing in the road. As soon as the car stopped, I jumped out and ran to him. My arms went around him and I began to sob again. We stood in the street for a long time, crying, holding each other close. "Come home," I told him, "Jason doesn't know yet."

Jonathan and I drove back home, but Jason had left for class two hours earlier. In those pre-cell phone days, we'd have to wait for him to come back. Jonathan sat at his desk in the studio. I went upstairs to my bedroom to cry.

It wasn't long before I heard someone coming up the stairs. A neighbor, Joanna. Our children had grown up together. We embraced and cried, sitting on the edge of my bed. I repeated what little I knew about the circumstances of Todd's death.

Jason soon came bounding up the stairs. "Dad said to come right up. What is it?" He looked apprehensive, surprised to see me crying and to see Joanna there.

I pulled my oldest onto the bed next to me and repeated the words I'd said to his brother. "Todd was struck by a car and killed."

Jason cringed, doubled over in pain, his eyes squeezed shut. As he sobbed aloud, I rocked him in my arms as I had when he was a baby and cried with him, our faces buried in each other's shoulder. Weeping, Joanna wrapped herself around both of us. She's grieving, too, she just wants to help, I told myself, but I wanted to be alone with my son and our grief.

It was Jason who extricated himself first, walked down the hall to his room, and closed the door. Joanna and I rose, too, and walked downstairs to Jonathan's studio.

"They've cancelled classes at Clarke Central," Joanna informed me. "They've brought in counselors to talk with students."

Numb, I only nodded. I'd not thought of Todd's friends. He seemed so alone these last few months. Joanna offered her help and I thanked her. "I'll let you know. It's too soon. We haven't had time to think."

"Where's Jason?" Jonathan asked after Joanna left. We were holding on to each other again.

"In his room. You should go up to him." He nodded and slowly headed up the stairs.

I heard the studio door close and Dane walked into the family room, eyes red, face wet. We embraced and he held me tight against his chest. "Jason knows?" he said.

I nodded. "Dad's upstairs with him now."

"How did it happen?"

He wanted to understand. He wanted an explanation. I had none, just the story of Todd running away. "I don't know how it happened." Nor did I want to know. Details meant more pain.

I heard Jason and Jonathan coming down the stairs. Dane released me and turned to his brother. "Hey, man." They hugged, then sat on the sofa against the windows. I sat down between them and took their hands. The "if onlys" in their thoughts sang in chorus with my own.

Grief hung in the air, noxious, constricting our throats. No one spoke. Jonathan entered the kitchen and poured a cup of coffee, then went back to his studio, his safe haven.

Finally, I rose and said, "I need to shower. We'll have dinner with Grandma and Grandpa tonight. They need us too, okay?"

Jason nodded. Dane sighed, "Okay."

After getting cleaned up, I went into the studio to find Jonathan. "Listen, I'm going to drive back to Mom and Dad's. I don't want Dad to go to the hospital alone. I promise, I won't go in. I just want to be there for Dad."

I drove back to my parents' house. Dad was hanging up the phone as I entered the kitchen. Mom informed me, "Everyone's flying down tomorrow. They should be here by lunchtime. Hannah and Mike are coming, too." My cousin Hannah had adopted Mom and Dad as her parents by then, and was like a sister to all of us. My eyes filled with tears again, grateful my family were on their way. I needed them. Jason and Dane needed them.

Mom and I went with Dad to the hospital. Dad drove. I was so fearful for him. If Todd were terribly mangled, I knew Dad would be haunted by what he saw. More tears. *My poor baby, did he suffer? Did he die in excruciating pain? If only I knew he didn't suffer, that he died instantly.* Thinking was torture, but there was no help for it.

At St. Mary's, Dad gave his name and purpose. And we waited. As we waited, I wrestled with the reality that Todd was dead. *What happened to the energy, the life-force that was my son? Energy is neither created nor de-*

stroyed. I had no religion, but I held on to that axiom of science; it became my mantra. I repeated it over and over and it gave me, the atheist, solace, even hope.

It was nearly an hour before a hospital representative came to talk to us. When he said, "The police have decided an identification isn't necessary. You're free to go," I was so relieved, for Dad's sake. I didn't know then how unusual it was not to require a positive identification. I would have done it. I was burning to kiss my son one last time. Or to get one lock of his hair. I wanted it so badly, but I didn't ask, honoring my promise to Jonathan.

Much of the rest of the day is a blur. I remember a fellow school board member taking me for a walk around my parents' neighborhood. It was such a beautiful day, one of those good-to-be-alive kind of days. And yet my son was dead. It didn't seem real. I couldn't cry with people around, but people would come. I let them do whatever they thought would help. But we all knew nothing would.

Jason, Dane, and I had dinner with Mom and Dad that night. We went over Todd's last hours with them, his nervous energy, his desire to leave, his fight with Dad. I apologized for the terrible position I'd put them in, and I apologized for Todd. He didn't know what he was doing. He loved them.

Then we talked of what needed to be done when the family arrived, and began to prepare for the funeral.

When I returned home, Jonathan met me at the door and we held on to each other and cried. I told him of the day's events, that Dad didn't have to identify Todd after all, that his friend Mike and all my family were arriving tomorrow. Then I went upstairs to my room.

Crying again, I held on to my dresser, leaned into it to hold myself up, and sobbed. I felt like my guts had been torn open, my heart exposed and raw. How would I go on?

The certainty came that whatever I decided in that moment would determine my path for the rest of my life. There was no escaping the choice: *This grief could kill me, settle in my bones and kill me.* There was so much to reproach myself for.

But by some grace, in that perilous moment, I surrendered. Blaming myself was the path of death and endless sorrow. I wasn't in control, never was. So I chose not to punish myself. Instead, I vowed to make some good come out of Todd's death, to find a purpose worthy of the memory of him and the love I bore him.

I will not hide the cause of Todd's death. He had tried to make it appear an accident, but I knew it wasn't. Substance abuse of some kind was the real cause of his despair and his death—I knew this. The world would know, too, his friends and their parents would know, all the students at Clarke Central would know. *Let my grief be a warning.*

Then it hit me: *Today is my birthday.* I moaned. Todd died on my birthday. He didn't mean to give me such a gift, but he did.

My first life is over, I realized. *This is what death is.* Compared to the pain of losing my beautiful son, death held no terror for me. How could I fear what he had so fearlessly chosen? I was perversely in awe of his courage.

This is the first day of my second life. And I swear, my second life will be different. All my life, I'd put others ahead of what I wanted for myself. I'd sacrificed the life of my dreams twenty-two years before, to give Jonathan the life of his dreams. *But what about my dreams? Am I any less deserving of happiness than any other soul on this earth? This is my life! Don't I deserve to live the life of my dreams?*

And so I swore: *In my second life, I will do what gives me joy.*

Exhausted, I climbed into bed, overwhelmed by grief, but also an inner determination. And that, I realized many years later, was Todd's true gift.

CHAPTER TWELVE

Ashes

I thought I would get to Mom and Dad's before my family on Saturday morning, but they were already there when I arrived. My brothers, Eddie and Robert, met me outside. Robert grabbed me in a fierce embrace, as if he could fend off the terrible thing that had brought us together, then passed me to Eddie. We kissed and hugged each other and went inside. Tears and hugs expressed the love and sorrow words could not.

Jason and Dane needed family there as much as I did; they spent most of the weekend with their uncles. Jonathan still wouldn't set foot in my parents' house if he could help it, but was missed and asked for. In fairness, he was physically as well as emotionally exhausted, still recovering from his open-heart surgery. It appeared to me that he wasn't drinking, a significant milestone for him. I hoped it was true.

That afternoon, Mom joined Jonathan and me at Bernstein's Funeral Home, where we arranged for the wake on Sunday and funeral on Monday. Since Todd was being cremated, I knew a Catholic funeral wasn't possible. The funeral home director offered to contact his pastor at Athens First Baptist Church about holding the funeral there, and made an appointment for us to meet Reverend Appleton that evening.

That night, Todd's friends held a candlelight vigil at the site of the accident on Timothy Road. Jason, Dane, Dad, and all my family attended, while Mom, Jonathan, and I went to meet with Reverend Appleton.

I felt awkward at first. Jonathan and I had agreed to be up front about our beliefs: we weren't religious. But these things didn't matter to Reverend Appleton. We were suffering; we were in need. He was gracious and kind and listened sympathetically. I told him Todd's troubled story, and that I didn't want to hide the role I thought marijuana had played in his death, that it wasn't harmless. I wanted his friends and their parents to know. I wanted to expose the code of silence that kept others in Todd's life from telling me whatever they knew about the risky choices he'd been making.

"Todd was not a victim," I stood to emphasize the point as I sobbed the hard truth, "Todd must take responsibility for his death."

Reverend Appleton took my hand, kissed it, and said, "I honor you."

His gallant gesture surprised me, and I knew I'd found a friend at the darkest time of my life. He generously agreed to hold Todd's funeral at First Baptist, and would lead it himself, and handle all the details of the service.

"Ryan's mother offered to help," I said. Ryan, Todd's best friend since middle school, and his mother, had called to offer their help.

"Then I'll call her tomorrow," he promised.

"But I'm going to choose the music. I'll make sure you have the CDs by tomorrow," I said as we left.

For the wake, Jonathan, Jason, Dane, and I arrived at the funeral home early. There was no casket, or any sign that Todd had died, only a large board filled with pictures of him, covering the short span of his life.

The rest of my family arrived, as did so many others: Todd's friends and classmates from elementary, middle, and high school, their parents, Jason's and Dane's friends, classmates and their parents, many teachers, principals, and administrators from the Clarke County School District, and fellow school board members. I was overwhelmed by the outpouring of compassion and support. Two visitors stand out in memory. First, Mary, with whom I'd worked at the construction company and hadn't seen in two years. "Mary, it's so good of you to come, thank you," I greeted her as we hugged.

"Anne, I'm so sorry. I don't think you know, but I lost my son, too. He was killed two years ago."

"Oh! Mary, no! I didn't know. How terrible! I'm so sorry."

"I have something for you." She put a gift-wrapped box into my hands. "Whenever I want to talk to my son, I take a bath and light a candle and say thank you Jesus for the gift of William and the life we shared for fourteen years. Sometimes I light up to fifty candles at a time."

I could see she wanted me to open her gift, so I did. In the box was a Waterford crystal votive candleholder. "Thank you, Mary, you're too good. We're members of the saddest club, you and I, parents who've outlived their children." We embraced again.

The last person in line was an African-American man whom I'd never met. He stood before me, tears streaming down his cheeks. "I'm the driver," he said.

All I could do was put my arms around him. I knew his name from the newspaper stories about the accident. "Brian, I'm so sorry. I know it wasn't your fault." We stood there, crying together. "Thank you for coming. This must be so hard for you."

Brian nodded. The woman standing next to him then introduced herself as his mother and said how sorry she was. We spoke briefly, then parted. Too painful.

After three hours, for the first time, I noticed my surroundings. Jonathan had left my side hours earlier, unable to stand for a long period. Since his surgery, he had aged ten years. His hair was stark white. He seemed to have shrunk three inches in height, his shoulders rounded and stooped to protect the chest that had been split open. I could see outside that the sun had set. Inside, the room had emptied. Only Jonathan, Mom and Dad, Jason, Dane, and Reverend Appleton remained.

Reverend Appleton urged me to go home and rest. He must have realized how draining the funeral the next day would be. Jonathan, too tired to resist, went back to my parents' house with me for some dinner. Then we did return home.

Earlier in the day, my brother Jim had taken the list of music I had chosen, purchased CD's, and delivered them to First Baptist. That night, I asked Jason and Dane to each write their own words for Todd's funeral. Jason wrote two paragraphs, but Dane was unable to write anything at all. Men find it so difficult to put words to their emotions, and my sons couldn't speak with me about their sorrow and regret.

It was important to me that they say a formal farewell to their brother, but I forgot that Ryan's mother was organizing the ceremony; they weren't included in the program. I regret that to this day.

Early Monday morning, Jason, Dane, Jonathan, and I all arrived at my parents' to have breakfast with the family before the funeral. After breakfast, I changed into my hurriedly purchased black dress. We were running late; the limousines from Bernstein's waited outside. I remember thinking, *They can't start without us*, and not stressing that we wouldn't be at the church by eleven on the dot.

As we entered the vestibule of First Baptist, I could hear the first movement of Beethoven's "Moonlight Sonata," sad and mysterious. The men from the funeral home organized us into a line to enter the church. As we walked in, everyone rose and I watched from afar as I lived the nightmare from so many years before, the dream that one of my sons had died and I was walking down the aisle of a church filled with hundreds of people staring at me.

When the latest repetition of "Moonlight" ended, Reverend Appleton greeted the congregation and read an opening scripture. Then three of Todd's friends shared their memories of him. When it came time for Reverend Appleton to speak, he told of a young man, beloved by his family and friends, and the terrible choice he had made. He spoke directly to the many, many Clarke Central students present, to warn them against experimenting with drugs, and against keeping silent when they knew of others using them. At times his words were harsh and hard, so hard I could no longer hold up my head, but laid it lightly on Jonathan's shoulder. Athens's *Flagpole Magazine* later published the sermon, but by then Appleton had revised it. The published version carried the same strong message, with the fire and brimstone excised.

Reverend Appleton led the congregation in singing "Amazing Grace," and concluded with a benediction and an announcement that there would be no receiving line, and that the family was leaving directly after the service was over. I was surprised by this, and concerned that there'd been no announcement that we would receive friends at my parents' home. Would the people attending know they could visit with us there?

After the funeral, I embraced Jason and Dane and whispered, "From now on, whenever we hug, there will be three of us. Todd will be with us, too."

I needn't have worried. A small group of friends stayed with Jason and Dane that afternoon, while neighbors and friends came by Mom and Dad's. Jonathan didn't stay long, but returned home with his friend Mike. Reverend Appleton stopped by later in the afternoon, and we found a quiet corner in the living room to talk.

"You said exactly what I wanted Todd's friends and parents to hear," I told him. "Thank you."

"I've done funerals where the parents sweep it all under the rug," he replied. "I admire what you've done. It's a true service to this community."

"I don't know how yet, but I'm going to try to get through to kids and their parents, that they're not telling on a friend, that they might be saving a life when they see someone using."

"I'm sure you'll find a way. How are you holding up?"

"I'm okay." He looked at me disbelievingly, so I added, "I do my mourning alone."

Then I changed the subject. "My lifeline these last few days has been 'Energy is neither created nor destroyed.' I'm holding on to that. The energy that was Todd, that was his life-force, it can't just become nothing, so where has it gone? I read this book a few years ago, called *Many Lives, Many Masters*, written by a psychiatrist about a patient he healed through hypnosis and past-life regression. Do you think reincarnation is possible?"

Reverend Appleton skirted the issue of reincarnation and spoke instead of Christ's message of love and redemption. I listened and thought that our two ideas weren't necessarily in conflict, but held my tongue. He soon rose to leave.

I walked back to the kitchen and family room to rejoin my brothers and sisters. They would leave in the morning and life would go back to what? Normal?

Normal was gone. The only normal that remained was the inevitable arrival of tomorrow.

* * *

And it came. Tuesday: Nothing to do but mourn.

Todd was dead, gone forever. My son had vanished overnight, fled to some distant place, and I'd never see him again.

Shock turned to disbelief. How could this be happening? Todd's death forced me to abandon the story of my life—the fairy-tale life of the Family, my family—where all turned out well in the end, where I and all the people I loved lived happily ever after. I had cast Jonathan into the role of Knight and Father, and yet still I was unprotected. Even worse, I was the Mother who could not protect her Child, a mother who had outlived her son in unnatural order. I had struggled for so long to bear the burden of betrayal, disease, and divorce, and refused to break. But Todd's death broke me. I surrendered to its overwhelming force.

Had I believed in God, I could have blamed Him for the tragedy that had befallen me. But I didn't. That crutch was denied me. What was I going to do? How was I going to bear it? I could only surrender.

Powerless in the face of death, the ultimate, inevitable mystery, I was nonetheless amazed at the courage of my son to choose it. Whether he had run out in front of that car consciously or in a state of panic, I believed his death a suicide, and I was crushed that so great was his despair, he decided dying was better than living.

I went to his room to search for answers, straight to his desk. Somehow I knew, even before I opened the top drawer, that I would find a note. It read, "The life has gone out of me and I can't get it back."

I doubled over and sobbed aloud. *That's what he did when he ran out of the car and back to his room. He wrote this note.* My last words to him had been chiding and exasperated. Was that when he gave up? What terrible thing had happened to him that he couldn't recover from? I reproached him for not trusting me enough to tell me what was wrong, for not believing that I would love him, whatever he had done. And I reproached myself for not saying that out loud to him that day.

And then I had to go on living. There's the rub. Jason and Dane needed me. Though they were going back to class, back to work, back to life as usual, I could see they were struggling. Their hugs were so tender and protective of me, unspoken promises that each one wasn't the last, and they lingered, held on just a few moments longer than their wont. They winced when Todd's name was mentioned. And when I asked, neither wanted to talk about him or what had happened. The wound was too fresh.

Like some doubting Thomas, I fingered that wound every morning to remind myself: *He's dead, he's gone.* Every morning, I woke up the same way I went to bed— crying. In between I got through the day.

My first task was to take food to the homeless shelter. Friends and acquaintances had sent us more than we could possibly eat. We had requested that, in lieu of flowers, donations be made in Todd's memory to the school district's Foundation for Excellence in Public Education, but many sent plants and flowers too, and I had hundreds of thank-you notes to write. Cards and letters came in for weeks expressing the sadness and grief people felt. Many thanked us for not hiding the cause behind Todd's death. It seemed his death had struck a nerve with students and their parents. I became convinced that no family was untouched by some form of substance abuse.

Clarke Central students sent letters and poems to express their grief and loss and to ask "Why?" They recalled a friend who had always made them smile, who was kind and thoughtful and cool. It wasn't until many years later that Ryan told me that he himself had been arrested for underage possession, at a UGA football game the Saturday after Todd's funeral. He said the police officer kept badgering him, asking "What are you drinking for?"

Finally he said, "My best friend died last week."

"Yeah, who was that?" the officer asked as he stuffed Ryan into the back of his cruiser.

"Todd Cooper."

"Are you shittin' me?" the officer cried, unbelieving. "You're the second kid today who told me that."

That same week, our insurance agent, a neighbor, called us to come to his office to sign for the insurance check he had from the life insurance policy we'd taken out on the boys years before. I could scarcely believe that Jonathan had made the policy payments through all our financial woes, and to this day believe Tommy kept up the policy for us. The same afternoon we received the check, we picked up Todd's remains from the funeral home. It was horrible to feel like we'd profited from our son's death, and his ashes weighed heavily in my lap.

But that unexpected check enabled us to catch up financially and make our own gift to the Foundation for Excellence in Todd's memory. The remainder we decided to split between Jason and Dane, as a gift from their brother. My thought was that they could put it toward their education. I should have known from my own eagerness to get rid of that money that it was a terrible mistake. Within six months, both Jason and Dane wrecked their cars, and then had to use those funds to get them repaired. Not only could they also not profit from their brother's death, they unconsciously punished the instrument that caused it.

Neither Jonathan nor I knew what to do with Todd's ashes. We hadn't bought an urn, so they were still in the cardboard can from the crematorium. The funeral home had put the can in a Christmas bag with a picture of an angel on it, and a caption that read, "I bring you tidings of great joy." I set the bag in the center of Todd's dresser in his bedroom. He was home for good.

* * *

Friends would call to get me out of the house. I remember walking with a girlfriend around the lake at a local park. It was Indian summer. A warm sun pushed us forward to seek the shade of trees leaning over the path in front of us. It felt good to be walking, even though we were walking in circles. While we walked, I argued aloud the question that dogged me.

"What happens to the energy that's stored in the body when someone dies? What happened to the energy, the life-force that was Todd? Science says energy is neither created nor destroyed, so it has to go somewhere. I wonder if it stays as organized as it was when it animated someone."

No one, including my friend that day, had an answer for me. Perhaps they simply ascribed it to the desperate ramblings of a grieving mother. But for me, the search was on.

Another friend told me about the Compassionate Friends, a support group for parents who'd lost a child, and she urged me to go to a meeting. I promised to try it, and attended an evening meeting the following week.

Some of the parents there I recognized: the mother of a little boy who'd died of a malignant brain tumor just five months earlier, and the coach whose adult son recently drowned. I was warmly welcomed by everyone and invited to share. I told them about Todd's last day, the irony that he died on my birthday. Did I mention the energy question? I don't remember. I remember what the coach shared: he urged us all to read *Talking to Heaven*, a book by James Van Praagh, and spoke of the comfort he'd taken from it. I'd never heard of James Van Praagh, but made a mental note. I do remember being horrified by the mother whose son had died nearly twenty years before. Her grief was raw and new, unchanged by time. She frightened me.

I had no intention to dedicate my new life to grief. The Compassionate Friends, I decided, wasn't for me. What could I offer them; what could they offer me? Someday I would be healed. Grieving, living with loss, finding solace—that was inner work, done alone.

CHAPTER THIRTEEN

Making a Life

Like so many others before and after me, I wanted to give meaning to the loss of my child by trying to spare other parents the heartbreak I suffered. For me, the issue was substance abuse, and I threw myself into what came naturally, community organizing. Joined by the mothers of Todd's friends and other volunteers advocating for substance-abuse prevention in Athens, we organized a campaign.

The shock of Todd's death was still so new that the boardroom of the school district's main offices was filled at our kickoff meeting. I spoke of my struggles with Todd and invited those present to join me in the goal: to break the silence that made alcoholism and addiction a secret wound that families hid in the darkest recesses of their homes, the secret blight the school system hid for fear of public reprisals, the secret burden students hid for fear of rejection or punishment by those in charge.

The first step would be a daylong conference at Clarke Central, offering workshops facilitated by community professionals, including school counselors, teachers, and parents. "Everyone is welcome," I told the audience, "and for anyone who wants to be part of the organizing committee—there's a sign-up sheet at the back of the room."

October dragged into November. Busy as I was planning the December conference, I found the days long and wearisome. Nights were the hardest. I'd promised not to punish myself, but I felt the full weight of my failure, and cried for what could have been. My heart had a hole in it that would never heal. Would I ever get used to it?

The one-month anniversary of Todd's death approached, thirty days since I'd seen his beautiful face. How would I bear it as days became years, years decades? Was this how that poor woman in the Compassionate Friends marked time, with anniversaries of her loss? I kept the house in order, made meals for Jonathan and Jason, and cried every day and every night.

One night in mid-November I had, as usual, cried myself to sleep. I'd come to think of crying as a nightly cleanse, bathing me body and soul. All the tears I shed for Todd were tears I never shed for my marriage or myself. Would I ever wash away the pain of those defeats? Death, disease, and a divorce still looming, the big three, had forced me to surrender. There was no more resistance in me. Whatever came into my life, so be it.

Hours later, I became aware that I was asleep but not dreaming. I was conscious of my body lying in bed. I felt the weight of the blanket on my limbs and the sheets on my skin. I knew I was sleeping, yet somehow I was also alert and present. Then I felt myself embraced, skin touching skin, the warmth of another pressing against me, a pressure so real, that so startled me, I sat straight up in bed, gasping. I looked around the room. "Todd?"

I knew instantly it was him. He'd hugged me. But there was no one there. The bedroom door was closed. *What the hell?*

I couldn't deny what had just happened; the experience was so visceral, so palpably physical. Wonder overwhelmed skepticism as love for my son vibrated through me. *He loves me.* Simultaneously grateful and thunderstruck, I tucked the memory away. *One day,* I promised, *I'll make sense of it.*

* * *

The December conference at Clarke Central was widely attended by students and adults. Most significant was a closing discussion led by the Athens-Clarke County police chief, during which he revealed that the superintendent barred police officers from coming onto school grounds to make drug arrests. School property had become a safe haven for drugs, for those who sold or used them. The reversal of that practice was the first meaningful outcome of the campaign.

In addition to meeting with my core group of volunteers, I was also attending organizational meetings of Family Connection and Community Connection, large umbrella organizations in Athens that brought together local, state and federal agencies, nonprofit organizations, the school system, churches, and the business community. Various initiatives and grant proposals were in their budding stages, and alcoholism and addiction were often seen as the root problem of a host of issues, from home-lessness to unwanted pregnancy. Because of this, sub-stance-abuse prevention and treatment were critical to developing real solutions to many problems. Eventually, I would apply for and receive grants for the program we were creating.

At the time, however, I gave little thought to the fu-ture. How I was going to support myself wasn't an issue to which I gave much thought, but in early December, one of my old bosses from the construction company I'd worked for called to ask if I'd consider working part-time. She had a project on the property management side of the business she didn't have time for, and needed help. It was perfect timing, and I accepted gratefully. I needed to get out of the house, and I needed the income. Jonathan and I still lived under the same roof, under the old agreement that I purchase the groceries, and I need-ed to do my part. I started work the following week.

My little committee of mothers tacitly agreed to pause our efforts as the Christmas holidays approached. At Thanksgiving dinner with my parents, Jason, Dane, and I agreed that our first Christmas in Athens without Todd would be too sad to be borne, and we decided to fly up to New Jersey to join my parents and the rest of the family there. Jonathan chose not to fly up with us, holding on to his old grudge against my father. I knew the boys felt guilty that their dad would be alone for Christmas, but I was proud of them for letting that be his choice, not theirs, and doing what was best for themselves.

We stayed with my sister Mary and her family. Their big house was where the entire Capone clan congregated for Christmas dinner. I couldn't help but remember earlier, happier Christmases there. Todd had loved staying at Mary's during the holidays, and I remembered his wish that he lived there, too, and that his parents were rich.

That first Christmas without Todd, it was all the same: the light-hearted love and laughter of his aunts, uncles, and cousins, the amazing food and wine, the wall of presents. Only he was missing. Throughout the week, there were tender moments when he was called to mind, with tears and smiles and gentle embraces for me and his brothers.

Jason and Dane flew back to Georgia the day before New Year's Eve. They wanted to be in Athens to celebrate with friends. I chose to stay and see in the new year with my family. One thing that weighed on me was the impending discussion of divorce with Jonathan, and how we would handle the division of property, essentially the house. A friend had talked me into seeing a divorce attorney in November and somehow, Jonathan found out about it. The attorney had a winning reputation and, never one to be outdone, Jonathan let me know he'd retained his own attorney. That surprised me. I didn't want an acrimonious, combative divorce. All I really wanted was a clean break, without a big fight over "stuff."

When I broached the subject with him in January, I tried to talk him into seeing the advantages of selling: not having a large house and yard to care for, living in an apartment with lower rent and expenses. He wouldn't hear of it.

"I'm never going to be in a position to buy a house again, Anne," he said. "I don't want to sell. I want to stay here."

"And I don't," I told him. "But I don't want a fight." I'd given a lot of thought to what was possible in terms of our finances. If we agreed to sell the house, we could pay off the remaining mortgage and might even be able to recover our deposit. But Jonathan didn't want to sell.

"If you pay me half of what we invested in this place," I told him, "then I'll sign the house over to you."

"Okay," he agreed.

"How are you ever going to pay me without selling?" I asked. "I don't want this to take forever."

"I'll refinance."

"Refinance?" I said, incredulous. "You really think you can get a new mortgage and fifteen thousand dollars?"

"Sure, we have a lot more equity than that in this place," he said.

We had an agreement, but not a timeline. And I wondered how he was going to prove sufficient income.

That same month, I reconnected with an old acquaintance, Terry Daly. She was one of the teachers of "Talking With Your Kids About Alcohol," the lifestyle risk-reduction program Jonathan and I went to years ago. Terry was a registered nurse and led the substance-abuse-prevention unit for the Northeast Georgia Mental Health Center, known today as Advantage Behavioral Health.

Terry joined our alcohol-and-drug-prevention group. As I learned more about lifestyle risk reduction from her, I became convinced it was the way forward for our task force. With Terry's help, I wrote our first grant proposal. My hope was that we would eventually be able to persuade the school district to incorporate the risk-reduction program into the middle and high school health classes. I submitted the grant proposal in March, but wouldn't learn if we would receive funding until October.

In the meantime, I had become fully employed, if you counted two part-time jobs as full employment. Another friend, the executive director of the Samaritan Center, a nonprofit that provided psychotherapy and spiritual counseling, asked me to be the organization's part-time office manager and bookkeeper. The assignment was quite similar to the project I was working on for the property management company, figuring out why numbers from two different systems didn't jive and fixing the mistakes. I readily agreed.

That March, my sister Edna called Mom and Dad to tell them that Hannah, our cousin, was in the hospital and not going to make it. Hannah had struggled valiantly against breast cancer for five years, but the end was near. We flew up to New Jersey the next day, but Hannah died before we could see her. Edna had left her side the night before, and a friend who went to visit her in the morning found her dead in her room. The staff never even noticed. We were horrified: another loved one dying alone. I wondered if Hannah and Todd were together.

When I returned home to Athens, Jonathan was angry and resentful. "Don't you think it's time you moved out? How long do you expect me to go on supporting you?"

"You want *me* to move out? I still own half this house."

"Why not? I'm the one paying the mortgage, you're not. I'll live up to my part of the deal. You know that. I'm working on getting a new mortgage. When I get it, I'll give you a bank check and you can sign a quitclaim deed."

"Fine," I said, but I was still angry. How could he make me feel like a moocher? Who was cleaning the house, doing his laundry, and cooking his meals? The thought must have occurred to him too, because a day later he informed me, "I'll probably remarry. I don't see myself staying single."

I stifled a laugh and made no reply, except in my mind: *Right. What woman could resist all this fun, living hand-to-mouth and cleaning up after you? If that's supposed to make me jealous, it's not working.*

I made an appointment the very next day to see a one-bedroom apartment in the same complex I'd once pointed out to Todd. It was quiet, catered to professionals and graduate students, and was located on the west side of town, less than a mile from a grocery store and no more than ten minutes from my parents' place. The ground-floor apartment the property manager showed me had decent natural light, a small outdoor patio, fresh paint, and immaculate carpeting. I signed a lease that day and paid a deposit, and would move in over the last weekend in April.

"I'm taking my bed and dresser and night table," I informed Jonathan. "I'll split all the kitchen stuff with you, but I'm taking the set of china my brothers and sisters gave us for our tenth wedding anniversary. And I'm taking the car."

"Take whatever you want," he answered.

His offhand answer gave me license, but I didn't take much beyond what I had told him. He kept the business phone number and I kept the home phone number. I took my favorite piece of his mother's artwork, some books, my Airdyne stationary bike, an antique sideboard my sister Mary had given me, and two shabby antique loveseats with beautiful lines that I would eventually have reupholstered. I took the big box of family photographs, too, with a promise to give him a share after I got them organized.

There were no goodbyes. The day I moved out, Jonathan disappeared without saying a word to me. I borrowed a neighbor's truck and in a light spring rain, with Dad and Dane's help, moved into my new apartment.

For the first time in my life, I lived completely alone. It was so quiet, so peaceful. I loved coming home to find it exactly the way I left it. I wasn't lonely, but I felt bereft, the mother who'd been unceremoniously dumped out of the nest. There I was, without Todd, in the place where I thought we'd be making a fresh start together. Every day after I came home from work, I laid down on my bed and cried. Why couldn't he have given us more time?

Reminders of him were constant. Two weeks after moving into the apartment, I had to attend the high school's graduation ceremonies. All school board members were expected to attend. I almost didn't go, knowing it would be terribly painful. And I was late getting there. The chorus was just finishing a song as I slipped into my chair on the stage, and a board member leaned over to whisper that the song had been dedicated to Todd and another student who died that school year. I felt guilty then, to have missed their tribute, and cried even more that night.

A few weeks later, Todd's friend Jenny called to ask if she and some friends could come see me. "Of course," I told her. We set a date for a Saturday afternoon in early June.

When the doorbell to my apartment rang, I hardly knew what to expect. There were seven or eight of Todd's friends at the door, some unknown to me. I knew Jenny, Jesse, Daniel, and Chip, but I was meeting Ruchi and Taryn for the first time. I invited them all in and apologized that there was nothing to sit on. My furniture was out getting reupholstered.

We spread out on the carpet in the living room. I offered them chocolate chip cookies I'd baked that morning, but no one ate any. They were eager to give me their presents. First, a copy of the 1999 Clarke Central yearbook. It had been signed by all of them and many other Clarke Central students, with messages of love for Todd and his family. Then Jenny handed me a wooden box.

"We took up a collection for a memorial, a bench and tree for Todd," she said. "We collected over two hundred dollars and want you to have it." As I opened the box, she continued. "See? We etched our names on the wood inside. And we collected all our pictures of Todd for you to keep."

My eyes filled with tears. "I don't know what to say, my heart is so full. This is so good of you. Thank you so much." I opened the box and saw a small photo album and cassette tape inside. "What's this?" I picked up the tape.

"We made a tape of songs for you that remind us of Todd," Taryn explained, "and we typed out the lyrics, too." She handed me a set of cardstock sheets, tied with gold ribbons. I looked at the song titles. Some of them I didn't know, but soon would: "Crazy Life," "Far Behind," "Angel," "Shame," "Friends," "Free Bird," "River," "You Were Loved," "Walls," and "Testify to Love."

"I can't wait to listen to it," I said. *They're still grieving, too*, I reminded myself.

We went through the photos together. They told me stories of Todd and made me laugh. I was learning new things about him, which almost made it seem as if he were alive again, and I was so grateful.

Jenny pointed to one of Todd standing next to a car. "This is one of my favorites. Look at his eyes," she said, "don't they look like they have flowers in them? We all were crazy about Todd's flower eyes!"

There were pictures of Todd at soccer games, and pictures of him with his buddies. There were photos of him standing proudly between Jenny and Emily, an arm around each, and one of him hugging Ruchi. Ruchi was smiling, a half-eaten apple in her hand, and Todd, towering over her, looked far-off into the distance, as if he knew he wasn't long for this earth.

And then there was the close-up of him, shining and golden in bright sunlight, looking over his left shoulder directly into the camera with a knowing smile, as if anticipating the moment I would first behold that wondrous image. He was so beautiful I could hardly breathe.

"Do you know who took this?" I gasped. "I need the negative for this one. This is how I want to always remember him. And I want his dad and Jason and Dane to have a copy, too."

Jenny said she knew who'd taken it, and promised to get the negative for me. Everyone got up to leave soon after, with hugs and promises to keep in touch. I thanked them again; they were such a gift to me.

True to her word, Jenny followed through with the negative of what I've come to think of as Todd's portrait. I had prints made and gave them to the entire family as Christmas presents that year. Jonathan had the photo blown up into eight-by-ten glossies and framed as Christmas presents for Jason, Dane, and me. I hung mine in my bedroom, next to the bed, and would stare at it for long periods, my eyes locked on Todd's, imagining him watching me when I cried.

* * *

One evening, soon after I settled into the apartment, the phone rang. "Hello?" I was loading the dishwasher, so held the phone to my ear with my shoulder.

"Anne, it's Jonathan."

I jerked myself upright, and the phone fell in with the glasses. "Sorry," I said after I picked it back up. "Is something wrong?"

"No, not at all. Would you have dinner with me Friday night? Six o'clock? We can meet at the Arch and decide from there."

"Dinner? Um, I guess so."

"Great, I'll see you then." He hung up.

Why had I agreed? We weren't enemies, but I didn't think of him as a friend either.

Friday night at dinner, I found myself with little to say and listening, as I always did, to his stories about clients and projects, of rooting for him and vicariously celebrating his wins. Falling so easily back into that pattern scared me.

The following week, he called and asked me to dinner again. It was hard for me to say no, so I agreed. "Where do you want to go?" he asked.

"I like East-West," I offered.

"Sounds good," he replied. "Can I pick you up at seven?"

"No, I'll meet you there," I told him. I didn't want him coming to my apartment. It was mine, separate from my old life.

Dinner this time was awkward and painful. I didn't have anything to say. I didn't want to share my new life with him. He was from the life that had died with Todd. *Why am I here? What does he want from me?*

Then I realized: *These are dates. He thinks we can start all over again. He doesn't accept that we're never going to be a couple again.* So the next time he asked me out, I told him no, it was too hard. I needed time to be alone and heal. I didn't want to go out with him. He stopped calling.

On a Sunday not long after, I arrived at Mom and Dad's for dinner. As we sat down for a glass of wine and hors d'oeuvres, Mom told me that Jonathan had called them the previous week. I was astonished—he hadn't spoken to them in five years. "What did he want?" I said.

"He asked us to take him to an Alcoholics Anonymous meeting," Mom said.

"Good for him," I replied, not hiding the bitterness I felt. It wasn't merely that he decided to go to AA only *after* our marriage had been destroyed, but that he'd asked my parents to take him. I knew instantly what he was thinking: if he won them over to his side, they would pressure me to go back to him. He knew my mother was a powerful ally, and he was calling on her again. I was furious.

"He loves you, Anne. He's really trying," Mom said. "He'd do anything to win you back. He said, 'I've lost her, Mom.'" Mom looked at me, her argument made.

"He's right. He has lost me. *I am done*," I replied. "I begged him to stop drinking for years and he wouldn't. Now that I'm gone, he's stopped. If I go back, he'll start again. That's what codependency is."

Thus I made my declaration of independence from Jonathan and, harder still, from my mother. I loved her, but her fear for me living on my own was no longer my fear. I was a woman who had made promises to herself. I was making a new life that would be very different from the old one.

CHAPTER FOURTEEN

Sense of Direction

Driving around town in the summer of 1999, I noticed a song getting a lot of airplay on the radio. The first time I heard "You'll Be in My Heart," I was at a four-way stop. As I listened, my eyes filled with tears, in direct contradiction to the song's opening plea to stop crying. I sat at the intersection and wept until the toot of a car horn reminded me to move on.

I loved that Phil Collins song. But I was often disappointed too, because I usually caught only the end of it. I wouldn't cry then, but would hang on to every word, every last, beautiful note, and feel my heart swell with love for Todd. I ached from missing him. Did he know how much? The question stayed with me always, and kept the hole in my heart fresh and raw.

* * *

In August, the director of MBA Admissions at the University of Georgia called me. The dean wanted him to start an evening MBA program in Gwinnett, and he accepted on condition that he could hire a part-time assistant director to help him. Was I interested? I certainly was, and he invited me to his office to talk. I started working for him soon after.

The timing of the move to UGA was ideal. I'd finished the project my old boss had hired me for and gave my notice, promising to keep in touch and thanking her for all she'd done for me.

Having graduated just a year earlier, I already knew the MBA program in great detail, which I expected to be an advantage as I began working for the Terry College of Business. But I soon realized that, pulling back the curtain, I had a great deal to learn. The technology, for example: Terry had its own homegrown system—primitive, looking back on it from today's vantage point—though it got the job done. The rankings game was another part of the equation: how to promote the program, how to attract the best candidates, how to make financial awards, and how to entice applicants to enroll after being admitted.

I sat in on candidate interviews with my new boss and was soon interviewing on my own, reading application files—essays, resumes, recommendations, and transcripts—and making admission recommendations. I loved the work. It was fulfilling to open doors, to give people an opportunity to achieve their goals, or at least to accelerate them along their path.

Updating the MBA viewbook was another of my assignments. In those pre-website days, a twenty- to thirty-page picture book was an essential marketing element and the program mailed out hundreds every year. My boss promised to introduce me to Patt, the graphic designer he used. As soon as we met, I wanted us to be friends.

It had been such a long time since I had girlfriends. I was still learning how. I felt as though I wasn't very good at it—I'd been so isolated living with an alcoholic husband. My job had been to hide his problem from the world, so I had no close friends other than family. I didn't know how to share myself with another person, or for that matter, how to have fun. In many ways I still saw myself as the awkward, bookish schoolgirl I'd been growing up, the one no one thought to include when they hung out on the weekend. I wanted my new life to be different.

Earlier that summer, I was invited to go blueberry picking with Connie, Lacy, Kitty, and Madelon, all mothers of Todd's closest friends. "We're going early Saturday morning before it gets too hot," Connie told me.

It felt good to be included, and I looked forward to it all week. We gathered at Connie's as planned and were among the first to arrive at the farm. We fanned out, each taking one side of a row and working the bushes in our little territories. The early morning breeze soon evaporated in bright, hot sun, and we became flushed and "moist," as proper Southern ladies referred to perspiring back in the day.

It took nearly three hours to fill our two-gallon buckets, pay for our berries, and dump them into our bags. A table filled with paper copies of blueberry recipes sat on the front porch where we paid.

"They're free," Connie told me. "Take whichever ones you want." Greedily, I took one of each. As I read, I realized I was getting hungry; we all were.

No one was in a hurry, so we piled into the van and drove to Thomas Orchards. Its open-air store fronted a large peach orchard and sold bushels of peaches, tomatoes, seasonal vegetables, rustic knickknacks, and fresh peach ice cream. I bought a single-scoop cone and a bucket of peaches and mentally made a note to take half to Mom and Dad the next day.

Gradually, we gathered around an outdoor table and sat down to eat our ice cream. We talked about what our kids were up to, who was traveling where over the summer. The conversation soon drifted to the doings of friends in common, many of whom were known to me only by name. I wondered at myself, having lived twenty-three years in Athens, yet having such a small group of friends. I listened for clues, but remained mystified. Would it have been different if I'd belonged to a church? Lived in a different part of town? Why did I still feel like an outsider?

Another friend, Shannon, whom I'd last seen at MBA graduation, called me that summer to reconnect. Fifteen years my junior, I'd met her and Gwen on the first day of MBA orientation, and watched enviously as they became close. I was drawn to both of them, yet I remember not sitting with them after that first day, ostensibly to meet other people, but as I look back, really to prevent intimacy—if I spread myself thin, going deep was impossible.

That summer was a good time for us to renew a friendship. Shannon and I were both recovering from codependent family relationships. Healing physically, emotionally, and spiritually was a path we would walk together for a time and, without consciously under-standing any of this, I nonetheless felt blessed.

After graduation Shannon had moved to Atlanta to work for Delta. She and her boyfriend lived in a rental house in Brookhaven, part of metro Atlanta, and I began to venture out of my geographic comfort zone, driving into Atlanta to get together, which made me feel both brave and happy, because I was doing something I'd al-ways wanted to do. Growing up barely twenty minutes from the George Washington Bridge, I had always want-ed to become a pro at navigating New York's streets and subways, but never had. Little by little, I was learning my way around Atlanta instead.

It was the time before cell phones and GPS. All I had was a map, which I tried to memorize before get-ting into the car. But invariably, I'd get lost. Gradually I learned to always go in the opposite direction from what seemed logical, and then I'd find what I was looking for. Losing my way made the world so much bigger, too. It helped me connect where I was lost to what I was seek-ing. It was hard for me to let go of what I thought was the right way, but once I did, I became a better navigator of the unknown.

When Shannon and I first reconnected, her body was suffering from the after-effects of old habits, con-suming lots of Diet Coke and fast food, and she'd begun a cleansing, gut-healing regimen called the "Body Ecology

Diet." I, on the other hand, had been raised from child-hood to eat a good diet, rarely consumed fast food or soft drinks and, adhering to that old pattern, was basically healthy. I never gave much thought to what I ate.

The pursuit of really good food, good for the body, became a shared adventure for Shannon and me. I bought a copy of *The Body Ecology Diet* to understand its prin-ciples and the regimen Shannon followed, and adopted it myself. One day in late summer, we got together at her house in Brookhaven so she could teach me how to make coconut kefir, a key ingredient in the Body Ecology Diet.

"The fermentation process consumes the sugar in the coconut water," Shannon explained as she used a hammer and nail punch to make holes in young co-conuts to drain their liquid. "All that's left is vitamins, minerals, and probiotics. I drink it morning and night with a little flavored stevia. I've begun craving it."

"What do you do with the rest of the coconut?" I asked. I hated to see anything go to waste, a habit my mother engrained in all her children by reminding us there were people starving somewhere whenever we wanted to throw food away.

"When I'm feeling really ambitious, I break them open and scrape out the young meat. It's a lot of work." She showed me how to break the coconuts open with a hammer and chisel, scrape out the gelatinous meat, and puree it in a food processor with some kefir to make a fermented pudding. After a time on the diet, I began to crave the kefir and pudding, too, and to my great satis-faction, dropped a few pounds. The diet also taught the importance of food combining, that it was fine to eat proteins like meat, fish, and eggs along with the complex carbohydrates of vegetables, but never to mix proteins with simple carbohydrates like bread, potatoes, pasta, or rice.

A change as fundamental as diet, the foods I chose to eat every day, became the outer sign of the inner changes I hoped to make. I was my own science project, and it led me to explore unknown territory, connecting physical and emotional health. Intuitively, I knew that emotions were connected to physical health. I remembered the choice I made on the day of Todd's death, not to let my grief kill me, and the migraine I suffered when I was under such stress from Jonathan's and Todd's afflictions, and realized that my doctor had tacitly acknowledged a causal relationship, too, when he prescribed an antidepressant as a preventive measure.

Shannon was dealing with her own grief—her father, suffering from alcoholism, had died recently. It was another bond between us. Sipping kefir in her living room, we talked about loss and grief. "How can emotions make a person sick?" I asked. "They're not real, not in the way that bacteria and viruses are real. So how can they have a physical effect?"

"Because they're energy," Shannon answered. "We have an energy system in our body, just like we have a circulatory system and a nervous system. Have you ever heard of the chakras?"

"No."

"The chakras are energy centers in the body. They're connected by energy channels that run through the body. I just finished reading a book ..." She got up from the couch and went into her bedroom. In a moment she was back, and handed me *Anatomy of the Spirit*, by Caroline Myss. "Read this," she said. "It describes the chakra system and how our emotions can make us sick."

Intrigued, I took the book home with me. That night, I curled up on the loveseat in my parlor with a cup of tea and began reading. In the opening of *Anatomy of the Spirit*, the author described herself as a medical intuitive, a term new to me. In 1982, she began getting impressions—how and why she didn't know—of a person's physical health and the emotional energy behind it. Word of her uncanny insights grew, and she eventually honed her diagnostic and intuitive skills through practice and by working with respected physicians.[1]

According to Myss, the author, a medical intuitive perceives the energy of life, a skill anyone can learn. Energy pervades all living things and, in the body of a human being, it generates a measurable electromagnetic field that extends an arm's length in every direction. Myss described that field as "an information center and a highly sensitive perceptual system" through which messages are sent to and received from other people, other living things, and the Universe itself. Intuitives, she wrote, are able to perceive those transmissions and read the content stored in someone's electromagnetic field or "aura."[2]

Myss further explained that all our experiences, both positive and negative, generate emotional energy that becomes encoded in our body and influences the formation of cell tissue. She cited the work of neurobiologist Dr. Candace Pert, who proved that "neuropeptides—the chemicals triggered by emotions—are thoughts converted into matter. Our emotions reside physically within our bodies and interact with our cells and tissues." According to Pert, our emotions affect not just our brain but our entire body because, "The same cells that manufacture and receive emotional chemistry in the brain are present throughout the body."[3]

Even more fascinating was an excerpt from Pert's appearance in the Bill Moyers documentary, *Healing and the Mind*, which Myss quoted: "Clearly, there's another form of energy that we have not yet understood. For example, there's a form of energy that appears to leave the body when the body dies."[4]

What happened to the energy, the life-force that was Todd? I jumped up from the loveseat and stepped into the kitchen, unable to sit still, such was the intensity of the emotional charge that ran through me.

Late as it was, I had to read more. I knew I'd never be able to sleep until I did. I flipped ahead, skimming through pages, and was disappointed to find that Pert's comment on energy and what happens at death was a small aside, not at all the focus of Myss's book. Rather, *Anatomy of the Spirit* was a guide to learning the symbolic language of spirit, and to understanding how we create health or illness in the body. My old philosophy course kicked in. *Wasn't it Aristotle who said when the soul is sick, the body suffers?* Impatient, I put that thought aside and kept reading.

Myss organized her book around the chakra system. According to Eastern traditions, she explained, we have seven chakras, aligned from the base of the spine to the top of the head. Each is an energy center associated with a different set of organs or glands and with a corresponding set of physical, emotional, and psychological issues.[5]

I couldn't help but apply what I'd read to myself. I saw that the primal concerns of the first, second, and third chakras—family and survival, money, sex, and personal power—had dominated my first life. I married for security, out of a sense of powerlessness and self-sacrifice, and put Jonathan's needs and desires ahead of my own, as a good Catholic girl should. Self-sacrifice is a woman's work.

Looking back, I saw that I had lived my last ten years in a constant state of panic, fight or flight, and I wondered why I wasn't more sickly. What had protected me? I began to appreciate myself for what I'd accomplished. Although I felt like an abandoned child, I hadn't responded like one, or played the victim. I reacted to my circumstances in ways far more powerful than I'd given myself credit for. Despite all the problems, I gave my sons the normal childhood and family life I wanted for them. When Jonathan crashed, I provided the income that sustained the family. I stayed connected to my larger family and the emotional support they could give. I'd also stayed connected to the larger community and a sense of purpose through volunteerism.

Then, at the turning point of my life, during my personal "dark night of the soul," when Todd died on my birthday, that first life ended and the second began.

Birth, death, and rebirth. Ten months after his death, I was living on my own, supporting myself, creating and sustaining new friendships, and leading a community initiative. My sons loved and looked up to me, and my parents, brothers, and sisters loved and empathized with me. My "energy leak,"—if I had one—was grief, the ever-present wound I wasn't particularly interested in healing, because the pain reminded me of Todd, of my love for him, and kept me connected to him.

I finished the book in the wee hours, and went to bed in the midst of a mental sea change. Myss's book pointed to a spiritual understanding of life and the universe completely foreign to me, yet I could see how many facets of it applied to my life. She was careful to connect her work with cutting-edge science and medicine, which left me asking, *What am I missing?* I believed in science. How could science support a spiritual explanation of the universe?

Before I finally fell asleep, I wondered if anyone had proven a connection.

* * *

In the fall, I decided to go to an acupuncturist. Dr. Pan's office was in Watkinsville, the next town over from Athens. I'd begun to suffer from hot flashes and wanted to avoid taking the hormones a traditional doctor would undoubtedly prescribe. Plus, I was curious. If Caroline Myss was correct about our emotions having energy that could heal or sicken us, then acupuncture, which uses needles to stimulate the flow of chi, could affect both emotions and the body. I wanted to experience the connection between my energy and my physical body.

My first appointment was so unlike anything I'd previously experienced in a doctor's office. For the first half hour, Dr. Pan interviewed me about my health, diet, exercise, and life circumstances while he took my pulse at different points on both wrists. I explained that I didn't have any health complaints other than hot flashes, but wanted to prevent problems if I could. I told him about the losses I'd suffered the previous year, about Todd's death. He listened attentively, without comment, and then showed me to a treatment room, where I removed my outer clothing for my first acupuncture treatment. The needles were not at all painful and I gradually relaxed, even dozed a little over the next hour, until Dr. Pan returned to remove them. Then he instructed me to get dressed and meet him in his outer office.

I sat down at the small desk where he waited with several bottles of Chinese herbs, pea-sized black pellets. He told me one was for digestion and the others for hormone support, and prescribed the number to take every morning and evening. He also recommended I take Tai Chi classes with him at the church down the street, and gave me the schedule. I thanked him and made my next appointment. Then he handed me the business card of a grief therapist, and recommended making an appointment with her. I told him I'd think about it.

Even though I worked part-time for an office of therapists, I never considered going to one. My intuition told me I would heal in my own way. I trusted that inner voice. My path would be different.

On the other hand, I did follow Dr. Pan's advice to join the Thursday evening Tai Chi classes. The building, a church, had been converted into community space and living quarters by an architect I knew, and I felt I had a connection there. The instructors were Dr. Pan's student teachers. Tai Chi was such a peaceful, centering practice that I did it almost every day, stepping my way across the length of my apartment. Eventually I noticed that I could feel the chi, the life-force, between my hands in the opening movements, an interesting sensation of a charge without heat.

That same fall I learned my grant proposal had been funded, and I began recruiting instructors. They would have to commit to learning a curriculum called *PRIME For Life* and teaching for two years in exchange for free training. Once they became certified, they would be paid for co-teaching evening and Saturday classes.

Terry Daly, who led the substance-abuse prevention unit of the regional mental health system, had become a good friend as well as a colleague. Together we met with school district administrators and the juvenile court judge to set up new systems by which teens with alcohol or drug infractions would be required to take our *PRIME For Life* classes. University students who went into Athens's pretrial diversion program were already mandated into a UGA-based *PRIME For Life* course, but there were no such classes for high school students, nothing to influence their thinking or choices about alcohol or drugs. That was what I hoped to change. By teaching *PRIME For Life* to that group, we'd give students who were experimenting with the sensations of being drunk or high life-saving information that could prevent tragedy. Their parents would be required to attend too, so they'd know how to support their sons or daughters.

Changing the heavy-drinking culture of Athens was an even greater challenge, but our parent task force had the support of both the local district attorney and police chief. A new task force was formed to find ways to prevent underage drinking, one that included members from every facet of the community. The county commission prohibited bars from reopening as dance clubs after they closed at two in the morning, thus ending the "early training period" of high school students in the downtown bar scene. The bar owners eventually agreed to hospitality training for their employees, too, on how to detect fake IDs and to recognize and cut off those who'd had too much to drink. At the end of the training period, the police department ran sting operations to enforce underage drinking laws. In addition to fines, establishments with more than one offense risked losing their liquor license.

During this time, Ray Daugherty, one of the coauthors of the *PRIME For Life* curriculum, visited Athens to address a conference at UGA, and I had the opportunity to have dinner with him, Terry, and Lacy, who had become one of my new instructors. Naturally, the conversation turned to our efforts in Athens, and Terry and I described the resistance we were encountering, led by a very vocal and influential beer distributor.

"That reminds me of the time we were working with a large national fraternity organization," said Ray. "We were piloting the program with them and the president was encouraged by the results. He wanted to make it part of the fraternity's national initiative. He hoped to get funding from a national beer producer, and asked me to accompany him and some students to a meeting with the company's CEO. I was curious to see how the CEO would respond, so I agreed to go.

"The CEO was very polite and listened attentively to the students' presentation on *PRIME For Life*, and how it influenced people to make low-risk drinking choices. At the end, after the students made their request for financial support, he leaned back in his chair and said nothing. He was thinking. The students leaned forward in anticipation. Finally, he said, 'Hmmm, this just might work,' and rose to his feet. 'We won't be funding it. Thanks for coming.' Then he escorted us out of his office.

"So I'm not surprised that you're getting resistance," Ray concluded, smiling. "People who make low-risk choices are not good customers for anyone selling alcohol."

The following January, five instructors, including myself, attended a week-long *PRIME For Life* training class held at Advantage Behavioral Health, led by Terry and a co-teacher from the Prevention Research Institute, PRI. The course had changed tremendously from what I remembered of "Talking With Your Kids About Alcohol," the version Jonathan and I had taken so many years before. I found it fascinating to learn how the material had been designed to gently persuade without triggering someone's defenses, and I loved the fact that it was updated every five years to incorporate the latest research on drinking, drugs, and the brain.

I took the challenge of becoming a good instructor seriously. PRI's research showed that the percentage of students in any class choosing to make low-risk choices by the end of the course was directly correlated to the instructor's effectiveness. The training was emotionally challenging, too. I so wanted a "do-over" with Todd. I knew so much more now.

I began memorizing the script in the teacher's manual. I wanted to be as good as Terry, who knew the material so well that, when she taught, it sounded like she was having a personal conversation with each individual in the room. I loved to co-teach with her because it was both a refresher and the motivation to get better.

My most memorable experience was teaching with my friend Lacy at Clarke Central. I was teaching the marijuana section and quoted research showing that, in rare instances, marijuana use could trigger schizophrenia.[6]

"I think that's what happened to Todd," I told the class with whom he'd have graduated.

"It wasn't marijuana," murmured a young man in the front row. "It was LSD."

I was so startled that I just stared at him. Lacy, my co-teacher, quickly began talking to gloss over my astonishment.

Years later, I had the opportunity to talk with Ryan, Todd's best friend, about the drastic changes in Todd the last year of his life. The pain of talking about him had been muted by time for both of us. We could both reflect on the past without debilitating sorrow or guilt. We met for lunch.

"I've thought a lot about Todd. We really were best friends," he said. "His whole personality changed overnight. I think he was becoming schizophrenic."

"I didn't understand what was happening to him then and I'm trying to understand it now," I said. "Todd grew something like ten inches between freshman and sophomore year, plus he was going through puberty, so his hormones were crazy, too. Schizophrenia never occurred to me back then. Do you think Todd ever used LSD?"

"No. At least not with me," he replied. "And we hung around together all the time. We'd been best friends since Clarke Middle.

"When we got to Clarke Central, Dane was one of the most popular kids in the school," Ryan continued. "Dane was awesome, and I got to hang out with him because I hung out with his younger brother. And then Todd became one of the most popular kids in school, too. Todd was ambitious. He was a social climber. I remember him telling me once about a time he got to hang out with some really cool, older kids. I was like, 'Dude, why didn't you call me?' And he was just like, 'Hey, we all have to make our own way.'"

"I didn't realize Dane and Todd were so popular," I told him. "But then, I always had to talk to a neighbor's daughter to find out anything about my sons' social life. The three of them were always so closemouthed with me." I went back to my original question. "So Todd never told you he tried LSD?"

"LSD was around Clarke Central then, but I don't think Todd ever tried it. I never saw him use it."

"But he did smoke pot," I said, wanting confirmation.

"Yeah, we did. But it was crazy. I've never seen anything like it," Ryan answered. "When Todd smoked marijuana, he would pass out."

"What?" I'd never heard such a thing. "You mean he blacked out?"

"Yeah. I remember one time, three of us smoked together, and we went to a drugstore for candy. Suddenly Todd hits the floor, out cold. Me and the other kid were scared shitless. We dragged him out of the store as fast as we could, before anyone could see and call the police."

I was dumbfounded. I'd never heard of anyone blacking out from pot. But if Todd had been that sensitive to its effects, then perhaps it *had* triggered schizophrenia in him. My denial of the seriousness of Todd's mental state grieved me anew. I was so sure he would get better if he just did as I asked. I never doubted that I could right his world if he would just let me help him. Why had I not seen it?

In the backup research in the *PRIME For Life* teacher's manual, I learned that in some people—especially those with a family history of psychosis—marijuana can cause delusions, violent outbursts, panic attacks, and depression, all symptoms that Todd had presented. If I had only known.

It all made sense now. Todd's favorite song, which he used to play over and over, was the Geto Boys song "Mind is Playing Tricks on Me." Jason told me he had once asked Todd what was wrong with him, but all Todd said was, "I've lost my shit." And then Todd's note, "The life has gone out of me and I can't get it back." *Finally,*

I thought, *I understand everything.* But I had so much more to learn.

CHAPTER FIFTEEN

Chrysalis

I returned from New Jersey, where I had celebrated Christmas and welcomed in the new millennium, in good time to attend the first board of education meeting of the year. It was my fourth year on the board. Since the previous summer, I'd come to the conclusion that it was time for a change in leadership, and it had gradually become apparent over the rest of the year that I wasn't the only board member who thought so.

It was a difficult decision to make, because I knew some of the people who had helped me get elected, and whom I'd come to think of as friends, would see it as a betrayal. The superintendent was African American, the first in the history of the Clarke County School District. It was a point of pride for many in the black community, and it sometimes made me wonder which was more important to them—having an African-American superintendent or seeing children succeed in the classroom.

Voting to remove the superintendent wasn't in my political best interests—I would be running for reelection in the fall. And it simply was hard to fire a person. But I felt a responsibility, first to the children, and then to the parents, teachers, and principals—they deserved better. Looking back, I think my greatest contribution as a board member was to open up the system to new leadership and new possibilities, though it did ultimately cost me my seat. As much as that felt like a loss at the time, a withdrawal from the public eye also felt right. I wanted to be at home by myself, where I could lick my wounds and cry in peace.

Another teenaged boy died while I was on the board, but I couldn't be a comfort to his parents. One year after Todd's death, my own sorrow was still too raw and deep. I stayed away from funerals, not only to protect myself from the pain, but also to not distract others from the pain of those newly stricken parents. I look back now at the generosity and compassion bestowed upon me at the time of Todd's death by mothers who had lost their own children, and I am humbled—deeply humbled—and so truly grateful.

There were to be other changes as the year 2000 began. The dean had appointed my boss to be the director of the evening MBA program, which left an opening for director of MBA admissions. My new boss, Mel, asked me if I would be applying and, thinking of my responsibilities to the grant I'd received and the substance-abuse prevention work I was doing, I told him, no, I didn't think so. However, I talked over the opportunity with the director of operations for the school district, and he urged me to reconsider. John had become a mentor and a friend. A position with the university offered benefits and a pension as well as a secure income, he argued. Why wouldn't I try for that?

So I asked myself that same question, and realized I was falling into an old habit—trying to save the world without thinking about what was good for me. Did I see myself living on grants for the next thirty years? Would it give me the career, financial security, and life I wanted? The answer, I realized, was no. Jonathan's entrepreneurial venture had soured me on the lifestyle. I wanted never again to have to worry about where my next paycheck was coming from.

I told my boss I'd be applying for the director of admissions position after all. I interviewed, and was hired at the beginning of March. While my decision meant I had to give notice at the Samaritan Center, I realized I could continue my prevention work on the side. It was the interaction with teens and parents that I really wanted to hold onto. I received a renewal of the grant for the following year, and hired my replacement for the coordinator position, but continued as a *PRIME For Life* instructor on evenings and weekends.

The third big change in the year 2000 was the official end of my marriage. Jonathan had gotten his new mortgage, I my payment, and the two of us, our uncontested divorce. I invested the money to give myself time to think about what I wanted next—to stay in my worry-free apartment or buy my own place.

Soon after, Dane phoned me to say that he, Jason, and Jonathan wanted a family meeting to talk about what to do with Todd's ashes. Instantly, I knew that Jonathan was using Dane as his go-between. Jonathan, not Dane or Jason, was the one who wanted to meet. Of course I didn't say that to Dane, just listened as he continued.

"Jason and I went hiking with Dad and his friend Drew in North Carolina last weekend," Dane said. "We spent the whole day there. At one point we stood on a cliff that looked out over this beautiful valley. It might be a good place to spread Todd's ashes."

"Really? North Carolina? I don't know about that."

"We can talk about it," Dane said. "Jason's coming in from Atlanta on Sunday. Can we meet at Dad's then?"

Convinced this was Jonathan's idea, I was furious that he would use Dane that way. I felt violated too, that Jonathan was trying to manipulate me. And I felt cornered, like I had no choice. "Okay, I guess so."

"Thanks, Mom." Dane sounded relieved. "Can I pick you up? We can go together."

We met early the following Sunday afternoon, in Jonathan's studio. I remember sitting on the sofa, with Dane and Jason on either side of me, as Jonathan, seated in a folding chair before us, opened the question in his best holier-than-thou manner. "I always tried to be a good father to Todd," he said, "and I feel like I'm neglecting my duty as a father by letting his ashes sit upstairs in his room."

I said nothing, but felt strangled by anger. Not only had Jonathan conveniently forgotten that he and Todd used to live in an almost perpetual state of war with each other, but he was also implying I was neglecting my duty to Todd, should I object. I saw the real reason behind our meeting—Jonathan wanted Todd's ashes out of the house. They made him uncomfortable. *He's kicked me out*, I thought angrily, *now he's kicking Todd out, too.*

"Jason, Dane, and I just came back from a trip to North Carolina," Jonathan solemnly continued. "On our hike, we came across a good place, very beautiful, to release Todd's ashes. That's why we're here today." He stopped and looked at me. It was my turn.

"I don't agree. That place meant nothing to Todd. And it's so far away. I want to be close to him, in a place that had meaning for him."

Dane and Jason remained quiet. With my eyes on the carpet, I said, "What about Todd's garden?" My mother and I had created a small garden in her backyard with some of the plants and flowers given us when Todd died.

"At your parents' house?" Jonathan asked. "What if they sell it?"

"Why should that matter? You're ready to dump them over some cliff somewhere."

"It doesn't have to be there," Dane offered. "What about the lake?"

"That's better," I conceded, "at least we have memories of being there together."

"When do you want to do it?" Jonathan asked. "Today's a nice day."

I began to cry. "I'm not ready! I'm not ready to let him go. I can't bear it!" I stood up to face Jason and Dane. "This cannot happen again, do you hear me? If anything happened to you, it *would* kill me. Do you understand? *I go next.*"

I turned to Jonathan. "I'll take Todd's ashes home with me. You won't be bothered by them anymore." Then I walked out of the studio and up to Todd's bedroom. The ashes were just where I'd left them, in the center of his dresser, in the Christmas gift bag. I took them downstairs with me, held them in a hug at my belly.

"Let's go," I said to Dane as I walked back into the studio. "I'll see you later," I told Jason. We were having dinner together at their grandparents' house. Then I turned and walked out to Dane's car, still weeping with anger and sorrow.

When I got home, I put Todd's ashes at the corner of my dresser, directly across from his portrait. It comforted me to have him with me in my sanctuary. I placed a photo of myself on top of the can so we would always be together, even when I wasn't there.

Our divorce might have been a quiet, peaceful affair, but my reaction showed me that I hadn't forgiven Jonathan and was still angry with him. Except for flowers and chocolates from a "secret admirer" the following Valentine's Day, I didn't hear from him again for two years. But I did send him a message, a hurtful message, just once, through Dane, so he could see how it felt. It was an awful thing to do to Dane, for which I apologized much later.

Forgiving Jonathan wasn't a priority, though. Our paths never crossed and the only time I thought of him was at the holidays, when I might have to share Jason and Dane with him. Mom and Dad invited him to dinner from time to time, but that was their affair. I admired their compassion. I had none. With time and distance,

I hoped my anger would wane and forgiveness take its place.

Two years later, however, when Jonathan sent me a letter of apology—one of AA's twelve steps—I could barely bring myself to read it.

Dear Anne,

The contents of this letter are things I wanted to tell you and I debated about asking to meet with you but came to the conclusion that you would feel uncomfortable or not meet at all. Letters are safe and hard to put down sometimes. I hope this one is.

Mike's [Jonathan's friend–AC] only comments about the time he spent with you was he made you laugh and cry. He did the same thing to me. He shared how terribly disappointed you were in Jonathan. [Jonathan often referred to himself in the third person when talking about an emotionally difficult subject.–AC] Disappointed doesn't quite cover it—but there has been enough time and distance for me to hold an honest court in my mind and to better understand "disappointed."

You were betrayed pure and simple. The marriage was betrayed. Jonathan betrayed himself. Then Jonathan was angered and hurt. The hurt will recede but remain. The anger is evolving into understanding, which hopefully becomes a tool for me to understand me. (When does one finally grow up!) I don't have any idea of what to do with the embarrassment, but evidently I'm doing something. Mom's invited me to dinner twice.

Each time I was awed by their love. Pretty soon I'll find enough courage to give your parents a verbal version of this letter.

When Mike told me you'd be over to pick him up, I got quite upset. While you picked him up I was conveniently taking a shower, thinking that I cannot look that woman in the face after what I have done to her. The shame and guilt are overwhelming sometimes, but I will not close the door on the past. Honestly understanding the past and realizing what and why I insisted on the course I took is the future and this is probably one of the hardest assignments I will ever have. There is no final goal, but a process.

In trying to understand the past I was surprised how much my concept of you influenced me. Not necessarily your relationship with me (I take—you give) but your relationship with yourself. I have come to greatly respect and admire you as a person. Where you have been, where you are now, and where I think you will go. How does she do it?

I am forced to look at the past with an honest eye to glean what I can to answer that question and there is an abundant amount of lousy past to choose from. It is a tool to help me understand me. I remember the good times too. I'm proud to have been your husband. My heart approaches you the same way it approaches Todd. "Thank you for sixteen years, at least I got that out of life anyway." Thank you for twenty-four years, Anne.

For some time I have realized that I have got to sit down with Jason and Dane and speak candidly about filling wine bottles with water, stealing change out of their piggy banks, and explaining why our marriage dissolved. I'll probably have them over for dinner in the spring. I am thankful to have the loving relationship with them that I do and this will make my amends somewhat easier.

One of the recent conclusions I have come to is that using Jason and Dane as a go-between for messages to you is terribly wrong and I have vowed never to use the words "Tell your mother" again. I did once that I remember and realized when the act was returned, how stressful it was on Dane. If it is important to intrude on you with a communication, I'll contact you directly—shame or not.

I wrote this letter for me as well as for you. In reading it, I realize how pitiful I am at conveying my thoughts in writing. I have neither the elegance nor talent to express my innermost feelings but in the most basic arrangement of letters, I hope someday to earn your forgiveness.

The most basic arrangement of letters: I am truly sorry,

Jonathan

I scanned the letter quickly. The lines that caught my eye, "You were betrayed pure and simple," and "I take—you give," and "How does she do it?" penetrated my defenses. The rest could have been pure gibberish. I was astonished at my reaction, that I was still so angry.

I reread the letter several times, and hoped to unearth some compassion in myself for the writer, but found only exasperation and resentment.

I felt manipulated again. *Great, so now I have to respond with my own letter.* But then I realized I didn't have to respond in kind, I had a choice. So I emailed Jonathan to acknowledge receiving the letter and promised to answer when I felt ready. Then I put it away.

Yes, I felt I owed him an answer, but not right away. I'd get back to him when the time was right for me. My priority was myself. For the first time in my life, my only responsibility was to nurture and heal myself. I took a weekly meditation class at the Athens Yoga Center in addition to my weekly Tai Chi class, but it didn't take. I wasn't ready for meditation, but I was ready for something.

* * *

In that first year as admissions director, my life revolved around work and it felt good. I recruited two classes per year, one for the eleven-month program that began in late May, and another for the two-year program that began in early August. The work, though cyclical in nature, was creative as well, and I moved the office toward a paperless system as quickly as computer and Web technology allowed. The part I enjoyed most was opening the door to people who wanted to make big changes in their lives. Orientation for each new class of students was, in part, a celebration of their transition to a new life.

Friendships were also blooming. Jan and Chris, both new additions to the MBA staff and single like me, had made big life changes themselves, moving to Athens and starting over. The three of us began having lunch together, and would occasionally go out on the weekend for dinner or a movie.

One Friday afternoon in February 2001, we all went for lunch to a Creole restaurant, to celebrate the birthday of another staff member. I ordered shrimp and grits, the thought of which today still makes me slightly nauseous, though not for the reason you might think. After lunch, a bunch of us decided to go to a movie together after work.

My stomach felt unsettled all afternoon. I assumed my entrée simply didn't agree with me, so I skipped dinner and met Chris and Jan at the movie theatre. I couldn't bring myself to eat anything there either. My indigestion persisted. As soon as I got home, I went straight to bed.

I awoke at midnight in gut-wrenching pain. I was vomiting a bit, not nearly on par with the nausea I felt, and concluded I must have gotten food poisoning at lunch. *Once that meal is out of my system*, I thought, *I'll feel better*. But at five a.m., the pain was worse. Desperate for relief and realizing I was unable to drive, I called Mom and Dad and asked them to take me to the emergency room.

Is it emergency room protocol that you must wait a minimum of an hour before someone sees you? We'd waited at least that long before I asked Mom to push the receptionist to get me in front of a doctor. I was finally examined by a nurse, who asked about what I'd eaten and felt around my abdomen. I couldn't tell if the pain was emanating from my right side. All I knew was that it had me doubled over. I was sent for an abdominal X-ray.

The diagnosis was appendicitis, and I was scheduled for immediate laparoscopic surgery. The pain by that time had gotten worse, even worse than labor, rendering me eager to be unconscious. When I awakened from the anesthesia, relief washed over me. The pain was gone and a tiny incision, no more than an inch, was all that was left of it. A quick recovery, and I was working half-days by the middle of the week. But I knew enough to be gentle with myself, and to take some time to understand what just happened.

What was my body telling me? I reflected on Myss's *Anatomy of the Spirit* and another book Shannon had turned me onto, Christiane Northrup's *Women's Bodies, Women's Wisdom*. They helped me explore the question.

The appendix is a second chakra organ. According to Northrup, most young adults unconsciously move into the roles of their second chakras and choose the partner that fulfills their second chakra needs. Women tend to marry for physical security, money, children, social status, and out of fear of abandonment.[1]

Learning this, I saw that the drivers of the most important decisions I'd made in my first life, as I was moving toward graduation from college and looking about for what I would do next, had been unconscious ones. Lacking the confidence to live on my own, I'd married Jonathan instead, an easy answer. As much as I had looked forward to a career, I chose to be a mother and a homemaker. The longer I stuck to those safe choices—for I knew deep within that I wasn't being true to myself—and the more I ignored the truth and promised myself that I would find happiness and fulfillment in

loving Jonathan and my children and doing for others—
the more life piled on, until I surrendered to the truth I
knew in my heart and soul.

For years, the energies of fear, anger, betrayal,
shame, and dependency had percolated in my body in
varying degrees, finally to be expressed in its most vul-
nerable part. Fortunately for me, the appendix. Of all
the second chakra organs—appendix, uterus, ovaries,
vagina, cervix, large intestine, bladder, lower vertebrae,
pelvis—only the appendix can be spared without major
health implications.[2] And that was where my negative
energies had settled. I felt immense gratitude that my
body had stored my second chakra issues there.

And what of the grief and anger I felt—still felt—toward Todd and Jonathan? I still cried every day. I'd come
home after work, lie down on my bed, and give full voice
to my grief—choking, loud sobs from deep inside of me.
I wondered if I would ever wash it all away.

Gradually, however, I felt my energy changing. For
the first time in my life, I was not only independent and
living on my own, but I also felt financially secure, professionally competent, and connected to other women.
I had shed a marriage that had tied me to a man who
needed more than loved me, in which I gave more than
I received, and where I felt responsible for everyone and
everything, but ultimately had no control. Moreover, I
had shed the belief that my needs always came last and
that I wasn't worthy of living the life I wanted. Self-
sacrifice was not my life's purpose after all. Was it any
wonder then, that I had shed my appendix?

Spring was coming to Athens. It was March. Each week, a new wave of color washed through town. First yellow, as forsythia adorned what had appeared to be naked piles of sticks, and daffodils bravely broke through the earth despite the cold nights. Then the shock of white-blossomed Bradford pear trees warming into pink-flowering cherry trees and rosy crabapples. Lavender wisteria choked the wild places with thick clusters of blossoms. Then a final mass of color as the dogwood trees, azaleas, and pansies piled on with the coming of April.

I decided I wasn't going to renew my lease, and gave notice to the apartment complex manager that I'd move out at the end of May. I contacted a former co-worker, asked her to be my real estate agent, and began looking for a place to buy. I wanted a townhouse. There wasn't much of a selection in Athens, but I found exactly what I was looking for right across the Clarke County line in Oconee County.

With the help of Dad and the boys, I moved my few things into my very own place. I had big plans for renovating the kitchen, but had to put those on hold until I could afford them. But paint was cheap! I'd painted Jean's house, rental houses, the Westgate house—now finally, I was painting my own house, mine alone, and no one could take it from me.

The front room first, then I worked my way from the main floor to the three bedrooms and baths. It took hundreds of hours, spackling, sanding, and taping off trim, but I enjoyed every minute. It was mindless and relaxing and a way of making my new space my own.

It was healing, too, the application of color to my new life. I was nesting again, making space, for what, I hardly knew. I knew only that it would be true, true to the heart of me, mine, and mine to share. In my bedroom I hung my sister Edna's graduation present, the print with the Jayne Relaford Brown poem, "Finding Her Here."

> I find her becoming,
> this woman I've wanted,
> who knows she'll encompass,
> who knows she's sufficient,
> knows where she's going
> and travels with passion.
> Who remembers she's precious,
> but knows she's not scarce—
> who knows she is plenty,
> plenty to share.[3]

CHAPTER SIXTEEN

Connection

One perk of working in higher education is having the week off between Christmas and New Year's Day. My girlfriend Chris had gone to Indiana to celebrate Christmas with her family and see friends there, but came back a couple days before New Year's Eve. We got together for dinner to exchange presents and, since her birthday was right after Christmas, to celebrate that as well. As our conversation turned to the year ahead, Chris asked, "What's in the works for 2003? Are you making a New Year's resolution?"

"I haven't thought about it," I replied.

"What might it be?" Chris liked to push me out of my comfort zone. She was good for me that way.

"Hmmm." I leaned back in my chair to think. Perhaps it was the Christmas spirit that affected me, because it came to me quickly what my resolution should be. "To have more fun!" It felt so good to say it, I knew it must be right.

"Excellent!" Chris said. "How will you do that?"

"I don't know yet," I said, "I'll see what the Universe brings." I had adopted that parlance somehow; it had become a comfortable way of referring to unknown possibility.

Chris smiled, satisfied by my answer. And she didn't let me forget it. A week later she forwarded an email to me, an invitation to a gathering at someone's home in Atlanta, to meet with a visiting California psychic and learn from our "angel guides." I laughed out loud at my desk.

At lunch, she brought up the email. "So what do you think? Want to go?"

"You're serious?" Chris was the most grounded, matter-of-fact person I knew, hardly the woo-woo type.

"Yes, I'm thinking of going," she said. "Come with me."

"To hear from my angels?" I chuckled. "I know who my angels are. One's sitting across from me now."

She laughed. "Okay, don't give me an answer yet. Think about it."

At the end of the day, I reread her email. It was for Friday night, so we'd have to leave directly from work to make it in time. *What the hell*, I thought, *I'm not doing anything, I'll go.* So I emailed her back.

The two of us arrived just as the program was getting started. The hostess greeted us at the front door and ushered us into the living room. There were five other women there, seated in a semicircle around the psychic Alexa, tall, blond, and dressed in a flowing white robe, just as I imagined. Chris and I took our seats.

The program was like a self-help workshop, learning to listen to your angels—what I'd call my intuition. Nothing particularly memorable, until the end. Alexa announced she would go around the circle and give each woman a short reading. When it was my turn, she said, "I see a red flower blooming up and through you. Claim your power. Let your soul guide you to love yourself. Go into your heart, it knows. I see increased health and energy. There's writing—a lot—and inspired. It will be a benefit to you and others."

Alexa had caught me with the image of the red flower. I did feel like I was blossoming into something new, that I was claiming my power. But writing? I had a love-hate relationship with writing. It was the hardest work I knew and I didn't do it voluntarily. I couldn't picture myself writing anything; it took too much time and effort. So I asked her, "I work full-time. How will I find the time to write?"

"Trust you have the time for it," she answered.

"Will it be published?" I asked, joking. "Fiction or nonfiction?"

"Even if it's presented as fiction, it will be nonfiction," she replied. Then she moved on to Chris.

I was intrigued, but resisted being impressed. By the time we got back to Athens Chris and I were famished, so we stopped for a late dinner at a restaurant on the Atlanta Highway. While waiting for our meal, we sipped our wine and discussed the evening.

"That was an interesting reading Alexa gave you," Chris observed, "did it ring true?"

"Some of it," I admitted. "I loved the red flower part. That felt true. But I've never thought of myself as a writer. That part is hard to believe."

"Do you ever write? Keep a journal?"

"The only writing I do is for work. I can't remember the last time I wrote for myself."

I watched her sip her wine and asked, "What about you? Why did you want to go tonight?"

"I'm interested in spirituality."

"Have you ever done anything like this before?"

"Yes, once, with a girlfriend, back in Fort Wayne."

"Tell me about it."

"Well, my friend was very depressed and I was really worried about her. Her parents had both died within six months of each other, and she couldn't get over losing them. I wanted to get her out of the house. She was becoming a recluse. So I invited her out to dinner and had to talk her into going. I took her to this restaurant I knew that featured a woman who walked around and read palms.

"During dinner, the woman stopped at our table. She looked at my friend and said, 'Your mother is very worried about you. She wants you to stop grieving and get on with your life. She says it's beautiful where she is and she's very happy. She plays the piano and sings with your father all day long.'

"My girlfriend couldn't believe it. She said, 'That's how Mom and Dad spent their Saturday nights! Mom played the piano and she and Dad sang their favorite songs.' After that, she recovered. She stopped grieving and started living again."

If it hadn't been Chris telling the story, I wouldn't have believed it. But it was Chris, and I respected and trusted her.

Visiting a bookstore soon after, I ran across James Van Praagh's book, *Talking to Heaven*. I remembered the one and only Compassionate Friends meeting I attended, how the coach who'd lost his son had urged us to read it. My conversation with Chris made me curious about psychics, so I decided to buy another of Van Praagh's books, *Healing Grief*. That seemed a more realistic goal for me. Talking to heaven was not in my line.

At least that's what I thought at the time. Later, I wasn't so sure. The early pages acknowledged the pain of losing a loved one and described the stages of grief so familiar to me, identical to the materials in the big three-ring binder that Bernstein's Funeral Home had given us along with Todd's ashes. I knew all those stages intimately: shock, denial, anger, guilt, and sadness or depression. The one that eluded me was acceptance.

The grieving process varied with each individual, Van Praagh wrote,[1] and from the first, I knew instinctively that I would go through mine alone, without resorting to negative behaviors and without turning to therapy or established religion. I stayed connected to family and friends, but grieving was the conversation I held solely with myself.

I was unprepared to accept Van Praagh's ultimate worldview of a wise and loving Universe/God Force within each of us.[2] He advocated surrender, however, and that I had done—I'd had no choice. I no longer suffered from the illusion that I had control over anything or anyone. Jonathan and Todd taught me well.

The rest of the book I read with a suspension of disbelief. I devoured the stories of Van Praagh's experiences as a medium, of his apparent ability to connect with the spirits of those who had died. They were like fairy tales that I wished were true.

Van Praagh's discussion of suicide caught me, however, and made me wonder. He said that spirits who committed suicide usually say they regret it, and that frequently they had committed suicide in a past life.[3] I thought about Todd and Jonathan's daughter Ryder, about how they had both died so young, and wondered about their connection. *Poor Jonathan*, I thought, *now I know his pain.*

Other souls who commit suicide have mental and biochemical imbalances, and these souls, Van Praagh explained, aren't fully conscious of their decisions. Was Todd fully aware of what he was doing when he ran out of his grandparents' house? Had some terrible fear, stemming from marijuana-triggered schizophrenia, driven him to run, just run without looking, without judgment? Van Praagh wrote that these souls receive restorative care on the other side before they move into the higher realms.[4]

Todd's last year, the bubble of confusion he lived in, that we both lived in, his terrible unhappiness with himself, my own terror and overwhelming sense of helplessness, all rose up before me. I had forgiven him at the time of his death, but sorrow, anger, and regret weighed me down. The acceptance that signified healing felt forever out of reach. Van Praagh recommended meditation—on healing myself, healing the sense of loss, creating what I wanted for the future.[5] I was already building a new life, but taking a leap of faith—in a God Force, in actual life after death, based on his stories about contacting loved ones on the other side—that wasn't a leap I was prepared to make.

* * *

That same January, Chris and I started taking a yoga class at the Healing Arts Centre in Athens. The Centre, originally the home of Athens's Unitarian church, had been renovated into an herbal pharmacy, yoga studio, and bottom-floor alternative therapy office suite. We went straight there after work on Thursday nights. I fell in love with yoga and continued taking classes even after Chris stopped going. It felt familiar, like a homecoming, and I practiced faithfully each evening at home after work, repeating the same asanas in the same order as that week's class.

Meanwhile, Chris was having some health issues and was searching for a solution. She would become faint during the day and thought she might be hypoglycemic. She consulted a doctor and a nutritionist, changed her diet to eat every few hours, but felt no better. I tried to interest her in the Body Ecology Diet, but it sounded too difficult to her—Chris was no cook. So then I recommended Dr. Pan; she started seeing him and slowly began to feel better.

It was early February when Chris came to my office to tell me about a new experience she'd had at the

Healing Arts Centre. "I had a reiki massage last night after work. It was amazing!"

As she raved about how much her energy had changed, she laid a gift certificate on my desk. "Here, I want you to try it. The therapist's name is Melissa Moulder. Make an appointment and tell me what you think."

I was surprised and touched by her gift, given for no other reason than friendship. I promised to go as soon as I could find time. In the college admissions business, the first quarter of the year is the busiest and though I had an administrative assistant, I was essentially a one-person operation. I took files home to read almost every night of the week and did candidate interviews all day long.

So it wasn't until the middle of March that I remembered the certificate. I called the Centre and made an appointment with Melissa for a week later, a Saturday, which happened to be the day before Easter, at one o'clock. My plan was to have the reiki massage, go home and shower, then pack a bag for an overnight stay at my brother John and his girlfriend Lori's new house in Roswell, a town just outside Atlanta.

I arrived promptly at the Centre at one for my appointment. I'd just sat down in the waiting room when a young woman entered. She was my height, at least twenty years younger, with large brown eyes and shoulder-length brown hair. "Anne?" she said.

"Yes. Melissa? Good to meet you." We shook hands.

"Come in." She turned and brushed through the curtained entrance to a hallway, and I followed her into a treatment room, small and snug, dominated by a large massage table in the center, with barely enough room to walk on either side.

I handed her the gift certificate and said, "Chris swears by you. She gave me this months ago. She can't wait for me to try reiki."

Melissa smiled. "So what are you interested in," she asked, "reiki or reiki massage?"

Feeling both skeptical and adventurous, I asked, "What exactly is reiki?"

"Reiki is a way of manipulating energy to increase the flow of chi in the body," she explained. "It increases energy and helps the body heal itself."

"And what's the difference between reiki and reiki massage?"

"In a reiki session, I work directly with your energy. You've had a massage before, right?" I nodded. "Or I can give you a full body massage and add some reiki wherever I find your energy is stuck."

"Let's do straight reiki. I know what massage does for me, I'd like to see what reiki does by itself. What do I do?"

"Nothing, just lie on the table. I'll start at your head and work my way down the length of your body. Do you have any health problems?"

"No, I'm pretty healthy."

"Okay, then I'll step out and let you take off your street clothes. But before you do, pick out the colors that you're drawn to." She laid out a rainbow of scarves on the table. I picked the blue and purple ones. Melissa added red, orange, and yellow. I learned later that the scarves corresponded to the colors of the chakras. Red, orange, and yellow are the colors of the first, second, and third chakras, the ones that were such a challenge to me. Blue and purple are for the sixth and seventh chakras, representing voice and spirituality.

"After you undress, get under the sheet and lie face-down on the table. I'll be back in a few minutes," Melissa said. Then she left the room and closed the door.

I stepped out of my sandals, slipped off my shirt and slacks, and climbed up on the table. Feeling chilled, I was thankful for the sheet over me. As I placed my face in the headrest and shifted side to side to find a comfortable fit, I wondered what was going to happen and how it would feel. The skeptic in me wondered whether I would feel anything at all, but the explorer was excited.

I heard Melissa come back in the room and close the door. She placed the scarves at different points on my back. Then she walked to the top of the table, stood in front of my head, and began. I focused intently on what was happening. Not much, it seemed. I tried to re-lax and open up to the experience while Melissa touched me lightly, tapping the top of my head and the top of each shoulder. She then moved to the side of the table and continued whatever she was doing on my back. I felt nothing, but there was a sense of calm in the room. I was relaxed and peaceful.

I didn't know how much time had passed, but grad-ually I realized that Melissa was working somewhere on my legs, below the knees. I couldn't see what she was doing. It seemed that at least an hour had gone by, and I started wondering when she would finish. She didn't

214 • ANNE C. COOPER

touch me, but I could sense her. Sometimes I could hear her take a breath. She was taking a long time.

More time passed. Suddenly she began to sing quietly, in a language I didn't recognize. Her song was sad and mournful and my eyes filled with tears, though I didn't know why. Finally, she laid her hands on my legs and told me to get up. "We'll talk after you get dressed," she said, then left the room.

I hastily put on my clothes and sat down. I could tell from looking out the window that it was late afternoon. I wondered what had just happened and why I had teared up. I grabbed a tissue, wiped my eyes, and blew my nose. Melissa returned a few minutes later and pulled up a chair to sit across from me, her shoulder almost touching the table.

"How do you feel?" she asked. Our eyes met.

"I don't know. What was that song?"

"I was chanting in Sanskrit, Shula Chandra. I guess you noticed that I spent a lot of time at your feet."

"Yes, what was that about?"

"My spirit guides told me to smooth your aura at your legs. And every time I did, I saw a child come tumbling at me."

Incredulity about spirit guides became alarm. I tried not to see Todd tumbling under a car.

Melissa looked at me and hesitated, then said, "Sometimes, when I work on a client, I find an energetic connection with someone close to them who's died. When a husband loses his wife, for instance, I'll find that they're still energetically connected. Have you lost someone recently? Has someone close to you died?"

Every hair on my neck and arms was standing at attention. I said quietly, "My son, Todd. Five years ago this coming October. He was hit by a car and killed." My vision was obscured by tears. I tried to reabsorb them before they could spill out by closing my eyes.

Melissa rested her hand on my knee. She said nothing, simply sat quiet and still. I waited. "Get back up on the table," she said. We stood up together and I started to lie down on the massage table again. "No, no, sit Indian-style," she instructed. Not knowing what to expect, I sat on the table, swung up my legs, and crossed them in front of me.

From a small table at the long end of the room, opposite the door, she picked up a string tied to a long, tear-shaped crystal prism. Then she climbed up on the massage table and sat across from me. She held the string with the crystal between two fingers, her elbow out in front of her torso, so that the crystal could swing freely. It hung between us, not moving.

She said a prayer aloud to her spirit guides. I listened as she asked them for guidance and thanked them for allowing her to be present with me. Then she began asking questions, but not of me.

"Do I have your permission to work with Anne?" The crystal started swinging back and forth between us, but I couldn't detect any movement on Melissa's part. I watched carefully.

"Is it appropriate for me to work with her energy?" The crystal continued its movement.

"Is there another being in Anne's energy field?" The same swinging.

"Do I have your permission to work with the being in her field?" It continued swinging back and forth.

"Is this being connected to Anne energetically?" The crystal's movement continued.

"Does this being need to be attached to her?" The crystal's swing shortened, then began swinging side to side, left, then right.

"Is this being a drain on her energy?" The side-to-side movement continued.

"Is this being related to Anne?" I watched Melissa's arm and shoulder; they were perfectly still as the crystal's swing shortened again and changed. It returned to swinging back and forth, from her to me.

"Is this her son, Todd?" The crystal's motion didn't change. Yes. A shock rushed through me.

"Did Todd stay on the earth plane after he died?" The back-and-forth swinging continued.

"Is Todd connected to his mother?" Yes, the crystal said. Tears ran down my cheeks.

"Does Todd need to be attached to Anne?" The crystal gradually changed to a side-to-side motion. No.

"Has Todd chosen to stay on this earth plane?" Again the crystal slowly changed direction. It began swinging back and forth again.

"Does Todd want to go to the Light?" The crystal slowed until it had no clear movement. Melissa continued. "Is there a reason that Todd has not returned to the Light?" The crystal swung back and forth. Yes.

"Is this reason connected with Anne?" Yes.

"Is Anne the reason Todd has not gone to the Light?" Yes.

"Is there a benefit to Todd for remaining on this earth plane?" The crystal slowed and swung left to right. No.

"Does Todd remain for Anne's benefit?" Again the crystal slowed, then began swinging back and forth. Yes. I pressed my lips tight to hold back a sob.

"Does Todd remain to stay with his mother?" Yes.

"Does he stay of his own choice?" Yes.

"Does he stay to take care of her?" Yes.

Melissa lowered the crystal to her lap and looked me in the eyes. I was weeping silently. "So my guides are telling me that Todd stayed on this earth plane after he died to take care of you, rather than return to the Light. He must love you very much." She handed me a tissue. "It's difficult for a soul to straddle two planes. But he wants to do it." She paused. "What do you want?"

I was stunned. Love for my son vibrated in every part of me. I choked on my words. I felt so cherished and so grateful, just at the thought that he had stayed with me, to take care of me, to help me through my grief. I couldn't answer right away. What did I want?

Energy is neither created nor destroyed. My hope that the organized energy that was Todd still existed somewhere, somehow, had been just that—hope. I never believed that an afterlife existed, or that there were other planes of existence outside of the four-dimensional one in which I lived. But if there was an afterlife, I wanted Todd to do what was best for him.

"I want to tell him how grateful I am and how much I love him. I miss him so much. I want him to know that I'm okay. I'm strong. I can take care of myself—I'm in a

good place now. So if there's a way, I want him to continue to grow and develop. I want him to continue on his
journey, whatever that is."

I broke down then and sobbed. I loved him so much.
I wanted to hold him, kiss him. Part of me didn't want
to let him go. I didn't want another separation. But I also
wanted what was best for him. I wanted him to grow—
growth was life, life that overcame death.

"Lie back down on the table," Melissa said. She slid
off and stood next to me as I lay facedown again. She
moved, to my feet I imagined. She continued speaking.
"When we love someone, we connect with them energetically, through our chakras. A chakra is like a lotus
blossom with long tendrils at the center. That's where
our energies connect. The tendrils coming out of your
chakra are joined energetically with Todd's. To discon-
nect you from him, we'll have to separate your tendrils.

"Picture those tendrils in your mind's eye. Imagine
you're holding them with both hands." I pictured a lotus
flower, its long, thin tendrils intertwined and connecting me to Todd. I saw my hands closing over them, each
hand just a short distance from the other. "Now imagine
that you're gently, ever so gently, pulling them apart, so
they're no longer connected." I saw my hands holding
the strands gradually moving apart, the strands disen-
tangling and disconnecting from the ones in the other
hand.

"Now fold up Todd's tendrils and carefully tuck
them back into the center of his chakra." She waited.
"Have you tucked them in?"

"Yes," I sobbed.

"Good, now do you see the tendrils you're holding? Those are yours. Roll them up and gently tuck them back into the center of your chakra."

I saw my hands tucking the strands into the center of a lotus flower. I waited. Melissa must have continued doing reiki, because it was some time before she spoke again. She said a prayer of thanks to her spirit guides, then touched my shoulder. "You can sit up now."

I rose and sat on the edge of the table. She handed me a tissue and I dried my face. *I must look a wreck*, I thought. *I feel like I've been crying for hours.* I felt completely drained, exhausted.

"Are you okay?" she asked.

"Yes, just give me a minute." I blew my nose again and wiped my eyes. "What time is it?"

"I don't know." She walked over to the table at the end of the massage table and looked at a small alarm clock. "It's almost six." She came back and stood in front of me. "Are you going to be able to drive?"

"Yes, I'll be okay. Just give me a few minutes. Listen, I'd like to write you a check—you've spent your entire afternoon with me."

"That's generous of you. You don't have to do that." I took out my checkbook and began writing as she asked, "What are you doing tonight?"

"I was supposed to go to Atlanta for the weekend, hours ago, actually. I'll have to call when I get home. I'm not up to driving there now."

Melissa nodded. "Good. When you get home, I want you to take a warm bath. Get a picture of Todd and a candle and put them where you can see them. Tell Todd everything you want to say to him, and when you're ready, blow out the candle. His soul will be released and he'll go to the Light."

"I will," I promised and handed her the check. "Thank you." We hugged. "I'm overwhelmed."

"Let me know how you do."

"I'll call you next week. You'll see me again!"

I opened the door into the hallway and made my way outside. It was dusk. I walked in a daze to my car, opened the door and sat down in front of the steering wheel, incredulous. *I'm an ordinary person. Miracles don't happen to everyday, ordinary people like me.* But one just had. At least it felt like a miracle; I had no other explanation.

I felt so loved, not just by Todd, but by something greater. How could this be? Very hard to believe. While my heart accepted it completely, my head was searching for an explanation. I'd never met Melissa before. But I had just spent five hours with her and everything, everything had changed, even my grief. Was it joy?

Driving home, I recalled how the Phil Collins song, "You'll Be in My Heart," used to come on the radio, and how I'd connected it to my sorrow. Then it dawned on me: I had misunderstood the message entirely. That was Todd, comforting me! He didn't want me to cry, and was telling me he was there to take care of me. I remembered too, how often I started up the car just as the song was ending. That was Todd, too, through the closing words to the song, telling me he was right behind me, that he would always be with me. I remembered that terrible morning on Timothy Road, screaming to him, "You can't leave me!" And he didn't.

When I got home, I called Lori to let her know that I wouldn't be driving over until the next day. I told her briefly about what had happened and that I'd see everyone tomorrow. Then I went up to the bathroom and turned on the hot water for a bath. While the water ran, I lifted the framed picture of Todd off the wall next to my bed. It didn't have a stand, but I could lean it against the wall and the hot water knob on the ledge of the tub so he would be looking directly into my eyes when I got into the water.

The water was too hot when I tested it, but the tub was only half filled. I turned on the cold and regulated the temperature. Now for a candle. Then it occurred to me—Mary's gift, the crystal votive candleholder, on the bookcase in my bedroom. I'd never used it, but I remembered her card and what she'd told me the night of Todd's wake, that she would take a bath, light candles, and talk to her dead son. Coincidence? It felt planned.

The candleholder went next to Todd's picture, then I turned off the water, undressed quickly, and lit the candle before stepping into the tub. Gradually I eased into the water. Fully immersed, I looked into Todd's eyes. Our eyes met. My heart felt as if it filled my entire chest. What did I have to tell him? Everything he already knew. How much I loved him. How much I missed him. How sorry I was. If only I could go back. If only I knew then what I knew now. If only he had given us more time. How blind I was. How much I had wanted to trust him. How overwhelmed I was to know that he hadn't left me when he died. That he stayed. That he loved me that much. That he wanted to take care of me. I felt treasured, cherished. I was dear to him. He was still with me. I closed my eyes and focused on our connection, and the love we felt for each other. I prayed for all good things to come to him and for the mysterious journey he was making. I told him I wanted him to continue on his path, to grow.

My mind reviewed the last three days: the sadness of no longer celebrating his birthday, the memory of him dying on my birthday, a Friday, his Good Friday, and the miracle revelations of the day, Holy Saturday, the day before Easter and the celebration of rebirth.

Birth, death, rebirth. The Catholic in me couldn't help but notice. Yes, Todd had died on my birthday. So much had died on that day. My son. My first life. And my second life had begun in pain and suffering. Birth, death, rebirth. Coincidence or pattern? I couldn't dismiss it. Something was at work and wanted me to pay attention.

The bathwater had grown cold. Time to go. Would he really be gone this time? *So hard to let go. But it's time. Todd darling, you need to move on. You know how much I love you. I'm so proud of you, and so grateful. Thank you, sweetheart, I love you.*

Lifting the candleholder's hurricane shade, I looked at the flame. Tears welled up again. I closed my eyes and blew out the candle. Before my closed eyes, a tiny pink heart floated away. *I don't care if I'm imagining it,* I thought, and blew him a kiss.

I rose up out of the tub, dried off, and put on my robe. I reached for Todd's picture and hugged it close as I walked into the bedroom, then rehung it on the wall next to my bed. His beautiful face beamed down at me. *Good night, sweet.*

It was only nine o'clock, but I was exhausted. I climbed into bed, still marveling at the day, and fell asleep immediately.

CHAPTER SEVENTEEN

Wanderings

Trying to make sense of what had happened with Melissa, I was lost. I read about reiki on the internet and discovered that medical and science-oriented sites dismissed it as a pseudoscience related to "healing touch." That reminded me of the seventy-year-old woman I'd met and connected with during my last campaign for school board. We'd both lost our sons. Her son, suffering from severe depression, was shot and killed by the police in an incident at her home. As a result, she trained local police officers in how to deescalate confrontations with the mentally ill. Formerly a nurse, like Melissa, she practiced healing touch. She struck me as the archetypal wise woman, called a crone in many cultures, venerated for her healing power and judgement. So to my mind, the comparison of reiki to healing touch wasn't necessarily a bad thing. It just raised more questions.

After my session with Melissa, I remained in a state of suspended disbelief. The experience made my ideas about life, death, and how the world works obsolete.

Like old maps depicting some other time and place, they no longer corresponded to where I lived. I let go and wandered into unknown territory, full of strange ideas I would have dismissed in my first life with a snide, patronizing comment.

Science, not religion, was my point of departure. I had read a couple books on Einstein's theory of relativity and, with a lot of reading and rereading, grasped the basic concept, that time and space were relative to the position and speed of the observer. Quantum physics, the study of subatomic particles and forces, was where I disconnected from modern science. I was completely ignorant. All I knew was that Einstein had problems with quantum theory, which postulated that subatomic particles, the basic building blocks of the universe, were fundamentally indeterminate. We can know a particle's position or its speed, but not both. Probabilities, not cause and effect, more accurately described how subatomic particles behaved. Einstein objected: "I, at any rate, am convinced that [God] does not throw dice."[1]

So I perused the science section of my favorite bookstore for a book on quantum physics that was accessible to a layperson like myself. There I found a book, published in 2002, just a year earlier, called *The Field: The Quest for the Secret Force of the Universe*, by Lynne McTaggart. As I read it I realized that very little of the science McTaggart illuminated in it, some of it nearly one hundred years old, had ever been integrated into our Western worldview.

The Field prompted me to examine the framework within which I thought. Simply reading the prologue, I saw that my everyday way of looking at the world—like that of everyone I knew—was bounded by a three-hun-dred-year-old paradigm based on the work of Newton, Descartes, and Darwin. I thought in terms of cause and effect, of a material world constrained by space and time, operating predictably and mechanistically according to certain basic, inviolable scientific laws.

My second life was not of that world. Todd and my experience with Melissa had cut me loose. But what world was it? I was living in a state of perpetual won-der. In my small, quiet life, a miracle had occurred; I had found love that survived even death. I couldn't explain it, and I wanted an explanation.

Reading *The Field*, I learned that a contingent of scientists was applying quantum principles and process-es to the world as we know it, not simply to subatomic particles. These principles seem to contradict common sense and even our experience of reality.

> As the pioneers of quantum physics peered into the very heart of matter, they were astounded by what they saw. The tiniest bits of matter weren't even matter, as we know it, not even a set some-thing. ... And even stranger, they were often many possible things all at the same time. But most sig-nificantly, these subatomic particles had no mean-ing in isolation, but only in relationship with ev-erything else. ... You could only understand the universe as a dynamic web of interconnection. Things once in contact remained always in contact through all space and all time.[2]

But even if everything in the universe is interconnected, how did Melissa discover that Todd remained connected to me after he died? This line I read hinted at an explanation avoided: "A coherent theory of the spiritual implications of quantum physics remained beyond their [the pioneer physicists'] grasp. Niels Bohr hung a sign on his door saying 'Philosophers keep out. Work in progress.'"[3]

As I read and reflected on what I was learning, my worldview began to shift. I learned, for example, that most scientists dared not go where the quantum pioneers feared to tread. As McTaggart discovered in the process of writing *The Field*, many physicists were unwilling to discuss the implications of their research.[4] Throughout the twentieth century, mainstream scientists have kept their heads down to study their one little corner of a mystery and refrained from looking up and out to see what it might mean.

The discoveries of Newton, Darwin, and Einstein, on the other hand, transformed the thinking, literature, art, and music of their times, and the worldview of living men and women. Contrast that with quantum physics, isolated from our everyday understanding of the world. It applied, scientists said, only to the subatomic world, which we can't see or touch, and which most of us never think about. So we operate in our day-to-day world with an obsolete understanding of the universe. This is one of the tragedies of our time and we suffer for it.

Quantum physics, like the Bible before Gutenberg and the Reformation, has been positioned as too far beyond the capacity of normal, everyday people to understand. Better to keep it in the official realm of science, and definitely not apply it to anything but subatomic particles. Neuroscience, biology, biochemistry, genetics, theories of human perception, remain confined to a fundamentalist Newtonian paradigm of a mechanistic, material universe.

This prohibition hasn't stopped individuals, governments, and companies from profiting from the application of quantum physics to new technologies. Even now, supercomputers are being designed that exploit the quantum property of entanglement to instantaneously exchange information between subatomic particles—defying Einstein's axiom that nothing can travel faster than the speed of light. But our understanding of the transformational physics behind that technology—and our perception of the way the world works—lags behind.

The scientific establishment punishes scientists who dare connect their discoveries to spiritual meaning. If they do, their research and credibility are instantly and irrefutably tainted. So we're stuck in a world where science and religion are positioned as adversaries, and the search for meaning in our time has devolved from existentialism and nihilism into the cult of celebrity and the search for momentary fame.

The Field delves into the discoveries of the scientists who bravely ventured beyond conventional thinking and applied quantum principles to areas outside of particle physics. The key element was the inclusion of the zero point field in their equations and their thinking. The zero point field is the energy that remains in a vacuum, the background energy that pervades the entire universe, a sea of energy where subatomic particles pop in and out of existence and connect everything in a great universal web.[5]

This intellectual leap allowed maverick scientists to explain some of the greatest anomalies of classical physics:

- Why an electron stays in its orbit around the nucleus of an atom (and why the atom and, therefore, all matter is stable).[6]
- A unified theory, integrating gravity with relativity and electromagnetism, the Holy Grail of modern physics.[7]

Yet no one seems to have noticed. By comparison, Einstein's breakthroughs made headlines around the world when he published his theory of relativity.

Chapter by chapter, McTaggart recounts how some scientists crossed the line into living systems and how, as their research unfolded, they discovered that living cells functioned according to quantum processes, too. Our cells communicate at the quantum level instantaneously through the zero point field. Other scientists explored mind, memory, and perception, which led them to theorize that the human brain uses quantum processes to function—in fact, uses wave interference, the language of the zero point field, to process information from the senses.

> Perception occurred at a much more fundamental level of matter—the netherworld of the quantum particle. We didn't see objects per se, but only their quantum information and out of that constructed our image of the world. Perceiving the

world was a matter of tuning into the zero point field.[8]

What we perceive as matter is actually a three-dimensional construct created by our brains. We don't see or feel matter; we perceive its energy pattern. We don't actually see or feel a chair; we perceive the chair as a chair because our senses pick up its wave interference pattern, its "quantum information," and our brain uses quantum processes to translate what our senses perceive into a chair.

Why does it matter? Because we, too, are energy— not mere flesh and blood! Armed with this new understanding of our quantum universe, I better understood why emotional energy can create sickness or health. Carolyn Myss's book, *Anatomy of the Spirit*, took on a new level of meaning for me. It made sense that, in addition to circulatory, pulmonary, digestive, and nervous systems, we have an energy system with energy centers or chakras. Myss's ability to see a person's aura, to see their energy, hinted that there really was a "sixth sense," an ability to perceive energy directly, not merely through our five senses.

And finally, what happened to the energy, the life-force that was Todd? I could almost hear the words I'd read in Myss's book: "Clearly, there's another form of energy that we have not yet understood. For example, there's a form of energy that appears to leave the body when the body dies."[9] Let there be light indeed!

* * *

The next time I drove to Atlanta to visit Shannon, I told her about what had happened with Melissa, and tried to interest her in reading *The Field* so we could talk about how it applied to my encounter with Todd. But Shannon wasn't interested in a scientific explanation of what she already believed to be true. "The last time I went up to North Carolina," she confided, "I had a session with a psychic. She told me about my past lives, and it's helping me understand how to heal."

Past lives? More new territory. I remembered *Many Lives, Many Masters* and wondering about reincarnation and past lives, but I had never embraced those ideas as actually true. And yet here was one of my best friends, whom I knew to be a highly intelligent and capable woman, accepting such fantastic ideas on faith alone. Astonished and mystified, I asked myself, *How can Shannon not need a rational explanation when I am so driven by the need to understand?*

I saw Melissa once a month, and learned more about her as we became better acquainted. Melissa had the wanderlust, and insufficient funds to gratify it. She had arrived lately in Athens after traveling through the Southwest and studying with a Native American shaman. How exotic, I thought. I wondered how she'd been able to live for as long as she did without regular employment. Melissa was very close to her grandfather; he was her rock. Her mother, on the other hand, didn't approve of her strange beliefs and practices. But that had all changed after her session with me. "I'm finally able to talk with my mother about my work," she told me. "I had Easter dinner with her and told her your story. At the end, my mother said, 'Maybe there is something to what you're doing after all.'"

I agreed. There definitely was something to what she was doing. I needed to understand it.

Meanwhile, still true to my New Year's resolution of three years before, I was having more fun. I had gotten into opera, which surprised me a great deal. I'd gone to see Strauss's *Die Fledermaus* on a whim, just because I loved his waltzes, and fell in love with the voice as an instrument. The operetta was sung in English, and the chorus included local singers. In the party scene, the mayor and others I recognized were among the revelers onstage. I had so much fun that I began going to whatever opera came to Athens's Classic Center. I even dragged Jason and Dane to see *La Boheme* with me. For birthdays and holidays, we started giving each other experiences: theatre tickets to see live shows and musicals together. We saw *Footloose, South Pacific, My Fair Lady*, and one magical night, the day after Christmas, while we were visiting up north, my sister Mary gave us tickets to see the Broadway revival of *Man of La Mancha*.

Opportunities to travel cropped up occasionally at work. Recruiting fairs and professional conferences took me to cities I'd never visited: Washington, DC, Baltimore, San Diego, Boston, San Francisco, and others. I particularly enjoyed the annual conference of the Graduate Management Admissions Council, which always featured fascinating speakers on topics related to business or business education. One favorite was the conductor Benjamin Zander, from whose book, *The Art of Possibility*, I took inspiration: "In the universe of possibility, you set the context and let life unfold."[9] In New Orleans, the conference's city-themed dinner featured a tarot card reader, who used the shortest card-reading modality, a three-card set, so he could get to as many attendees as possible. I'll never forget my three cards: death, rebirth, and infinity. Those three cards turn up consistently—even today—whenever I happen to run into someone with tarot cards.

I confided to Shannon that one of my dreams was to take Jason and Dane to Italy and she, out of sheer goodness and generosity, surprised me with the gift of three Delta buddy passes to take us anywhere in the world we wanted to go. I could hardly believe it, but the boys and I were planning a two-week trip at the end of June 2003 to Rome, Florence, and Venice, with a side-trip to Cinque Terre, a string of villages on the coast of Italy. Amazing!

Shannon was nervous for us and warned me that we might not get a flight exactly as planned. She taught me the rules of flying stand-by with buddy passes. Not only did we not have a problem, we flew first-class both ways! My guys were totally impressed.

Our only mishap occurred during our first hours in Rome. After getting off the train from the airport, we were to walk one block to our hotel. But we couldn't find it and walked the surrounding area for over an hour in search of it. It was very warm and we were thirsty and tired and exasperated. At that moment, standing on a street corner and looking very much the tourists with our suitcases, we were accosted by two gypsy women, one with a tiny, newborn baby that she thrust at us as she and her friend pushed us up against a stone wall. I guarded my zippered pocketbook fiercely; it contained our passports and mine and Dane's wallets, but not

Jason's; he'd wanted to keep his wallet in a buttoned back pants pocket. As soon as they had pickpocketed his wallet and realized there was nothing more to be gained, the gypsies took off and Jason discovered his loss. Then, with the help of a cabdriver, we finally found our hotel.

Jason called his credit card company, then went to the police station to report the theft. When he got back to our room, I saw how upset he still was—we all were. I put my arms around him.

"I should have given you my wallet," he said.

"You gave me your passport, though. That would have been much worse."

He didn't answer, but threw himself on the bed in disgust and blinked back tears. I sat next to him and ran my fingers through his hair. "Let it go, honey. You can let this ruin your trip or you can let it go. It's only money. I'll give you whatever you need. It'll be okay."

To his credit, Jason did let it go. The following night, after a day touring the Coliseum and the Forum, we dined outside on a small veranda, the wine incredible and the food equally so. The waiters could tell I was neither guy's girlfriend and concluded I must be their sister, which made me feel as silly as the wine did. Walking back to the hotel, we actually found Jason's wallet, less cash and credit card, but still holding his driver's license. Eerie. We felt as if we'd gone back in time and followed the thieves. I hoped the money would help that miserable gypsy baby, tossed around so haphazardly.

In Florence, we met up with Jason's girlfriend Stephanie, who was taking a class in Italian with the UGA Study Abroad Program for the summer. She joined us for a bicycle tour through the city and into the countryside. The next day, at the Uffizi Gallery, Stephanie showed me a painting by Botticelli. "Who does this remind you of?" she said as she pointed.

I could hardly believe my eyes. "Jason!" Uncanny, but my oldest was a living copy of Botticelli's *Portrait of a Young Man with Mazzocchio*. I had to buy a postcard as a memento.

All through our amazing trip, I secretly mourned that Todd wasn't with us, that he hadn't given me the time to get our lives turned around, that he hadn't given himself the time to get better. He would have been twenty-one, even taller than he'd been at sixteen and a half, with the same golden head and sky-blue eyes. I kissed him in my mind—often—and told him how much I missed him. I'd learned so much; I understood more clearly how the negative energy of our family environment affected him, and wished he could have been part of the shift I'd made. I wished he could see how different, how joyful life could be.

CHAPTER EIGHTEEN

Readings

After our return from Italy, I went to see Melissa. For my forty-ninth birthday, and the fifth anniversary of Todd's death, she suggested an Akashic record reading. "And what are Akashic records?" I asked.

"It's your soul's history, the record of all your past lives and what you've learned from them. I had an Akashic record reading a few months ago from a woman named Jean Read."

Past lives again. I looked at her askance. "Seriously?"

"Yes," Melissa said. "Jean's amazing. She doesn't like to talk about your past lives unless it has some bearing on this one. She's more interested in helping people understand their present lives and future."

"Interesting. Is she here in Athens?" I asked.

"No, she lives in Missouri."

"Missouri? I can't go to Missouri."

"She can do it over the phone," Melissa promised. "It's all energy. You don't have to be in the same room."

That surprised me. "Oh." Then I let judgement go. "Okay, I'll give it a try. How do I make an appointment?"

"I'll email you her phone number."

The next day, I called Jean. She was in a rush; she and her family were moving to Colorado and although she didn't have time to answer questions, we agreed to an appointment time, Saturday, October 11, at nine in the morning. She promised to email me more information and a release form that I had to sign and mail back to her.

Two days later, her email arrived. I was surprised by how long it was and read it several times. But Jean's explanation made me feel like I knew what to expect.

Dear Anne,

Sorry I did not have more time to talk the other day about what all a consultation involves, but I trust this information will clarify things for you.

I prefer to know as little about you as possible, so if you have any questions prior to the consultation, keep them toward clarifying the process and as little as possible about what is going on with you personally. ...

Once you call me, I will ask if you have any questions before I open your Records. When we are through with any discussion, I will open your Records with the use of a prayer and your name. I will need your legal name along with its correct spelling.

Once your Records are open, you begin by asking questions concerning your current life challenges. ... I listen for the information and receive it either through clairvoyance, clairaudience, and/or clairsentience [extra-sensory sight, hearing, and/or feeling]. I then relay the information to you as clearly as I can express it. You may then ask more questions about the information received or go on to another question.

You should know that the Record Keepers only reveal information you are ready to receive. So for example, if you asked a question like, "What is my life's purpose?" the answer given today would be different from the answer given to you a year ago or a year from now. For many choices have taken place since a year ago and many are to be made in the coming year. So the information given at the time of the consultation will be appropriate for who you are on the day of the consult.

The Records can reveal past-life challenges and gifts you have brought into this lifetime. It can also reveal issues, fears, judgements, false beliefs, etc. that have been handed down to you through your genetic lineage as well as past lives.

It can also give you glimpses of future potentials. I say potentials only because you still have to play your part and take the steps to create your future. For example, if I told you that you have the energy of an advocate and would make a great politician and should run for city council and within five years you will be elected mayor, if you never pursue the opportunity until four years from now, you most likely will not be mayor in five years. Spirit is willing to help with the creation, but you must meet God halfway by doing what needs to be done in the physical world.

Anyway, back to the consultation. It becomes a question-and-answer session throughout the time on the phone. If you want more clarity, ask for it.

Since I will be in your Records, I respect the parameters of it. Accessing your Records is like accessing the halls of Congress and its libraries. There is no way we could read each book of each event in the history of your soul. Nor is it necessary. What is important is who you are today. What gifts did you come in with? What challenges continue to trip you up in your current life? Did you come in with unresolved issues with your family members, co-workers, or friends? You may have been Cleopatra in a past life or Mary Magdalene. Does that matter? Maybe. But only the parts (challenges, false beliefs, judgements, issues, gifts, and patterns) you have brought forth from those lives into this lifetime. It can be easy for some to become enamored with who they have been and quit showing up in today's reality.

Anyway, the consult will go on until one hour and fifteen minutes. At this time I tend to close the consultation. Through experience, I have found that you have asked most of your important questions by then and any more information can't be absorbed. You should be saturated.

Give the information time to settle in. Sometimes this takes moments, days, or months. Some of the information may never resonate with you. I do ask that you become familiar with your own lie detector in the middle of your chest. Listen to the information with an open heart. Feel the information that resonates immediately and shelve the information that doesn't. It may later have meaning when presented from another perspective.

I recommend that you keep a paper and pencil handy to record some of the information during the consultation. It takes on different meanings several weeks to even months later when you read over the material again.

I look forward to speaking with you Saturday morning. … Happy Birthday!

Many blessings,

Jean

Looking back, I'm surprised I didn't balk, but I was fascinated by these women I was meeting, with abilities that seemed to allow them to transcend life and death. Had I read about them, I would most likely have dismissed them as frauds. I had to experience them myself, in the moment, to know what was true.

The atheism of my first life, entirely theoretical, based on what I knew of philosophy and science, was crumbling under the otherworldly weight of my second life's unfolding. I wanted to understand the mysteries of the universe. I once thought that solely the realm of science, but I was discovering a spiritual path, one any scientist would undoubtedly scorn. Was I just a grieving mother desperate for consolation? I didn't feel that way. Todd had helped me move beyond that aching, hopeless sorrow. But I was still seeking understanding.

Following Jean's suggestion, I prepared my questions ahead of time and organized them in a notepad, with space left under each for her answer. I wanted to capture every word.

I phoned her Saturday morning, thanked her for her thorough email, and told her I had no questions about the process. I was eager to get started. Jean said a prayer to her spirit guides, asked for permission to open my Akashic record, and told me to begin.

I had organized my questions into sections, first about myself, then Todd, then questions about important relationships. (I ended up having two readings with Jean, six months apart. I've combined them here.)

"I took my first question from your list, Jean. What is my life's purpose?"

"You're one-third of the way toward accomplishing your purpose in this life," Jean answered. "Your role is a helper, to boost people up to climb walls. You're a behind-the-scenes person."

That seemed to fit. One of the reasons I enjoyed my role as director of MBA admissions was because I opened doors for young people to realize their potential, not simply in business, but in every part of life. I had always believed that with the right values and leadership, business held the means to improving the quality of life for humanity.

"What gifts did I bring into this life that I'm underutilizing?"

"Your voice. You need to speak up more. With voice comes vision. You have clarity, but you don't speak up. I have an image of you sitting with a small child. I think it means you must return to innocence, go back to the awe state. Open up to your inner child."

Inner child. I had heard that term before. Wasn't it part of the popular conversation in self-help psychology? I made a mental note to look into it.

"What is my greatest false belief about myself?"

"That you're always truthful, that you know the truth. Don't be so hard on other people because they don't see how you see. See others' ways of seeing. Give credence to others' sight."

Ouch. In my politics, my religious beliefs, my decisions, I always believed I was right. Had I ever considered the possibility that I might be wrong? I liked to think of myself as tolerant, but was I really open to changing my mind? More food for thought.

"What is my greatest fear?"

"True honesty. With others and yourself. Part of you is still hiding. You're afraid that if you let others see the core of your being, you will be abandoned. Fear of abandonment is behind your fear of total honesty."

At that moment, I felt like Jean was truly seeing into the heart of me. That was terrifying, but I also found it strangely comforting to be known. I screwed up my courage and continued.

"In what ways do I sabotage myself?"

"By not moving. Not taking a risk. You move as long as you're comfortable, then stop or backtrack. I recommend you try the Leap of Faith meditation. Envision yourself at the edge of a cliff. State your intention, let the questions come forth. Then let trust fill your heart and step off the edge."

I remembered the many times I chose to stay with Jonathan out of fear that I couldn't support myself and the boys alone, a big step backward.

"In what ways do I empower myself?"

"In your eating. Your self-discipline keeps your body in balance, it helps your emotions stay in balance. The Zone Diet plan would be good for you."

That was odd. And brief. When I reread my notes, I wished I had asked for more information on that question. Coming back to it so many years later, I understand completely.

For my birthday, Shannon gave me a gift membership in the Weston A. Price Foundation, a nonprofit that grew out of the research of the Renaissance man and dentist, Weston A. Price. Price practiced dentistry in the early to mid-1900s, and over time, saw a marked increase in tooth decay, caries, and the need for orthodontia. People's jaws were too small to hold their teeth. He began looking for answers and started, naturally, with what they were putting into their mouths, the food they were eating. His discoveries about nutrition, in particular his anthropological research comparing the diets of preindustrial native cultures with those of modern, industrialized civilization, revealed not only the answers for dentistry, but for a host of modern-day plagues.[1]

The Foundation carries on Price's work by supporting and publishing independent research untainted by big government, big pharma, industrialized medicine, and industrialized agriculture. In the first hundred pages of their cookbook, *Nourishing Traditions: The Cookbook that Challenges Politically Correct Nutrition and the Diet Dictocrats*, Sally Fallon, the Foundation's founder, and the nutrition expert Mary Enig, PhD, lay out the fundamentals of human nutrition and health. Those pages alone are worth the price of admission. The cookbook's recipes are wonderful, but even better are the eye-opening excerpts from books and articles printed on the outside column of every page. "Food is medicine," said Hippocrates over two thousand years ago and after reading *Nourishing Traditions*, I understood why he was exactly right.

I began drinking raw milk, making my own kefir, eating raw butter, raw cheeses, and eggs from chickens who scratched in the dirt and ate bugs out under the sun. More and more, I bought organic vegetables and meats. When the Food and Drug Administration and the Georgia Department of Agriculture forced the owner of a local food co-op to pour out four hundred gallons of raw milk on the ground—including mine—I joined him in a lawsuit, supported by the Farm-to-Consumer Legal Defense Fund. To my amazement, the FDA claimed in its brief that it had the power to dictate what people are allowed to eat. "If people let the government decide what foods they eat and what medicines they take, their bodies will soon be in as sorry a state as are the souls of those who live under tyranny," wrote Thomas Jefferson. The current state of American health proves just how right he was. I eat nutritional food, take no medicines, and create balance in my life, in part, through diet. Jean was so right.

"What false beliefs do I have about my relationship with Todd?" I asked Jean.

"That it was his fault."

I could not believe my ears. I had never doubted that Todd was to blame for his own death. Her answer was so psychically dissonant that I would not have remembered it if I had not written it down.

"You can speak to him," she said. "He's around you a great deal. Let him help with your inner child work."

"Did he fulfill his life's purpose?"

"Yes."

Another shock. I was just a third of the way toward accomplishing mine, but Todd had completed his in sixteen-and-a-half years? I could not believe it. "How did his purpose relate to me?"

"There were no unresolved issues. All were resolved in his lifetime. I see an image of you, dressed in medieval clothes. Todd is leaving you and you call out to him. As he leaves, he's smiling and waving. You are distraught. You think he has left you and that you will never see him again. You are astounded when he comes back to you with a child in his arms. Your inner child. Let Todd be your spiritual guide."

I *had* called out to him. And he *had* come back to me. His death was the turning point of my life, the beginning of a new life. Was that the child he gave me? My heart was pounding.

"Was his death a suicide?"

"His heart stopped from a loss of blood."

Non-answer. I felt sick. My poor son. I couldn't bring myself to ask if he suffered. I was too afraid of the answer.

"I'm trying to find closure with Todd's death. What were the lessons for me?"

"They're about forgiveness and the independence of each soul. There is no blame for an event that happens to someone else."

Forgiveness. I still had a lot of work to do. I had not forgiven Jonathan. In my heart, I blamed him and his drinking for the breakup of our family. Had I forgiven myself? And had I truly forgiven Todd? And how had his death not been his fault?

Jean continued, as if in answer to my unspoken questions. "If I hurt someone because I tell them the truth, because they asked me, I'm not responsible for their feelings. I may betray someone to be true to my own soul. Todd did this."

Todd's death became more of a mystery than ever. I thought I had it all figured out. I shied away from hearing more and changed the subject.

"Do I have any unresolved issues with Jonathan?"

"No, I see a child walking his path. He seems happy."

"Did I begin this life with a debt or agreement with him?"

"No debts, it was about inner peace. He is there to help you discover and explore it. Jonathan's at peace now. There's no strong bond between you, it's more like friendship, a brother and sister."

I had expected to hear that I had married Jonathan because of some karmic debt I owed him. To hear that his purpose was to help me explore inner peace seemed the exact opposite of what our life had been together. But I felt relieved to know I could move on and not feel as though I still owed him something.

"I had a dream the other night that was so vivid that I actually remember it," I said. "I usually don't remember dreams. I dreamt that I found a baby in the bottom of a bookcase, mixed in with the books. I rescued it and it hugged me fiercely. What does it mean?"

"You're giving your inner child permission to exist. You're letting your inner child be funny and playful. Give your inner child five minutes every day!" Jean said.

The inner child again. Play. Wasn't that the point of my New Year's resolution? I needed to get better at following through on that and play more. I was always so serious.

"I see you walking on a small footpath through a high pasture, with new grass and wildflower buds. Meditate on crossing that field, see what you experience, see where the path leads. This is a place where you can call forth divine guidance. Todd is saying 'Well done!'"

Then abruptly, she added, "I am concluding this session with a blessing from your spirit guides."

Ha! I had them, too. I'd not considered that.

"'Anne, you are growing and expanding. You are so deeply loved and honored. Take off your blinders, grow in compassion, and live in Spirit.' Ah, this is unusual—I see the infinity sign! Fully indulge in the experience of life."

Infinity again, like my tarot cards! I felt exhilarated. Could it be—anything was possible? And Todd was there at the end, too! "Well done," he'd said. *What exactly had I done*, I wondered. All I could identify was the unusual journey I was on. I read and reread my notes, but was unable to take in the full meaning of what I'd been told.

I put them aside. I focused on spending time with my inner child. I had just turned forty-nine and there was no time to waste. Time to have more fun!

CHAPTER NINETEEN

More Miracles

Soon after my reading, my sister Edna came down to Athens to visit. I wanted her to meet the other women in my life and invited them all to a "Goddess Dinner" on the weekend of her stay. I cooked a fabulous meal, the wine flowed, and there was chocolate mousse for dessert. We laughed all evening and discussed the books we were reading and what they meant in our lives—*Dance of the Dissident Daughter, The Invitation, Crossing to Avalon.* We celebrated throwing off the shackles of patriarchy and recognizing the power in opening up to the sacred feminine.

My inner child and I were playing happily together, but not in the way I visualized at the time. I imagined travel, adventure, carousing with the girls, breaking the "good girl" expectations that had defined me. It took me a long time to realize that true play for me and my inner child was through the books and ideas I was discovering.

Strangely, my love of reading had a primal connection to my inner child. My mother once told me that she had started potty training me when I was just nine months old. She would hold me on a little pot in her lap and read a book to me until I finished. Was it any wonder then, that I found books and the new worlds I could explore through them stimulating and deeply satisfying? My dream made perfect sense—my inner child was buried in a bookcase!

When I learned that Carolyn Myss had published a new book, I purchased a copy. At first, I read it as a continuation of *Anatomy of the Spirit:* people become ill if they avoid the lessons and experiences they designed for themselves. But the insights in *Sacred Contracts: Awakening Your Divine Potential* go much further. Much of the book is devoted to identifying and analyzing the archetypes with which we and our life experiences are most closely aligned. They are clues to understanding our sacred contract. Myss described how she came to see that we have an eighth chakra where our archetypal energies reside, that bridges "the personal unconscious with the collective unconscious … [and that] represents a continual current of cosmic intelligence that feeds into your psyche."[1] It is, she declared, the home of our sacred contract.

I wondered, *What is my sacred contract?* According to my Akashic record reading, I was one-third of the way toward completing it, but what was it exactly? The answer Jean had given me was very broad: "A helper, boosting people up to climb walls, a behind-the-scenes person." Two of the archetypes Jean identified fit with what I had achieved in my life, Justice and Liberator. I thought of my contribution as a board of education member, liberating the system to find a better leader. The archetype that Jean identified but glossed over was Artist or Artisan, and I wondered what that was about. (At that point in my life, I would never have believed I'd write a book.) Despite the lack of real insight, I felt like the exploration I was doing was part of my contract. That admission in itself was a leap of faith, though I'd never have admitted it at the time.

We can discover our sacred contract by identifying our archetypes and paying attention to the circumstances of our life, Myss wrote. Before we are born, we purposely design our lives to give ourselves choices and opportunities to grow spiritually.

> Our life is laid out in steps and stages arranged in such a way that we always have the opportunity for spiritual transformation, which is the ultimate goal of working with your Contract, ... dependent only on your willingness to pick up the subtle clues and cues that appear along the way. Dreams, intuitions, apparent coincidences, and "chance" encounters are just a few of the cues that will lead you on the path to genuine transformation.[2]

Were my encounters with Melissa and Jean Read part of a greater plan that would lead to my spiritual transformation? I had to laugh. The Universe was taking no chances on subtlety with me! But I also had to admit that I could no longer ascribe to a materialist view of the Universe. It was far more complicated than that. I began to let go of my atheism, too: an atheist's universe wasn't a place where Todd continued to exist. My experiences indicated that Todd did exist in some other form, that death is not an end, but a continuation. Untethered, I continued to explore.

* * *

After my Akashic record reading, everything I thought I knew about Todd's death was turned on its head. How could it not be his fault? The police report had concluded his death was a suicide. An officer told us other drivers on Epps Bridge Road that morning report-ed that he'd run out in front of them with no heed for his own safety. I had discovered his note. I learned after his death that he might have used LSD. And I knew for a fact that he had an extreme reaction to marijuana that had in all likelihood triggered schizophrenia. He probably had a flashback or a panic attack the afternoon before he died, when he'd run out of school to his therapist's office. He must have been in the same state the morning he died. Perhaps it wasn't his fault, perhaps he didn't know what he was doing, but it had been his choice to try marijuana, or even LSD—ultimately a fatal choice.

In all my musings on my sacred contract, I avoid-ed facing the meaning and role of Todd's death in my own life. It was a classic case of denial. I simply didn't go there—until September 2004.

That summer, Shannon emailed me information on a conference in New York City being hosted by the Omega Institute, the institute's "Women & Power" con-ference, and asked if I'd like to go with her. The con-ference was being co-hosted by Eve Ensler, author of *The Vagina Monologues* and founder of V-Day, and Elizabeth Lesser, co-founder of the Omega Institute. The list of speakers was stunning, from Eve herself, Gloria

Steinem, Jane Fonda, Geraldine Ferraro, and Sally Field, to women I'd never heard of with alluring and provocative resumes: Marion Woodman, Pat Mitchell, Carole Black, Johnnetta Cole, Julia Stiles, Rosario Dawson, Debbie Ford, and Sister Joan Chittister. After reading the website information, I registered for the conference and emailed Shannon: "Absolutely yes, I'm going." We agreed to share a room at the conference hotel and made plans to fly up together.

The juxtaposition of those two words, *women* and *power*, was in itself a radical act. Held September 10 through 13, 2004, nearly two thousand people participated in examining their meaning and the shift that occurs when they are connected, when the sacred feminine is given voice in the lives of individuals, nations, and the world.

Gloria Steinem, the first speaker on that Saturday morning, September 11, told us what we already knew, that we had come together for "magical, important, changeful days." Behind her, five banners of mythic goddesses, each eight feet square, painted in vivid primary colors with organic flowing lines, danced across the stage. "Have we liberated the Sheraton Hotel or what?" Steinem began. "The molecules in the air in this room are never going to be the same again!" We cheered, a high, musical cheer rarely heard, the cheering of women in the majority.

"A lot of us who were at the first conference last year on the Omega campus were concerned," Steinem continued, "that we wouldn't be the same without trees and grass. But I realized last night, and I see again looking at your faces, that we forgot that we are trees and grass, we are nature, and we are bringing that into this artificial space."

Steinem told us there was nowhere else on earth she would rather be on that day, in order to remember "the fragility of flesh and the durability of the spirit." She said she didn't know where it came from or who made the first one, but she was so proud of the many New Yorkers protesting the start of the war in Iraq, whose hand-lettered signs had read "Our grief is not a cry for war." She called for greater participation in voting by single women to oust the Bush-Cheney regime that had led the country into a war of revenge. Her observation that the common factor in serial killings, mass murders, and the recent school shootings—that the killers were one hundred percent white, middle class, and male—drove home the point that men, raised in the expectation of dominance and frustrated in that expectation, became violent and dangerous. She was amused that people in the media were surprised to learn that the September 11 terrorists had been middle class and well educated, and were unable to make the connection between terrorists and men raised in patriarchy.

As she recounted some of the women's movement's achievements over the last thirty years, Steinem traced a path I could claim as my own: the shift in consciousness that occurs when women moved from dependence to independence. The future she predicted and hoped for was a movement toward interdependence, when women had a meaningful voice in the halls of power; when the economic value of the work women did raising children and caring for elder family members was recognized in the GDP and by the IRS; when the responsibility for raising children was shared equally by men; when men, too, wondered how they were going to balance family and career as they planned their future; and when boys were not forced into independence as girls were into dependence. "We've raised our daughters more like our sons," she observed, "it's time to raise our sons more like our daughters."[3] She made me feel proud of how I'd raised my own sons, proud of the emotionally generous, tolerant, thoughtful men they had become. I was so grateful to hear her, the role model for my generation of women, and to be in communion with the women there that day.

We had no time to recover from the integrity, intelligence, and emotional honesty of Steinem's talk before Elizabeth Lesser was back on stage to introduce the next speaker. Dr. Marion Woodman, she said, was "the soul of our conference." She told of the first time she attended a workshop with Woodman, a Jungian analyst and author, and became mesmerized by her voice and her message. "Marion was the first woman I ever heard articulate how it's not just enough to gain power, but that we have to bring our feminine values along with us and change the very definition of power. ... Centuries of patriarchal thinking have stripped the soul from our inner and outer lives. We're suffering from a loss of soul, she says. Men are, women are, the earth is. And women are in a unique position to help the world reclaim its soul."[4]

Marion Woodman was a tiny woman who nearly disappeared behind the lectern. She had beautiful, long, wavy gray hair and a distinctive, slightly raspy voice. She began with a reflection on the day and the catastrophe of 2001, three years before. "Having been through loss myself this year, and realizing my age," she paused, then started again. "With each passing of someone we love, more of us is on the other side. And gradually, the reality of that other side is coming in and shifting our reality here, so that the suffering of the loss brings through the transformation." I was deeply moved, that she had so succinctly and accurately described the cosmic shift in reality I was experiencing as I mourned Todd's death.

In her talk, Woodman described the soul, symbolized by the Rose in Christian mythology, opening petal by petal. In its own time, the Rose enters the Fire. "It's the Fire that gives it its strength, the suffering that we go through." Can we hold the reality of our own Rose-soul, she asked, as we go through the Fire?

Individual suffering, and how it brings us through to transcendence and a whole new experience of soul, Woodman connected to what is happening at a cultural level in the world. Technology has made us one world, and we don't have the slightest idea what to do with it, morally or politically. But the rise of the feminine principle brings with it a new way of thinking. It sees connection rather than division. It takes the time to bear witness to suffering, to see, listen, and love.

Woodman reminded us that when she spoke of masculine and feminine, she wasn't speaking of gender. That is patriarchy, she said, a power principle that had become a parody of itself and done profound damage to men as well as to women. Rather, she was speaking of energy, the energy of shiva—creative, powerful, and life-giving—and the energy of shakti—receptive and loving. Shakti is the heart energy that can fill a room, the energy that holds presence. Even quantum physics has recognized the importance of presence, Woodman pointed out, and has proven that the act of watching affects the outcome.

Thus, the feminine principle, the presence that holds the soul in love, with no agenda, can change any situation. That, she concluded, is the great work before us, to bring the feminine energy of shakti into this present age of alienation and loss, when the Rose and the Fire are one.⁵

At the conclusion of Woodman's talk, Elizabeth Lesser announced a half-hour break, to see the exhibitors or to remain in the auditorium for a guided meditation with Debbie Ford, author of *The Dark Side of the Light Chasers* and *The Secret of the Shadow*, both of which Shannon had read. We decided to stay. There are times when the heart is wide open and, instinctively, I knew it was important to stay and listen to my heart. Ford asked us to close our eyes and guided us through a meditation to open to our shadow self. She guided us into the darkest places in our souls to bring what we found there out into the light.

What is my shadow? I found it, buried in the deepest, darkest part of me: *Todd died to set me free to begin a new life, a second life, and discover spirituality.* That was the sacred contract between us. I allowed it in, the recognition that I must have agreed to such a terrible thing. But I had to ask: *Was I so stubborn, so closed to the possibility of a spiritual side to life, that my son had to die to open me to it?* I was humbled. What was my greatest false belief? I prided myself on knowing the truth. I had so much to learn.

I shared my insight with Shannon. And then emotionally, let it go. I had cried for so long, bringing that awful realization into consciousness was all that was left for me to do to release it. What remained was discovery, the possibility that there was a spiritual side of life for me to explore.

Shannon and I got up from our seats, stretched, and walked out into the sunshine. We found an organic cafeteria for a quick bite, then returned to the Sheraton to walk through the exhibitions. We came across one exhibitor with a Kirlian camera that he claimed could photograph a person's aura, so I had mine taken just for the fun of it. My aura was bright green, signifying the energy of love, the heart chakra, with just a touch of third chakra yellow, self-energy, on the right and left, and a cloud of magenta, representing spiritual connection, at the eighth chakra above my head.

We also met the artist Janet Morgan, who had painted the gorgeous banners on the stage. She was selling prints but didn't have one of my personal favorite, the red-and-yellow banner of a goddess dancing atop the globe. I took her card. Maybe one day she would have prints made of it and I could buy one. Two years later, I contacted her again and bought the original to hang in my two-story foyer. It is fabulous, my reminder to live life to the fullest every single day.

The second half of the day was as powerful as the first. Shannon and I headed back to Georgia two days later wondering how we would use what we'd learned.

* * *

At the end of September, a week before my fiftieth birthday, my brother Robert and his family drove down to Athens for a week-long visit. They stayed with my parents, but naturally wanted to see my townhouse. I gave them the tour and proudly showed off the quiet haven I'd come to love. I was proud of my space, my Victorian parlor in particular. It was very feminine, a place where I often curled up with a book in the softly curved, channel-back loveseat I'd had reupholstered after I moved out six years before. The townhouse was my retreat from the world, calm, quiet, and all my own.

After the tour, we walked out my front door and across the grass to get into Robert's van to go to dinner in Atlanta with our brother John. I was about to climb in when I spied something shiny on the pavement directly below me. "Meredith, did you drop your ring?" I asked my niece as I picked it up.

"No, it's not mine," she said.

I turned to her mother. "Is this yours?"

"No," she said, "but it's beautiful."

The ring was silvery metal scrollwork in the shape of a butterfly. "I guess it's mine then." I smiled, feeling the touch of a miracle in finding it, as though it were left there for me. I remembered Debbie Ford's words at the Women & Power conference: "Your life will be transformed when you make peace with your shadow. The caterpillar will become a breathtakingly beautiful butterfly."[6] I put the ring on the middle finger of my left hand. It fit perfectly. I thought of Todd, the anniversary we shared, and wondered if he was still around me.

A week or so later, my friend Chris, who'd moved to Atlanta, emailed me a notice from the New Age church she'd started attending. Unity North Church was hosting an interactive art exhibit that Saturday, "Paintings That Heal." The artist was Brent Atwater, identified as a medical intuitive by Dr. Larry Burke, who, along with Carolyn Myss and Dr. Norman Shealy, was a founding member of the American Board of Scientific Medical Intuition. Did I want to go? I thought back to Chris's previous invitations, so critical to my new life. Of course I wanted to go!

Tickets to the exhibit were twenty or forty dollars, depending on the level of interaction selected by the attendee. At the forty-dollar level, attendees arrived at ten in the morning to participate in ongoing research on the energetic effects of Atwater's paintings. The twenty-dollar level was simply an afternoon of viewing the paintings themselves. "Let's do the whole thing," I said to Chris. She agreed, and I told her I'd pick her up so we could go together.

On Saturday morning, I arrived at her place promptly at nine. "You navigate," I said as she got into my Chevy Lumina. While she directed me to the church, she patted the Lumina's dashboard and asked, "When are you going to trade this baby in? Let Steve get you a Jaguar."

Jason and Dane's friend Steve, a Jaguar mechanic, had offered to find me a used Jaguar. Chris was teasing and serious; she wanted me to put myself out there more and thought a flashy Jaguar would catch a guy's eye. I wasn't in a hurry.

"I'm saving up for a new kitchen," I replied. "I need this car to last ten more years at least. It's fine. No dings. And who wants a car payment?"

"You should let him find you a Jag. What do Jason and Dane say?"

"They're embarrassed by my car. I know it's old. But they're guys. It doesn't matter to me."

When we arrived at Unity North, only a few cars were there. We walked to the front doors and into the vestibule. A man and woman stood at a table just inside. They perked up as we walked in. "Hi," said Chris, "we have ten o'clock appointments." She gave our names.

"Yes," the woman replied as she checked our names off her list. "Follow Tom and he'll take you to your stations."

Tom led us into the nave. About a third of the space had been subdivided into activity stations; the other two-thirds was filled with paintings, arranged in three large horseshoe shapes. The paintings' backs were to us. "You can start here at the aura station," Tom told me. "Then you'll go over there," he pointed, "to the Heart Math station. View the paintings, and then redo the aura reading and the Heart Math." He turned to Chris. "You can come with me." They walked off.

"Have a seat," said the woman in the aura station. A computer screen and a glove were on the cafeteria-style table in front of me. The glove was connected to a computer sitting on an adjacent table.

"Hi," I said as I sat in the chair across from her.

"Hi. Have you ever seen your aura before?" she asked.

"As a matter of fact, I have. At a conference in New York. I had a picture taken."

"Our equipment is probably a little different. Today we're going to measure your aura before and after you've viewed the paintings," she explained. "Put your hand in this glove."

I put my hand into the glove and watched the screen. The outlined human figure on the screen gradually acquired a shadowy, gold cloud around it. The field didn't extend very far from the outlined figure.

"That's your aura," she said as she typed into the computer. "When you come back from viewing the paintings, I'll take it again and read it for you. You can take off the glove now and go to the Heart Math station."

Obediently I walked across the room in the direction she pointed. Another table and chair with a computer and screen were set up. While the operator worked with the woman in front of me on the Heart Math program, I looked around for Chris, but didn't see her. I wondered what she was doing and why it was different from what I was assigned.

The operator finished and motioned me to sit down. She attached a sensor to my fingertip, and the graphs on the computer screen in front of me started to change.

"Look at you," the woman said, "you're already in the green. The red zone means 'fight or flight.' Green signals calm, no stress. It's where we want to be. See if you can concentrate and go deeper into the green." I watched the arrow on the computer screen and focused on feeling more relaxed. There was just a slight movement deeper into the green.

After a few minutes, the woman said, "Go view the paintings." I returned to the aura station at the far side of the room and the first half-circle of paintings just behind it. It was hard to believe that these images could heal. With hints of anatomy, distorted and putrid, the paintings looked like disease.

I moved on to the next half-circle. Lurid yellows and reds, dark greens that turned black, there was nothing pleasing about them. I saw that each had a name, the name of an actual disease: arteriosclerosis, breast cancer, congestive heart disease, mitral valve prolapse. The third and final half-circle displayed more diseases, entitled gallbladder, irritable bowel syndrome, hepatitis, acid reflux, arthritis. The last painting was the most bizarre: schizophrenia. How terrible to think that this gruesome painting portrayed the way someone's mind worked. It was a visual scream. *My poor son.*

As I walked away, a volunteer directed me back toward the Heart Math station. This time I didn't have to wait, and I held out my hand for the sensor. The needle on the screen dipped down into the red zone and stayed there. *Wow, those paintings have upset me.* I began to pay attention to my energy, which had obviously been disturbed. I took some deep, slow breaths and watched as the needle began to move up, out of the red zone. As I concentrated, the needle continued toward the green. But my time was up, a line had formed, and the Heart Math lady was ready for me to move on. As I stood, I glanced at the screen to see that I'd just barely reached the green zone.

I looked again for Chris. No sign of her. *Maybe she's looking at the paintings.* I crossed the room and sat down for another aura reading. I put my hand in the glove and watched the computer screen. My aura was much bigger this time, more than three times the size of the earlier reading. "Would you like me to tell you what I see in your aura?" the volunteer asked.

"Okay," I replied. "What do you see?"

"An injury to your left shoulder." She pointed to the image on the screen, where the aura around my left shoulder, neck, and arm extended out farther. I'd partially dislocated my shoulder two months earlier by carrying my laptop bag, over seventy-five pounds, with my left hand, as I struggled with a shoulder bag and suitcase with the other during a three-city recruiting trip for work. It still ached, and would take over a year to heal.

"And here on your left shin," she said and pointed to the aura there. That was a very old injury. Over ten years before, I'd fallen off a ladder and hit the corner of a brick planter on the way down. The bone had been bruised. Two bumps were still visible on my shinbone.

"God, that hurt! I remember that. I thought I'd broken my leg," I told her.

"The only other thing I see is a surgery." She pointed to the right side below my waist, and looked at me for confirmation.

"An appendectomy. Right again," I told her, impressed. "How does this work?" I gestured to the glove and computer.

"I don't understand it myself," the volunteer admitted. "I was trained to use the equipment and software. Unity North purchased the software from the developer." This seemed to confirm what I'd read in the exhibit brochure, that they were using a gas discharge visualization camera, developed by Russian scientists at the St. Petersburg State Institute of Fine Mechanics and Optics.

Just then Chris walked up. "How's it going?" I asked.

"Not good. They took me to some guy with a divining rod. I'm not sure what he was talking about. It was very confusing. He told me to go look at the paintings, but now they're telling me I wasn't supposed to look at them until after they read my aura." She sounded frustrated. "So now they want me to get an aura reading and do the Heart Math, look at the paintings again, and get another aura reading."

"I just finished with my second reading. Have a seat." I took my hand out of the electronic glove and stood. "It's pretty cool. They could see old injuries, even my appendectomy."

Chris looked at the woman behind the table, who beckoned her to sit down. Chris sat. "What do I do?"

"Place your right hand in the glove." The woman helped Chris put her hand inside the glove, then turned to the computer. The screen went blank. "Something's wrong. It's not working." She walked over to a guy a few feet away and pointed in our direction. They huddled over the computer and keyboard. Chris removed her hand from the glove, but the screen was still blank.

"We're going to have to reboot the machine," he said, "and see if that will fix it." He looked at Chris. "Do you ever have trouble with computers? Or electronics?"

"No," Chris said, feigning wide-eyed innocence. We exchanged looks and I stifled a laugh. At work, Chris always had weird problems with her computer, problems that never afflicted anyone else. She once confessed that an energy charge built up in her body over the course of the day, and the only way she could get to sleep at night was by taking a bath to discharge it.

"Sounds like you're going to be here a while. I'll wait for you outside," I told her. I turned and walked to a side door where another volunteer stood. "I think I'm all done. Is this the way out?" I asked.

"Yes, go through here," he gestured to the door. "Now you go to the transition room."

"The transition room?"

"Yes, down at the end of the hall."

I walked out the door into a small vestibule where two tables had been set up with books for sale. I wasn't in the mood for browsing, so I walked down the hall, which opened up into a large room. Just to the left of the entrance were two bulletin boards, covered with eight-by-ten, black-and-white photographs. Opposite the door, more paintings hung on the wall, from which a narrow platform jutted out and extended the full length of the room.

Much easier to look at, I thought, as I walked to the far right and began examining the paintings. They were abstract, some with silhouetted figures, some simple geometric shapes, in a style that struck me as innocent and unsophisticated. In the last four paintings, there was a shift in subject matter. The fourth-to-last one showed the silhouette of a man walking through a door shining with a bright light. Next came the portrait of an attractive man about forty years old. The last two were of a ghoulish, black-and-white exoskeletal creature holding a bloody heart in its hands. "How god-awful," I said to myself.

"Yes, I was painting my grief," said the woman standing next to me. Pleasant looking, with blond hair and blue eyes in a bright green dress, she turned to face me.

Oops, she must be the artist, Brent Atwater. I looked at her foolishly and didn't know what to say.

"Do you see this ring?" She held out her left hand to me. On her ring finger was a large emerald.

"It's beautiful," I said.

"My fiancé gave this to me when he asked me to marry him. The next day, he was killed in a car accident. I thought my life was over. I felt like my heart had been ripped out. I wanted to die, too."

My heart went out to her, but all I could say was, "How terrible for you."

"Then he came to me in a dream." Brent walked to the portrait of the man. "I painted him. He promised we'd be together again." She walked to another painting, this one farther to the right, that looked like a crescent-moon seesaw in a sea of vivid blues and purples. "I realized that it was true. Here we are dancing in the Light."

As she was speaking, I asked myself, *Why is she telling me this?* So I said, "I'm Anne, by the way, and I know how you must have felt. My son was killed in a car accident."

She stopped short and took me by the shoulders. "Oh Anne. Have you met Dwanna? You have to talk to Dwanna."

"Dwanna? What—who's Dwanna?"

Brent didn't answer, but took me by the arm and pulled me out the door into the hall. There was a door on the left. She opened it and drew me inside. There was no one in the room except a woman seated with her back to us.

"Dwanna, this is Anne. She has to talk to you," Brent cried as she drew me in front of the seated figure. Dwanna looked up and smiled a welcome. She couldn't have been more than five-two, slight and delicate, with very white skin, pretty features, and red hair. She looked to be my own age.

"How do you do?" She handed me her card. "Have a seat." There were four folding chairs in a semicircle around her. I sat in front of her. Brent exited the room.

"Do you know about me?" Dwanna asked.

"No," I said. "I came here to see the paintings and met Brent. She said I had to meet you."

"I see. Have you ever seen *The Jonathan Edwards Show?*"

"No," I replied, "but I've heard about it. He's a medium, right?"

"Right. I'm kind of like that. Images or symbols will come to me from the other side. I'll tell you what I think the message is. You tell me what it means to you.

That will help me keep the energy flowing and hold the connection."

I nodded that I understood and waited.

"I'm picking up depression, someone who has no energy, can hardly get out of bed in the morning. Is that you?"

"No, not at all," I replied. As I answered a heavyset woman and a teenaged boy came into the room and sat to my left. Dwanna repeated what she'd just said.

"Yes, that's me," the woman said. "That's why I'm here. My son wanted me to come see you, to see if you could help me. He's so worried about me. My husband divorced me a year and a half ago. I cry all the time, I'm so depressed, I don't know what to do." She and Dwanna conversed for a short time.

Dwanna turned to me again. "An older man, a heavy smoker. He died of lung cancer. Does that mean anything to you?"

"No," I told her.

She looked at the woman, who also shook her head no. Another woman entered the room and sat to my right. Dwanna repeated what she'd said.

"Yes," the woman said. "My grandfather."

"Sometimes the spirits are eager," Dwanna explained to us, "they anticipate events. Time is not the same for them." Then she turned to the woman. "Your grandfather wants to thank you for taking care of him to the end. You nursed him?"

"Yes," she said.

"You've been the nurse and caretaker for several members of your family. That has been your role, but your grandfather wants you to move on." She and the woman spoke. I didn't pay attention.

Suddenly Dwanna turned to me. "The phone rang in the middle of the night."

"Yes," I croaked, startled, stricken with the same horror I'd felt that morning.

"I see a road, dark, lined with trees."

"Yes, that's where it happened."

"Mother I'm so sorry, Mother I'm so sorry, Mother I'm so sorry. Mother I love you, Mother I love you, Mother I love you," Dwanna chanted.

I was overcome. Tears, sorrow, pain, and love flowed through me.

"Did he … did he suffer?" I asked. A dark terror, I never let myself go there.

"He was in a coma. He didn't feel anything. He called to you."

"I called to him!"

"He's spelling something. J-A-S—"

"Jason. His brother Jason."

"Yes, he says 'Jason has never gotten over my death.' He wants you to know."

"Jason and Dane never speak of Todd. They won't talk about it."

"He says you need to get him help."

"I will," I promised.

"He's spelling another name, M-A-R—"

"Mary, my sister Mary."

"Todd wants you to remember him to her. He wants you to thank her and give her his love. Were they close?"

"Todd spent a couple of weeks with her the summer before he died. They talked."

"He wants you to remember him to the whole family. Tell them he loves them."

"I will."

"He's singing to you. He's singing 'You Light Up My Life.' Mother, I love you, Mother, I love you, Mother I love you."

I choked and couldn't speak.

"He's showing me a room filled with presents."

"That would be Christmas up at Mary's house. He loved going there. There literally was a wall of presents."

"He says they're all for you. He has so many presents for you. Now he's singing 'Pennies From Heaven.' That's telling me that whenever you find something on the ground, it's from him."

"My ring! I found a butterfly ring on the ground at my house."

"Are you thinking of trading in your car?"

"No, I—we just talked about that on the way over here!"

"Yes," Dwanna said. "Todd wants you to know that he will *always* be with you."

Then, as suddenly as she started, Dwanna turned to someone else in the room. Done. I just sat there, stunned. Finally, I got up and walked out.

I walked back into the transition room and stood inside the door, dazedly staring at the bulletin board filled with photos. A woman began talking to me. At first, I didn't hear a word she said. Then I made myself pay attention and heard her say, "… and I noticed these small spheres of light in my photographs. It started happening after my son was killed in a car accident."

Another car accident. Another son killed. *All right already! I get it!* I cried out to the Universe. *You have my complete attention! Hit me over the head with it, why don't you?*

"I think the spheres are souls from the other side who've come back to visit this earth plane," the woman continued. "Would you like to try taking some pictures?" She offered me her camera.

"No." I was overwhelmed. "Thank you." Incredulous joy coursed through me. *He is still with me, he loves me, he's sorry, he loves me. Todd, I love you, I love you, I love you!* I felt so honored, so cherished, so blessed.

I looked around the room for somewhere to sit. No chairs, only the shallow ledge jutting out from the wall. I went over and sat on the edge. The photographer was walking around the room, taking pictures. But all I could think of was the last thirty minutes and the miracle that had just occurred. I memorized each moment, every word that Dwanna said, that I said. *I have to tell Jason and Dane.* Would they believe me? I could scarcely believe it myself.

The photographer walked over to me with her camera, one of the new digital models that had just come out, and showed me the photo she'd taken moments earlier— of me, sitting between the portrait of Brent's fiancé and the painting of the man going to the Light. At my right shoulder, in the corner of the photo, was a huge ball of white light. *Yes, he would be that big and bright and close. It's true: Todd will always be with me.*

CHAPTER TWENTY

Dwanna

I told Jason and Dane about my encounter with Dwanna. They respected me too much to think I'd gone off the deep end or was lying to them, but I could see they were looking for other explanations of what happened. They didn't believe in psychics. Jason didn't deny that he was still troubled by Todd's death, but his comment was simply, "What's the point of dwelling on it? It won't change anything."

"I know," I replied. "But burying your feelings can have a huge effect on your life. Your emotions can make you sick. Can you honestly tell me that, deep in your heart, you don't feel guilty about Todd? About how you two used to pick on each other?" He didn't answer, so I continued. "I want you and Dane to come with me to a session with Dwanna. It's important to me. I know you have your doubts, but humor me."

Two weeks later, Jason, Dane, and I met with Dwanna in a private home in Atlanta. Dwanna met us at the door and led us into the living room, dimly lit with candles. I saw Jason and Dane glance at each other and roll their eyes. They didn't even have to say it: *We knew it—candles.*

Dwanna invited us to sit and sat down herself next to a table with a recording device. We sat across from her, Dane to my left and Jason to my right. I explained that I'd met her at Unity North and asked my sons to come to a follow-up session. She nodded, but I could see that she didn't remember me.

"I've found it's helpful to my clients to have a recording of their session, so I'll be making a CD tonight," she explained. "Are you ready to begin?" We nodded and she pressed a button.

"I want to welcome all of you and say to you, this is a good night for everybody to feel as if they have their loved ones around them. You have come to hear from a loved one and you know that loved one has been trying to get in touch with you. He says, 'I made the transition very quickly and I know that each of you miss me. But I also know that when I communicate with you, I do it in a way that sometimes you don't know it's me.'

"There are many, many loved ones who come here tonight, but there's one that's most important, and he would say to you, 'I have no time to waste. I want to talk to you all.'" Dwanna laughed. "So it's like he's trying to get in as much information as possible, so I'm going to do my best.

"He says he would have been afraid of this. So it's like, 'I would have been afraid to have you communicate with me if you were on the other side.' So this is not something he would have known about before he crossed over.

"He had a lot of really good times with all of you, because you were really close. I'm seeing a lot of togetherness, and then he says, 'You brought me back and forth in your hearts, and I know that each of you has thought of me over and over again. Crying, asking for me to come back, I couldn't. But I know that each of you would want to know that I'm near you.'

"'Charming guy.' He said he was a charming guy. He had a lot of charisma. And he says 'I was very, very popular.' Does that make sense to you? In other words, he was popular with his peer group. And he also had a lot of enthusiasm about life. 'I got so far in school,' he said, 'because I really applied myself.' Does that make sense to you?"

"At the end, no," I said. But I wasn't being fair to Todd. He had always worked hard in school. He was an A-student until high school. And I didn't realize how popular he was until long after he died.

"He's giving roses to someone," Dwanna said, "and that's a symbol for me to say that there was a birthday. Whose birthday is it?"

I raised my hand.

"It's yours. So he is saying happy birthday to you. He knows you felt as if you had the rug pulled out from under you. But you also made yourself strong all through this. You stayed strong. And he says he's very glad that you had the support of everybody around you.

"He's also talking about," Dwanna chuckled, "I'm using this symbol, a tar and feathering. I feel it was you," she turned to Jason. "Did you two get in arguments, Jason?"

"Yes," Jason answered.

Hearing the grim tone in his voice, I glanced over to see his reaction. If he was surprised, he wasn't showing it.

"That's not unusual for brothers to get in fights or arguments," Dwanna said, "but he's saying, 'You used to keep me upset. You loved to do that.' I don't know what it was about, you picking on him or him picking on you, but it was like, you used to upset each other."

"Yeah, we'd upset each other," Jason said.

"He says, 'You just gave me hell when I didn't deserve it.'" Dwanna laughed. "That's how he says it. You gave him hell and he gave you hell. It was a kind of picking at each other and fighting. He doesn't want you to be concerned about that and wish you hadn't done it, because it's a sibling rivalry kind of thing."

I glanced at Jason again. Still he showed no emotion, no surprise. Would Todd be able to get through to him?

Dwanna continued to address Jason. "He says, 'You always just understood everything and I didn't understand it as much as you did.' There's a lot of energy with you, Jason, wanting to do something to change the world. Does that make sense to you?"

"Sure. I have a lot of plans."

"And they're good plans," Dwanna said, "but he says, 'Don't let yourself be overworked about it, because all those plans are going to take place. It's just going to take some work. And don't worry about whether you make it very big or not, just as long as you aim for that goal.'

"Something about calling you on the carpet. Was there anything about you being reprimanded for something just recently?"

Jason looked surprised, then sheepish, and kept his eyes on the floor. "Yeah, I got into trouble recently."

"Okay, because he's saying you've been called on the carpet. That means you've been reprimanded and you've waited it out to see what's going to happen. It's okay, everything is going to be okay with that."

"Okay," Jason said and shifted in his chair. I could see he was ready to change the subject. Afterward, I asked him what happened, but he wouldn't tell me. He was ashamed, he said, and didn't want me to know.

"You are going to need to do some extra work to make up for this. Does that make sense to you?" Dwanna asked.

"Yeah," he answered.

"All right. He says, 'You deserve a good pat on the back too, because you've tried your best, but sometimes you find yourself weary from struggling so hard.' Does that make sense to you?"

"I work hard, and sometimes I don't work smart. So I do a lot of work and then I figure out how I should have done it. So I do it again the right way."

"All right. Keeping yourself very busy, all of you. It takes a lot of time away from your family life. There's a lot of busy-ness with all of you. And it's not important that you stop being busy, but it is important that you make quality time for each other. Is there something about religion with some of you? Are you interested more in religion because of this? Or spirituality, one of you? You've questioned?"

"I have," I answered. "I'm much more interested in spirituality."

"Okay," Dwanna said. "Because he says this has prompted you to search more. He says it was sort of like a deal you made a long time ago, before you came into this earth plane."

"That was one of my questions, whether Todd and I had a contract," I said. I wanted confirmation of what I'd discovered at the Women & Power conference.

"Yes, but he says it wasn't known to you on the personal level. It's like having a son who has conspired with you before you came to this earth plane to learn some lessons. You weren't really agreeable as to how they would be learned. You were very disagreeable as to how this had to happen. He says he's sorry."

"That's something that tortures me still," I said. "Was there no easier way for me to learn this?"

"He says—"

Jason said, "Do you have a feeling that this is Todd, our dead brother, that you're talking to? I assumed you were going that way, but I didn't know who it was at first."

"Yes," Dwanna answered. "I'm talking with Todd, the guides are helping. I have angels, guides, all of you have them. So they work on questions you've had about your lives. You've had that question, Anne. You've wanted to know why.

"You're going to need a lot of counseling over this, is what Todd's saying, all of you, because it took a great toll on your lives. 'Although it isn't fun to be in this situation,' he says. He didn't have much fun either. He says, 'I used to be cantankerous.' Does that make sense to you? Hard to get along with in those last days, and so he's apologizing for that.

"He said he had a good time on this earth plane, too, especially when it came to putting himself into situations that he knew might cause you pain and worry, but he enjoyed himself.

"So Jason, he's saying that you found yourself in such shock you still couldn't believe it. He says, 'I know you said I'm sorry that we didn't get along so well.' So he says that he wants you not to worry about that. He says, 'I don't blame you for anything.'

"Shawn, Shawn, is there a Shawn? Who has a Shawn around them? Anybody?"

"I had a best friend named Shawn a long time ago." Jason answered. "I haven't seen him in years."

"Well, it's just a way of Todd connecting with you. He knows your friends so he speaks of Shawn. How long ago was that?"

"It's probably ten years," Jason said.

I glanced at Dane, leaning far back in his chair, his arms crossed, and wondered whether he was as impressed as I was, seeing Dwanna go straight to Jason to address his guilt about his relationship with Todd.

"He says you're working really hard to put power and meaning into your life. Does that make sense to you?"

"Sure," Jason replied. "I don't think I have a lot of meaning in my life. I'm just another guy working to be successful. I don't have a higher calling or anything. I have things I enjoy doing and I actually enjoy my work right now. But I guess it's all worldly things, you know, human comforts, that I'm after."

"You're not looking for anything deeper in meaning."

"Yeah."

"Well, it's all about using what you know. You have a great intellect. And you have something deeper than that, you just haven't touched upon it yet."

"Okay."

"You'll find it. You just have to sort of acclimate all of these ideas within you. Because you're a real idea person. You like to think of ideas in your life and what you can do with them. Sort of like an inventor. Does that make sense to you?"

"Sure, I go that way."

An understatement. Jason is one of the most creative people I know. He used to go to Saturday classes at the University of Georgia's Torrance Center for Creativity when he was in elementary school. They tested him and walked me through his results to show me just how off-the-charts creative he is.

"All right," Dwanna said. "Was there something about a Russ? Do you know who that is? A Russell. Can either one of you place somebody named Russell?"

"I just started working with a guy named Russell," Jason said. That question from Dwanna, Jason later admitted, made him reconsider his suspicions of her legitimacy. There was no way she could have known it.

"Okay, so your brother keeps talking to you about your work. He's talking about your success. Because you want to know if you're going to be successful."

"Okay."

"And your brother says, 'Yes, you will. Keep on with the ideas, but look for the deeper meaning.' He keeps talking about those deeper meanings. Have you ever thought that you were going to be an executive in a large company?"

"I never, ever planned that, but it's turning out to be the case," Jason said.

"Because it's going to happen to you. And you're going to have this wonderful feeling that your family is well taken care of. That's when you have your family. You're just trying so hard to be on top. And your brother says, 'That's okay, but always look for that underlying meaning of life, too.' You don't have to struggle so hard, because in life, it comes easy for you, all right? It might look like a struggle, but it really comes easy to you.

"Is there anything about you wearing your brother's shirt?" Dwanna asked.

Dane spoke up. "I wear Todd's shirts all the time."

"He says you have such a beautiful energy. And he wants you to know that you and he got along really well. Does that make sense to you?"

"Yeah," said Dane.

"'Done deal,' he says. 'It's a done deal. Please don't worry about me. I'm fine.' Is there someone named Margaret, or Marjorie, that you all know? Mary,

Margaret, Marie, that M-A-R sound, do you know who that is?"

"My sister, Mary," I told her.

"Okay, because I'm hearing him reach out to her, saying hello to her.

"He says not to say too much to everybody about this because nobody will believe you." Dwanna laughed. "It's like, 'They wouldn't believe that I can talk from the other side.' But he is saying hello to your sister."

Dwanna's lightning-quick patter kept me on edge; I wanted to help her maintain the energy flow, but it was hard to keep up with her as she jumped from subject to subject.

"He shows me the month of October," she said. "Does that mean something to you all? The month of October. Is that a birthday or an anniversary?"

"Both," I answered. "He died on my birthday."

"All right. He's saying October is an important time. He says that he loves you and that you did all you could to make him comfortable after his passing, so he's thanking you for that.

"He keeps saying, 'Mother I love you, Mother I love you. Please take my apologies. Please take my apologies for causing you so much pain.'

"He's talking about loving to sleep late and having no energy to get up in the morning. Do you understand that?"

"Towards the end, Todd was very depressed and had no energy," I responded. "He slept all the time."

"Was this a suicide?" Dwanna asked.

"He ran out in front of a car," I told her.

Dane said, "According to the police—"

"Oh. It was an accident?" Dwanna asked.

"It was … there were questions," I said.

"Okay, I'm not going to decide that one way or the other, I just hear what he's saying."

"Does he say it was?" I asked.

"He says he couldn't get up in the mornings, that he wanted to sleep a lot. And then you say he was depressed. 'I had no reason to be on this earth plane,' is what he is telling me. He doesn't want you to blame yourself though. 'Don't be worried about it one way or the other,' he says, 'because sometimes you wonder if there was something you could have done to change something.' He says, 'I cannot give you all the details of everything I thought, but I thought that life was a drudge. I wanted it to be better. I'm fighting with myself over so many things. I didn't know what I wanted to do.' He couldn't make up his mind about what he wanted to do in his life. He says, 'I couldn't find the right things to think, so I just followed whatever I felt was right at the time.'

"He says, 'I couldn't, for the life of me, decide if I wanted to continue to be like everybody else.' He wanted to be different. He thought differently than other people did. But he says, 'I couldn't make anybody else understand that.'

"Do you know if he loved BBQ or loved to grill out?" Dwanna hesitated, then asked, "Was he cremated?"

"Yes," I said.

"He's trying to be funny, but I mean, you wouldn't think that's funny. But he had a good sense of humor. He did show me that, which is most unusual, because they usually don't."

Todd was right about that—I didn't think him funny at all. "One of my questions is whether he had any preference about where … I keep his ashes—"

"Where you should put them," Dwanna finished my sentence.

"Yes."

"'My life,' he says, 'was spent with you. If you have them, keep them.'"

"That's what I want," I said.

"He says not to give those up because it gives you great comfort to be near him—I'm seeing computers, computer technology. Okay, so it's you," Dwanna addressed Jason. "He keeps going to you, because he says he needs to let you know how successful you're going to be."

"Okay," Jason said. I saw Jason was determined not to give Dwanna any hints or clues if he could help it. His face was expressionless despite Todd's encouraging words.

"He says you have this wonderful idea that someday you're going to get married. And he says it won't be that long in coming. You just have to find the right one. You haven't found her yet. You want that right one, because sometimes you feel as if you'll never meet her. Does that make sense to you?"

"Sure," Jason said.

"He says if you want to be successful in love, you have to give of yourself. Don't hold back that love. Sometimes you hold back, because you don't want to get hurt. Does that make sense? There's a lot of deep things here, maybe I shouldn't go so deep."

"I don't mind you going deep," Jason said.

"He says you've been hurt by someone. And you don't want to do that again, so you're holding out, you don't want to give all of yourself until the right one comes along."

"Right," said Jason, "exactly." Jason was very hurt when his girlfriend Stephanie broke up with him. It took him a long time to get over it and start dating again.

"And he says you'll have three children."

Jason smiled at this. "Okay."

"'Is that okay with you?' he asks."

"Sure, I want kids," Jason answered.

"He says that is something you've been wondering about. Will I get married, will I be successful, will I have kids? And he says all those things are true, you will. And he says, 'You'll have good memories of me.'

"He's also talking about trying to get enough money in his life. Was there anything about him wanting to be better off or he was having problems with money, because he's talking about that."

I glanced to my right and left and saw that Jason and Dane's eyes were on the ground. Neither seemed ready to confirm what Todd was saying. "We were struggling, it was a very difficult time," I told her. "When he died, we were poor."

"'Say hello to Dad,' is what he's saying. The dad's not with you all? Is the dad somewhere else? Because he's saying hello to the dad. He's also talking about his face being damaged, or something about his face and head. Does that make sense?"

"I didn't see him after he was killed," I told her.

"Okay. He called to you, he says. He says you thought you heard him calling you. You know that he was there with you."

"I called to him!"

"He says he was calling to you. He says he's sorry for the birthday being so sad. And he says you weren't a wimp. He keeps saying how strong you were. He says, 'I was guided by the family to come over to the other side.' He says you've gotten plenty of mail from him. And I feel like that's from your thoughts. He says he loves his brothers, too.

"He says 'I'm very, very strong around all of you, but I have to prove that I'm around you. And the only way I can do it is by little things that nobody else would know.' And so he's touching on those things. Who is the good cook here?"

"Dane cooks," Jason told her.

"It's more so since Todd passed," Dane said, raising his eyebrows and exchanging glances with his brother.

"Well he knows about your cooking. He's also talking about being blond, who's blond around you? Is somebody blond?"

"He was blond," Dane said.

"Okay, because he says 'blond and beautiful,' that's how he says it."

"He was golden," I sighed.

"Oh, no wonder, he keeps showing me this blond hair. And he's talking to you, Dane, when he's talking about blond hair." Todd was telling Dane about his future wife, blond and beautiful, but we didn't know—it would be nine years before he met her.

"He keeps saying, 'I used to primp a lot.' Like he would get in front of the mirror and groom himself. He liked to do that. And he said, 'I stood there for hours just looking at myself, trying to figure myself out.'

"He says he loved his family. He loved meeting you at home. So I'm just thinking the reason he's telling me that is that some of you were away from home when he crossed over. Is that correct? Some of you were living somewhere else when he crossed over? Were you living at home?"

"Yeah," said Jason.

"And you weren't?" Dwanna turned to Dane, who nodded in the affirmative. "Because he keeps talking about how he loved all the family to be home, but somebody was living away from home at that time."

Dwanna turned back to Jason. "And you thought you were dreaming, like you thought this wasn't real. And he says 'I know all of you felt as if something would change to bring me back. I love you. Please don't get mad at me for doing what I did.'

"He's talking to you," Dwanna said to Jason. Then, to all of us, "And is there anyone who cuts hair or who does hair?"

"I just had my hair cut," I said.

"Okay. Cause he's talking about somebody cutting their hair. He likes the way you've done it. And he says 'I see how you look now and you're so much better than you were months ago,' and not to put yourself in such a place of grief anymore. He keeps saying 'I don't want you to grieve.'"

"I have some questions," Jason said. Genuine puzzlement with a touch of wonder colored his tone. "Two questions. One, a few things have happened recently that I attach meaning to. For whatever reason, I've been thinking about spiritual things lately, maybe because Mom's gotten into it. So now when I look at some things, I wonder if there's a purpose behind them. A few things have happened that I'm just positive there's some kind of meaning behind, maybe somebody's trying to tell me something, but I have no idea what it is. I'm not getting it. I'm getting a signal, but I have no idea what they're trying to say ..." He stopped.

"It's just that you need to listen to your own heart," Dwanna answered. "Todd says, 'You're struggling too hard to be successful without knowing the meaning of life.' That's what he was telling you, so you can dig into the depths of yourself and start to find more meaning to what you are and who you are, and how you fit into relationship with yourself. He says it's not difficult to get these meanings across to you because you're so wide open to them."

"Okay," Jason said, wary.

"He says, 'You weren't always this way. My death has brought a lot of awareness to you that you wouldn't otherwise have.' Just like with your mother and Dane. But it also has put you in a position of thinking, what if I died? What happens to me when I die? And how is it that people can talk from the other side? 'You've thought all those things,' he's saying. But it's also something of a 'I'm not sure if this is real or not.' He says, 'It's real because it is you that is inside that body, that real you. That's what I am, the part that never dies.'"

"Okay." Jason leaned forward in his chair, his elbows on his knees, his chin in his hands.

"It's about this part of you that is infinite, this part of you that is spirit that never dies. The body will be given up, sooner or later, but you'll keep that consciousness of you. He says 'That's what I did, I kept the consciousness of me.'

"Now when things happen to you, they're not big things, they're subtle things you pay attention to. And he says 'I know you've struggled with the idea that I'm around you and how could that be?' And he says 'It is a matter of your thinking, I touch your thinking. That's how I communicate with you.' And not to be afraid of him, because he says, 'I'm not a ghost, I'm not a spook. I'm spirit. So if I were to appear in front of you, it wouldn't be me the way I was in the physical body, it would be me as I am now, as a light.'

"He says, 'I know you've dreamed of me. It's easy to dream of me because you're not thinking using normal everyday consciousness.' But there's a little bit of reserve with you, Jason. You don't get too enthused because you're not sure of the validity of it. So Todd says, 'You just kind of want to step into it, like putting your toe in the water, you just want to touch the water first, to see what it's like. And then you'll wade in deeper and allow yourself to learn more as time goes by.' You're a very old soul. Have you ever heard that saying? Old soul?" Dwanna captured Jason's eyes with her own.

"I've heard the saying," he admitted, "I don't know if I've heard it applied to me."

"It applies to you," she assured him. "And you're an old soul in this earth life, this time, and it's called an incarnation. And this incarnation is for you to grow as much as you can. It won't always be easy for you, because you have some resistance. But he says you'll see that resistance begin to drop away as you get more and more proof about this. Because you're somebody who wants proof, who needs to know if this is real. It's okay to be like that. Is March important to you?"

"It's Todd's birthday," he replied.

"Thank you, so this is Todd helping me out here. And he says, 'Man, it's not all a gravy train.' I don't know why he's saying this. 'You've got to work hard to get the growth you want. Living,' he says, 'is easy. It's dying that's the hardest part. Because you give up the physical body and then you wonder what in the world did I do that for, because it's so important to be there and learn.'

"'Boy, it's a big deal over here, I mean it's beautiful, but you're not going to come over here anytime soon.' He says you're safe. You know what, have there been times when you thought life wasn't worth living?"

"I've had my down moments," Jason admitted, "when you get upset with yourself, but that's about as far as I took it. I mean I'd never give up, I don't think I'll ever give up."

"He says, 'You are a fighter. You're not a quitter.' He says he wasn't a quitter either. He tried and tried at life. He says he's there for you, to inspire you to go forward. He keeps talking about that meaning to life. Find those meanings to life. Do you have another question?"

"Well, my other question is about him," Jason said, hesitating a moment. "I have my regrets about our relationship. And I know that regrets aren't going to get me anywhere, there's nothing I can do about what's in the past. Is there anything I can do for him now, is there anything I can do for him?"

I was so touched by Jason's loving heart. And I could have predicted Todd's answer, just as loving.

Dwanna replied, "He says, 'You can do everything for yourself. I honor that.' He doesn't want you to do anything for him because he says, 'It's not where I live anymore, on the earth plane.' And he's also saying, 'Whatever you decide to do, do it for yourself, for me.'"

"Okay," Jason said with a satisfied nod.

"He says that's how it works. 'My memory is important to you. Do something to honor that memory by doing something for yourself.'"

"Okay."

"He says, 'You think about me a lot,' and he says you wonder what it is that he would want most from you." Then she gave Todd's answer: "'Just listening to me, just knowing I'm there, that I am with you and helping you.'

She continued. "Is there something about—you feel as if his death wrecked your life in some way? Because he's saying to you, 'I know how it impacted your life and life's not the same for you. It's like taking your heart out and stepping on it. I know that,'" her gaze swept all three of us, "and he's talking to all of you. But he says it's something that's already happened, and he doesn't want you to feel sad all the time. He said coping is a hard thing to do when someone has died, and he said all of you have had to cope with this."

As Dwanna spoke her expression remained intense, but a smile appeared and widened on her face. Seeing our curious looks, she explained, "I'm smiling because I heard him say his name clearly to me just then. He says 'Call on me anytime, page me anytime. Call me,' he says, 'I'm here. Trying to be stronger.' He's telling me he's trying to get through stronger, because there are some spirits that are stronger than others. Todd is learning and he's trying to get through very strong. So as he talks he's like, 'I'm trying to come through stronger.'

"He says 'It's a wide place over here, it's a big place' and he's showing me that. But he says 'I have to work very hard in communicating with you all, because you don't always believe it.' He wants you to believe it. He wants you to believe that it's him.

"He says he has a lot of presents for you, Anne, lots of presents. He says 'Each and every one of them will be special, because you're special.' He says, 'I didn't give you the credit for doing such a good job for me,' so he's giving you that credit now. And he says, 'I know I capitalized on your goodness sometimes, and I took advantage of you.' And so he's apologizing. He says, 'You don't see it that way now, but there were times when you felt that I needed to do something for myself—' Another name, is there a Ryan? Do you know who Ryan is?"

"Todd's best friend," replied Jason.

"Okay, so he's saying 'Say hello to Ryan for me.' He's bringing up Ryan as we speak for proof again that he's talking to you, and to let Ryan know that he's here in the spirit. And he says, 'I want him to know, because when he hears from me, I don't want him to shut down.' Somebody needs to tell Ryan."

"We'll have to track Ryan down," I said.

"Okay, if you get the opportunity, he's saying, 'Please tell him.' It's also validation. He's saying, 'He'd be mad at me if I didn't say hi.'"

Dwanna turned to me. "And how about you—questions?"

A bit startled—I'd been listening intently—I replied, "My big question was about when I'll have love in my life again. I'd be interested in what the guides have to say."

"Okay. You are a beautiful human being with a lot of talent that you sometimes waste on worrying—is what Spirit is saying. But it's not unlike you to be concerned or worried over situations you have no control over. You're someone who wants to be in control of your life and the lives of others. But that's not always possible."

"Right," I said, nodding.

"But then there's that part of you that's a little afraid. You're not sure how much commitment you want right now. You have this wonderful sense that someday you're going to have someone special in your life, and you want that. But it's not because you went out and looked for someone. They just sort of happen into your life. Does that make sense to you?"

"Yes." That was exactly how I pictured it. Not being the socialite, not enjoying the bar scene, having a small circle of friends, I imagined that love would eventually show up again as I lived my life the way I wanted.

"You're very exceptional and that's what you need to see about yourself," she continued. "Let it fall into place. You're just about ready to find something new in your life. And that's about joy. Because you haven't had that until now. All this time, you've just sort of had this displaced feeling, as if you didn't know where you belonged. You felt that place inside yourself that was so sad you just couldn't find peace and joy. So, starting to blossom. Now I know you want certain feelings in your life to occur with someone, but it's better that you don't push this into being, okay? Let it flow. Let yourself open up to other relationships, too. Can you do that?"

"I think so."

"Okay! Because there's somebody so special for you out there, waiting for you, that hasn't even been in your life yet. It's just not going to be in the next year. You're going to feel on top of the world when it happens, okay?"

"Be patient," I summarized.

"Well, it's better that you be patient, let's just say that. You're taking yourself back and forth about, well am I going to be by myself for the rest of my life?"

"Yes! That's been the question," I said.

"Yes, you're back and forth with that. What you have to realize is that the rest of your life hasn't occurred yet. There's plenty of it left. And you're going to have somebody in your life who is going to adore you and love you more than anyone else has. And you're not at all an unattractive lady, you're very attractive, so it's not going to be hard for you to attract attention, okay? It's hard for your children to see that about you sometimes, but they also would say—"

"A good-looking mom!" Jason laughed.

"There you go." Dwanna grinned. "He said it! And I feel as if nobody is more abundantly open than you are with your energy. You're that person that just opens your energy and says look at me, I'm here, in a loving way, so you attract a lot of good things to you, and a lot of good people to you.

"Also, I see something about you having the title to your house, I see you having a house that's paid off, a house that's complete."

"I have a nice townhouse," I told her.

"Okay, that's going to be yours. You don't have to be worrying about what's going to happen to you in the future financially, because your finances look really good. Your health is good too. Did someone have a heart problem or have something with their arteries, a circulatory problem, in your family?"

My mind went immediately to Jonathan. "My ex-husband, their dad does," I said.

"Okay. Now your dad's in the living, isn't he?" She addressed Jason. "Because I'm hearing something about having problems with arteries, and I don't see that problem with any of you. Your heart looks great, you have a strong heart."

Then she turned to Dane. "You put a party together beautifully. I don't know what this is about. Are you good at planning parties, or good at planning social occasions? Because I'm seeing you do really well at that."

He laughed. "I'm a kind of PR man."

"He's good at attending them," Jason kidded.

"'Born to you because you asked for me.'" She looked my way. "Todd's saying 'I was a very wanted child, okay?'"

"I love him dearly and miss him very much," I said.

"And he's talking about saying prayers for him and thanking you for that. But he says, 'I've said more prayers for you than you said for me because you've been so hurt by all this.' He's just trying to reach you and tell you that he's okay where he is. He says he loves all of you. And he says he's not mad about anything. He wants you to know that, Jason. He wants to settle that once and for all. 'Whatever happens today,' he says, 'I hope that each of you will be healed by it.' He says, 'I'm not through with you yet. Do you think I would ever go away and let you all feel really sad? I'm not going to do that. I want you all to go away feeling happy.'

"One last thing, is there someone named Betty? Don't know who that is? What I hear him say—and I don't know why he's saying this—is 'Bette Davis eyes.' You know Bette Davis, she had those really incredible eyes. I hear him say 'Bette Davis eyes.' That's why I have to ask you if you know a Betty."

I knew instantly what he meant. "All the girls said Todd had flowers in his eyes."

"Okay, then he *is* saying Bette Davis eyes. I didn't know what he was talking about."

"Yes, he had incredibly beautiful eyes."

"Oh, the stars in his eyes! Thank you, we close this session."

* * *

Dwanna gave me two CDs, a full recording of our time with her. We thanked her and walked back to our cars. It was late and I had to drive back to Athens, so the boys and I didn't have much time to talk over our impressions. I could see that Jason and Dane were surprised by how much Dwanna had gotten right and that they weren't able to dismiss her abilities out of hand, but they weren't convinced she was able to connect with Todd. I could see the logical side of their minds at work, calculating and weighing what Dwanna told them versus what could have been true for anyone, not just them.

Did our session with Dwanna help his brothers get past Todd's death? I believe it took some of the sting out of it, particularly for Jason. The passage of time has helped too, of course, but none of us has ever been able to speak of him without that twinge of pain. We love and miss him. We always will.

CHAPTER TWENTY-ONE

Gifts

I was disappointed that Jason and Dane weren't more convinced by the reading with Dwanna, but their skepticism couldn't dampen my joy and sense of wonder. I wanted to hear "You'll Be in My Heart" again—I'd come to think of it as "our song," Todd's and mine, so I decided to buy the CD as a Christmas present to myself. I was surprised to learn that the song was from the soundtrack to Disney's *Tarzan*, Todd's favorite Disney movie. I remembered him telling me how much he loved it.

Years later, as I began writing this memoir, I decided I needed to see *Tarzan* for myself and thought, *I can borrow it from Mom. After all, wasn't that how Todd had gotten to see it?* She'd bought most of Disney's animated movies to entertain her young grandchildren, so I assumed she had a copy. But she didn't own it.

Confused, I wondered how else Todd could have seen *Tarzan*. I'd never taken him. But he'd told me how much he loved the scenes of Tarzan flying through the jungle, like he was skateboarding on huge palm tree leaves. I remembered the conversation clearly. We were standing in the family room of our old house back in Westgate. But on further investigation, I learned that the movie and the song hadn't been released until the summer of 1999, six months after his death. Our conversation had to have occurred after he died, either that or I was dreaming. Or both. He had come to me in a dream once before.

How is it possible, I wondered, for a human being to communicate with someone who has died? Dwanna said, "They send me symbols, they send me names, they send me all sorts of things trying to tell me. It's all about communication. He actually is here. Heaven is not some remote location out there somewhere. It's all right here. There is no empty space. It looks empty because you're looking at it from the human perspective. But physics tells us there is no empty space."

How could physics explain what was happening? I had wandered so far from what I'd ever believed possible. I was lost. How could these miracles turning up in my life connect to anything remotely scientific? My left brain wanted a rational explanation bounded by science and reason. But I was learning that my sense of direction, my logical, thinking brain, often led me the wrong way. So I ignored it. I played with my inner child instead. We played with books and ideas, reading what the Universe sent us and trusting we would find our way.

In a phone conversation with my sister Edna, I told her about Dwanna. She didn't doubt any of it and asked if I'd ever heard of Edgar Cayce.

"No, who's he?" I asked.

"He was a psychic," she said. "I'm reading a book about him. You should read it, too. And give it to Jason, then he might not dismiss Dwanna so easily."

I bought the book, *Edgar Cayce: An American Prophet*, and read it eagerly. I learned that Cayce was one of the most well-documented medical intuitives and mediums in history, who gave 14,256 readings, fully documented with verbatim transcripts. Ten thousand of those readings were for medical purposes. A small study of seventy-four cases, chosen at random, showed that Cayce had an overall cure rate of eighty-six percent. Even more impressive was that he was often the last resort of desperately sick people, people he never met or physically examined.[1] His diagnoses and prescribed cures came from a "Source" who spoke through him while he was in a hypnotic state. Cayce himself had no memory of what he said under hypnosis.

Cayce's Source also confirmed the Eastern belief in reincarnation by revealing that it consulted Akashic records, "the record that the individual entity itself writes upon the skein of time and space"[2] to document the past life and death experiences of a soul, and to provide insights that connected one's current life, fears, goals, and abilities with those of past lives so the individual may grow spiritually.

The central message being communicated was that life has purpose and direction, and that reincarnation could only be understood in the context of where man came from and where he is going—from the "First Cause" or God, and back to God. The primary object of all human experience, the Source said, was to become a worthy companion to God.[3]

The Source described the body as a "trinity," composed of the physical body, the mental or conscious mind, and the spirit, which it described as the subconscious or "mind of the soul-force."[4] Moreover, the Source said that psychic abilities were available to everyone, but one's degree of development determined how skilled one would be. "What is known to one subconscious mind or soul is known to another, whether conscious of the fact or not."[5]

But how were Todd and I communicating? Dwanna, like Caroline Myss in *Sacred Contracts*, had described symbols and archetypes as the language of a universal field of energy, a language in which psychics are adept. If I was receiving messages from Todd, was I developing psychic abilities? Was I learning that symbolic language, too?

* * *

Everyone stayed in Georgia for the holidays that year. After a Christmas Eve dinner with my parents, Jason and Dane, unmarried and unattached, followed me back to my townhouse. Waking up with them on Christmas morning was really the only present I wanted. My personal celebration of my sons, thoughtful, loving, warm, and affectionate, was proof positive that our little family had survived another year. They helped me not miss Todd quite so much at Christmas. I hated when it was time for them go back to Atlanta, but they had their own lives there, separate from mine.

Our New Year's celebrations were wholly separate. I'd hear tidbits about parties and carousing and I worried. Jonathan and I had both talked with Jason and Dane about their risk for alcoholism, and I shared the risk-reduction information with them whenever an opportune moment arose. And yet I knew for a fact that heavy drinking was a major element of any party they attended. Dwanna was right: I worried a lot about things out of my control. And she was also right about Todd having more gifts for me.

At the end of January, I attended a conference in Palm Beach, Florida with a young woman who worked under me, a conference hosted by the company that provided the software for our online application system. The company was rolling out an update and it was important that we learn about the changes to expect in the coming year. It was a two-day conference, Thursday and Friday, and we decided to stay an extra day to enjoy the sun and the beach.

We arrived at the beach around noon on Saturday. Melanie was a sun-worshipper and quickly settled herself on a towel. I did the same. I'd brought a book along with me, a Christmas present from my brother John's girlfriend Lori, entitled *Destiny of Souls*. The author, Michael Newton, was a psychiatrist similar to Brian Weiss of *Many Lives, Many Masters*, but Newton claimed that when he hypnotized patients, he took them back, not to their past lives, but to their time between lives.[6] It sounded farfetched, but I was willing to entertain the idea.

In the introduction, Newton explained that he was a traditional psychiatrist who doubted hypnosis could be used for past-life regression until he unintentionally "opened the gateway to the spirit world with a client."[7] His amazement grew into intellectual curiosity, and he conducted research with patients for many years. In his first book, *Journey of Souls*, he retraced the soul's journey from death to the afterlife. In *Destiny of Souls*, he constructed from the testimony of hypnotized patients "a working model of spirit world structure" and a detailed description of soul groups, master spirits and guides, how Akashic records are used, and how we develop our soul's purpose or goals for each lifetime.[8]

As I read, I compared Newton's descriptions with my own experiences with Todd, with Myss's books, and especially with the biography of Edgar Cayce. It shouldn't have been a surprise to discover they were all congruent, but it was.

Newton wrote, "There are souls who choose to remain at the scene of their death for a while ... discarnates who choose to comfort someone who is grieving."[9] He is clear that if a soul chooses to stay longer on Earth, its guides will allow it to stay. Brian Weiss wrote the same in *Many Lives, Many Masters*, and Edgar Cayce said the same while in a trance: "The Source said: 'The spirit of all that have passed from the physical plane remain about the plane until their development carries them onward."[10] If I wanted support for believing that Todd had stayed connected with me after he died, Newton, Weiss, and Cayce provided it.

In the second chapter, Newton described techniques, like somatic touch and dreams, used by souls to comfort those who are grieving. Somatic touch is a term Newton coined to describe how "discarnate souls use directed energy beams to touch various parts of an incarnated body [including the senses] ... to convince the person grieving that the individual they love is still alive."[11]

I relived the comfort and warmth of Todd's hug that sad November after his death. I recalled the connection I felt with him every time I'd heard "our song" on the radio. I remembered my mantra, "Energy is neither created nor destroyed," and wondered if that, too, hadn't been a message from Todd. I remembered the reiki session with Melissa and discovering the undying love of a son who chose to stay on this earth plane, energetically connected to me, to care for me in my grief.

Newton, like Melissa, confirmed the difficulty of Todd's remaining on earth: "The departing soul is anxious to get moving on their way home, as the density of Earth does drain energy."[12] So much of what Newton wrote aligned with my personal experience, I couldn't in honesty then dismiss his other discoveries about life on the other side.

After reading for two hours, tired of lying around, I felt restless and wanted to stretch my legs. When Melanie declined my offer of a walk, I said, "Okay, I'll be back in a little while," and headed down to the water.

The ocean was calm. Small waves bubbled and stretched up to where I stood, just at the line where my toes got wet. Gradually I walked into the water up to my knees. Then I headed south down the beach, directing my steps to where the sand was hard and compact from the water.

As I walked, my mind wandered to the last time Todd and I visited Florida. But that had been on the Gulf side. The Atlantic side was so different, the water gray instead of turquoise, the sand brown instead of white, and so coarse in contrast to the Gulf's fine powder. The sun was just as bright, however, so bright that I had to squint. My eyes were barely open as I picked up my pace. The beach was almost empty, so I didn't have to worry about walking into anyone with my eyes closed.

My thoughts drifted back to that last vacation at the beach, how Todd and I had collected shells together and kept only the best ones. There were no shells on the Atlantic side, only coquina, half-inch-long, oval-shaped shells, nothing very interesting.

All right, Todd, I said to him in my head, *forget about pennies from heaven. I want a shell so unique, so different, that I'll know it has to be from you.*

I stopped, opened my eyes, and looked down at my feet. A huge ribbon of shells had washed up on the beach. Directly in front of my left big toe lay a shell about the size of a quarter, wet and white and gleaming. I bent down and picked it up. It was round and perfectly white on top, and although it was structured like a nautilus, it was flat rather than conical, and covered on both sides with a spiraling pattern of parallel, serrated lines. The white side had an eight-pointed star in the center; on the opposite side, the pattern of parallel lines was repeated, but with tiny flecks of gold connecting them. Instead of a star in the center, there was just a tiny hole at the tip of the slight cone. Overall the shell was about a half-inch thick. It was marvelous. I had never seen anything like it.

And I couldn't believe it happened. Todd had answered me? *This cannot be, this is not possible.* I began looking through the wash of shells before me to see if there were others like it, or simply other interesting ones. *Surely this can't be the only one.*

But I saw simply a mix of broken shells, mostly coquina. The only unique shell was the one I held in my hand. I continued walking down the beach, looking for evidence to contradict what had just happened. I found none. My heart felt like it would burst. *Thank you, thank you, my darling!*

The second gift arrived about two weeks later. I was attending the GMAC Leadership Conference in St. Petersburg, Florida with my boss, Mel. There was a small exhibitor section, and as Mel and I walked through we stopped at the GMAC booth. They were collecting business cards for a drawing for a hundred-dollar gift card. We both threw our business cards into the large glass globe. As I threw mine in, I remembered Todd's old raffle advice—I should have wrinkled it a little to increase my chances of winning. *Oh well, sorry Todd.*

At the end of the conference, as people were leaving, the GMAC president ran back to the microphone. "People, we forgot about the drawing!"

He turned to an assistant who was bringing over the glass bowl, stuck in his hand, and pulled out a card. As he did, I said to Todd, *Pennies from heaven!* and chuckled to myself. After all, the odds were greater than a hundred to one and I never won drawings.

He read the card. "Anne Cooper! Is Anne Cooper still here?"

I gasped. Again? I was laughing, but shaking, too. *Oh ye of little faith! Todd, you're making a believer out of me!*

The weekend following the conference, Mom told me we would be celebrating Dad's birthday and that Jason, Dane, their friend Steve, and John and Lori were coming to dinner. Since Jonathan's birthday was the day after Dad's, she said she had invited him to dinner, too. I appreciated being forewarned, but it didn't help. I felt awkward at dinner and was quieter than usual.

I knew Jonathan still had feelings for me and I didn't want to give him false hope. His health was fragile; he was fragile. From the strong, muscular guy I'd married he had become a thin shadow of himself. I suspected that his finances were as challenging as ever, too—I even recognized his shirt. And I was embarrassed by my own good fortune and health.

Seeing him again, however, reminded me that I'd never answered his letter. He had bared his soul in it. I still owed him a response. By this time, I should have known a book would show up to help me. I found *Radical Forgiveness*, by Colin Tipping, while browsing in a bookstore.

The ideas in Tipping's book integrated seamlessly with the spiritual concepts I was exploring. He, too, agreed that we are spiritual beings having a human experience and that we're born to learn in the flesh the spiritual lessons that will allow our souls to grow. "Looked at from a spiritual standpoint, our discomfort in any given situation provides a signal that we are out of alignment with spiritual law and are being given an opportunity to heal something. ... Sometimes the message has to become very loud, or the pain extremely intense, before we pay attention."[13]

My marriage had ended in a crescendo of pain, disease, and death. I was determined to be right, to stay in control, and to ignore anything spiritual. I'd watched the man I loved and trusted betray our relationship and our family and damage himself physically and mentally. I blamed Jonathan for his choices, and for being unwilling to try to get better. I saw myself as a victim, abandoned and living in constant panic about the basic necessities. I struggled mightily to find another way of looking at that situation, and found it hard not to blame Jonathan for all our troubles. Tipping's advice was to look at my own beliefs. "We always create our reality according to our beliefs. If you want to know what your beliefs are, look at what you have in your life. Life always reflects our beliefs."[14]

Thinking back to what I'd learned in *The Field*, I connected Tipping's idea that we each create our own reality to the other fundamental principle of quantum physics, the observer effect: "According to experiment, an electron is not a precise entity, but exists as a potential, a superposition, or sum, of all probabilities until we observe or measure it, at which point the electron freezes into a particular state. ... What appeared to put a halt to randomness was a living observer."[15]

The Field provided many examples of scientific experiments that measured the effect of the observer, or consciousness, on random systems.

- Living beings, from humans to baby chicks, can change the output of a random number generator from perfectly random, 50-50 results, to nonrandom output through focused attention.[16]

- Ordinary humans can remotely influence other living things, from unconscious muscle and nervous system activity to healing, through their focused attention, including prayer or meditation.[17]

- Human emotions, particularly emotions shared on a global scale, such as the grief felt by millions at the death of Princess Diana or the attacks of September 11, greatly increased the nonrandom output of a worldwide network of REG machines (random event generators), suggesting that collective consciousness has an organizing effect on the world.[18]

In a Universe of infinite possibility, we the observers, through our beliefs and emotions, give shape and direction to our lives. But if we make agreements with each other, like sacred contracts, prior to reincarnating, didn't that imply that our fate was predetermined? *How could I have agreed to my son dying so I could be reborn spiritually? Had I no say in the matter? Was I fated to marry Jonathan? What of my free will?*

I remembered critical decision points in my life. In high school, I'd had a spiritual experience and chose to see it as a trick of the mind, an emotional mirage. What if I'd acknowledged it as a connection to Spirit? How different my life—and Todd's life—might have been.

What if I'd left Jonathan after his DUI? What if I'd trusted the Universe to provide me with the means of supporting three boys? In all the advice that Edgar Cayce ever gave, "There was always one underlying theme— a willingness to call on God's help through prayer and have faith that help will come. … [He said] 'never worry as long as you can pray. When you can't pray, you'd better begin to worry! For then, you have something to worry about!'"[19]

In my first life, I pitied those who thought prayer had power. Instead I tried to go it alone. I was in control. I believed I could make Jonathan change for me, and I fought to exhaustion. I surrendered only after Todd's death. I always had choices and I'd made mine of my own free will. Free will, according to Cayce's Source, "ultimately determined an individual's fate. No one, not even God, could conclusively predict events shaped by the free will of an individual. … A man's will is supreme."[20]

Why had I chosen Jonathan as my husband? I recalled the sensation of a door closing, of my destiny decided, the night we first made love and he told me the story of his life. I married him to give him the family he never had, but I'd also married him out of my own fear of the unknown: of what I wanted next, of being independent and responsible for myself. I wanted to grow, but was afraid of taking risks and living on my own. He was safe—my mother had told me so: "I knew from the first time I answered the phone that he was going to be your husband." I admired Jonathan's strength and determination to remake his life after his daughter Ryder's death, to leave his family and the security of a family business, to move to Brooklyn, put himself through Pratt, and find out how far his artistic talent could take him. Jonathan had courage, street smarts, and a wisdom about people that I hoped would rub off on me. *I chose him.*

It also occurred to me that, although risk reduction had taught me to understand Jonathan's alcoholism in theory, I had never felt compassion for what he suffered, especially as our relationship was ending. I only blamed him and felt sorry for myself. I remembered his stories of growing up and the terror he must have felt in foster care with his little brother and sister, the three of them abandoned by two alcoholic parents in rehab. I abandoned him, too.

Many times Jonathan had tried to stop drinking, but I'd been oblivious to the shame he must have felt when I discovered he'd gone back. I remembered his despair when the economy and his health conspired so that he couldn't support his family in the way he wanted. I remembered his pride in his powerful physique, his strong heart and lungs. He'd been so certain they would never betray him. I remembered his depression and desperation, and the desperation that pushed me into finding a job and getting an MBA. I remembered Jean Read's answer to my question about how I sabotaged myself: "By not moving. Not taking a risk. You move as long as you're comfortable, then stop or backtrack."

Jonathan, in the very depths of his addiction, had been a helpmeet to me—not consciously, of course, but as Tipping characterized it, as "a soul-to-soul transaction. His soul knows about your original pain and is aware that you will not heal it without going through the experience."[21] Jonathan forced me to become self-sufficient, independent, and capable.

I'd grown up in a fairy tale, in a world where I was protected from all harm, and as a result, I lacked faith in my own abilities. I didn't believe I could make it on my own and looked to others to define my purpose and even my identity. Even as Jonathan's health and professional career were falling apart, I couldn't see how I was holding it all together. I was working, going to graduate school, and running a household. I'd even earned more than Jonathan the year before Todd died, and yet I still didn't believe in myself, or that I could make it on my own. Even after Todd died I was stuck, living with Jonathan under the same roof.

I moved because Jonathan pushed me out—out of the role of wife, mother, and homemaker, out of the house, and out of my comfort zone. If that were Jonathan's contract with me, what did I have to forgive? It was as though Tipping, in his book, were speaking directly to me.

> Do you feel how much that man loves you—at the soul level, I mean? ... He was willing to do whatever it took to get you to the point where you could look again at your belief about yourself and see that it was untrue. Do you realize how much discomfort he was willing to endure to help you? He is not a cruel man by nature, so it must have been hard for him. Few men could have done that for you while risking losing you in the process.[22]

Gratitude overwhelmed me. I looked at my second life and saw that Jonathan had helped me find it. I decided that, instead of a letter of forgiveness, what I really owed him was the part of his life I'd taken with me when I left—our life together as a family. I bought three photo albums and put together a photographic history of our shared life with our three sons. I gave them to him the next time I saw him, on his sixtieth birthday, at Mom and Dad's again for dinner.

Part of the Capone birthday ritual was to open birthday presents after dinner, during dessert. But when Jonathan got up to leave right after dinner, I realized he wasn't staying for dessert. I got up from the table, too, grabbed the gift bags holding the albums, and caught up with him before he reached the front door.

"Wait!" I called. "I have something for you."

He turned around and looked his question.

"I never answered your letter," I said, "because I never knew what I wanted to say. But I have my answer here. Happy birthday." I handed him the gift bags. "Open one."

He pulled an album out of a bag and flipped through the pages. Before he could say anything, I said, "I promised you a long time ago that I would share these with you."

"Thank you, Anne, I'll enjoy these." We hugged gently, carefully, and then he left.

I had imagined a very different scene. When it came time to open presents, I pictured him opening the albums and sharing them with everyone there. Jason and Dane would look over his shoulder, and we would reminisce and laugh over good times together. But that emotional release was not to be. I was sad and happy at the same time. I knew Jonathan would pore over those albums for hours, just not with me.

I never saw him again.

* * *

A year and a half later, on the last Monday of July 2007, as I was driving through the gates of my subdivision on the way to work, I suddenly thought of Jonathan. *He's sicker than me, so he's probably going to die before me. That means he's going to see Todd before me.* I felt jealous, then laughed at myself. *What a weird line of thought.*

On Tuesday, my friend Chris came to Athens for meetings and three of us, Chris, Jan, and myself, went to lunch together. We were in a sandwich shop, waiting for our order, when my cell phone rang. It was my brother John.

"Jason and Dane have been trying to reach you," he said. "Jonathan died."

I was already sitting down, but I gasped, hunched over, and held the phone closer to my ear to hear him over the din of the store. "What happened? When?"

"A neighbor found him this morning. He must have died in his sleep."

He died alone. I felt sick and so sad. The tears came, but they were mostly for Jason and Dane. They would have wanted a last memory of their dad; they would have wanted to be with him. I ached for my sons. Another death in their young lives. And I, with both my parents living. It wasn't fair.

Jan and Chris brought over our order and we went outside to sit at a table. I told them the news. They were stunned, too. I stared blankly at the food in front of me. I'd said my goodbyes to Jonathan so long before, the pain of this final separation felt anticlimactic. My sons' pain, however, would be raw and new, and I couldn't protect them from it. All I could do was hold them.

"I have to go home," I told Chris and Jan. "Jason and Dane are on their way to Athens. I have to be with them."

"Of course," said Jan, "I'll tell Mel. Don't worry about anything. Just go."

So I did. I was waiting when Jason and Dane walked through my door. There were no words, just embraces and tears that ended with us around the dining room table.

"When did you find out?" I asked Jason.

"Mike Martin called this morning and told me," he replied. "He said he hadn't seen Dad at all yesterday, so he walked over this morning and looked in at the studio. Dad wasn't at his desk, so he knocked on the door. When there was no answer, he went around back to get inside. He found Dad in his bed. He must have had a heart attack in his sleep."

"When was the last time you saw him?" I asked.

"Two weeks ago. We took him on vacation with us. To Pensacola, for a week. We had a great time. We went to the National Naval Aviation Museum, on the same base where his dad was stationed during World War II. When we went scuba diving in the Gulf, Dad came with us on the boat, to where they sank the aircraft carrier, the USS Oriskany. We got to tell him we loved him before he went back to Athens."

Dane showed me pictures they'd taken on vacation. There was a terrific photo of the three of them at dinner, Jonathan smiling proudly, flanked by his two sons. Mentally I blessed the man for his timing—that Jason and Dane had such beautiful last memories of him, of fun times sharing their passion for all things aeronautical and WWII, and that he had made that their last gift to him.

"I'm so glad you had that time together!" I said. "I'm sure it meant a lot to your dad."

"I think he had an idea this was going to happen," Jason confessed. "He called me last week and left a message to call. He said he had something to tell me. I never got the chance." The regret he felt was palpable.

"He called me too," said Dane, "and said the same thing. I didn't get back to him either."

"You didn't know," I tried to comfort them. "You would have been with him if you could." I changed the subject. "Where is he now?"

"Athens Regional. They're doing an autopsy," Dane said.

"When they're finished, tell them to call Bernstein's," I told them. "I'll call there and make arrangements. They handled Todd's cremation. You know he wanted to be cremated, right?"

"Yeah," Jason said. "He said he wants us to throw his ashes into the Gulf of Mexico."

We all got busy, making phone calls and arrangements for the memorial service we decided to hold on Friday. I called friends and former neighbors to let them know. As I was getting off the phone with Shannon, she said, "Pay attention, Anne. Jonathan and Todd will reach out to you."

As soon as she said it, it hit me—the shock of recognition. "Oh my God, Shannon, they already have. *They told me they were together yesterday*—when I was driving to work—before any of us even knew!" I later learned from the autopsy that the estimated time of Jonathan's death was Monday morning, another confirmation of the message I'd received. I'd been jealous for a very good reason.

The memorial service was simple. Jason spoke first, with love and respect, of the father who'd taught him so much about life and other people. As he spoke, I glanced at his new girlfriend Kelly, quietly wiping her tears. So sweet, I thought, little realizing she was his future wife. As Jason drew his remarks to a close, he invited everyone there to share a memory of Jonathan. I felt compelled to speak so my sons could hear that their father and I had made peace. I walked up to the podium.

"Jonathan and I met over thirty years ago. It didn't take me long to realize he was a man who had overcome many challenges in his life, challenges that would have crippled a weaker man. Jonathan was a 'pull-yourself-up-by-your-own-bootstraps' kind of guy. He overcame great tragedy to remake his life—not once, but twice. Somehow he survived losing a son and a daughter. Jonathan was a great storyteller who rarely told the stories that made him who he was.

"Jonathan loved being a husband and a father. He loved his work as a designer and he worked hard to provide for his family. He has earned his rest. In his own good time, he'll make a fresh start."

A few weeks later, as I helped Jason and Dane clean their father's house in preparation for signing it over to the bank, Jason confirmed that Jonathan had died of a massive coronary, a comfort to the three of us to know he didn't suffer long. I wondered if he had maintained his atheism to the end, or embraced the Alcoholics Anonymous precept of a Higher Power. I took great satisfaction in knowing that he and Todd were reunited. Another happy thought occurred to me: at long last, he was reunited with Ryder too.

CHAPTER TWENTY-TWO

ReUnion

There once was a circle of seven women, Jean Read told me when I asked her about my friends. She said we planned to be together. I recognized six of them, including myself. The seventh, Donna Terrazas, entered the circle in May 2007. My friend Shannon found her. Donna was an acupuncturist who practiced kinesiology and a healing technique using kinesiology called ReUnion.

Shannon wanted to learn more about kinesiology, so she and Chris organized a workshop with Donna and invited a small group of friends to participate. I drove into Atlanta on a bright Saturday morning, ready for fun and an interesting day.

After everyone in the room introduced themselves, Donna introduced the topic for the day. "Basically, kinesiology is muscle testing. We're all connected to a universal field of energy that contains all knowledge and all experience, and we can use our body to tap into it. A simple muscle test can tell us if any statement is true or false. If the muscle stays strong, it's true. If it goes weak, it's false. The test will also tell us if something in our personal energy field is good or bad for us." She recommended reading David Hawkins's book, *Power vs. Force*, for a deeper understanding of how kinesiology worked. Of course I made a note of it.

"The best way to learn about kinesiology," Donna said, "is to do it. Everyone find a partner."

I turned to the guy to my right, Shannon's friend Lee, whom I'd just met.

"We'll start with a simple Yes-No test," Donna instructed. "One of you is going to be the tester, the other will be the testee."

I agreed to be the testee, Lee, the tester.

"Stand across from each other," Donna continued, "inside the other's personal space. Whoever's the testee, hold your arm straight out to the side from your shoulder so that it's parallel to the floor.

"Testers, put your hand on the opposite shoulder to help your partner stay balanced. Then say, 'Give me a *yes*,' and lightly press down with two fingers on the wrist of your partner's outstretched arm.

"Testees, you should resist the pressure as hard as you can. See what happens. Then try 'Give me a *no*.' Go ahead and do it with each other."

Lee and I began. When Lee said, "Give me a *yes*," I was able to resist the pressure on my wrist easily. When he said, "Give me a *no*," my arm collapsed.

"Do it again," I told him. I couldn't believe I wasn't able to keep my arm strong. He wasn't pushing that hard.

He did. "Give me a *no*," he said, and pushed down on my wrist. As determined as I was to keep my arm straight, Lee effortlessly pushed it down. "Do it to me," he said, and held out his arm.

I got the same results.

"Now test your name," Donna called out to the noisy group.

"Your name is Lee," I said as I pushed down lightly on his wrist. To my surprise, he went weak.

"Oh my God," he said. "Try Leejay."

"Your name is Leejay," I said, and his arm stayed strong.

"That's incredible!" he cried. "Growing up, my dad was always Lee, not me. I was Leejay, short for Lee Junior. Let's do you."

I put out my arm and he said, "Your name is Anne." My arm went weak, and it was my turn to gasp in amazement while he looked puzzled.

"When I was growing up," I said, "I was called Debbie. Deborah's my middle name. I changed to Anne after I got married, when I moved to Georgia. Try Debbie."

"Your name is Debbie," he said. My arm stayed strong. We were fascinated.

Donna called us back to order. "How'd you do?"

Lee told the group about our little discovery with our names.

"The bodymind instantly knows whether something is true or false," Donna explained. "It can also tell if something in your energy field is positive or negative. I've brought lots of different things for you to test. Come on up and pick out a few items, and see what you learn."

We spent the next hour testing different substances. It would probably have been more scientific if we hadn't known what they were, but at the time, it was enough to see that we all went weak with the same items, for example, aspartame, chlorine bleach, and a picture of Stalin, and that everyone stayed strong with Vitamin C tablets, extra-virgin coconut oil, and a picture of Abraham Lincoln.

At the close of the workshop, Donna invited everyone to stay for a ReUnion session. We lay on the floor in a circle, our heads toward the center, eyes closed, and Donna read passages from different pages in a large, three-ring binder. I can't remember what the group's healing message was; all I remember is that the sunny day turned dark, wind and rain lashed at the windows, thunder and lightning crashed in the air. The change, so sudden, was eerie.

The workshop left me eager to learn more about kinesiology, so I bought *Power vs. Force* and devoured it. I've read it several times since. Back in 2007, I read an early edition of the work, but today, reading the 2012 edition, I understand more clearly how Hawkins connected his work in kinesiology with developments in many fields of study. Each time I read it, I learn more. To say the work is dense is a profound understatement.

Hawkins had the largest psychiatric practice in New York for twenty-five years, then left it in 1978 to move to Sedona, where he researched consciousness using kinesiology and explored the perilous territory where science and spirituality overlap. In the thesis for his PhD, which he earned at Berkeley in 1995, Hawkins proved the validity of kinesiology and used it to develop a map of human consciousness.[1] He created a logarithmic scale, from the lowest energy level at which humans can exist—Shame, registering 10^{20}—to the highest level, Enlightenment, $10^{1,000}$. The critical point where the energy of human consciousness shifts from life-destroying to life-sustaining is at 10^{200}, Integrity or Courage.[2]

In *Power vs. Force*, Hawkins detailed his proof of kinesiology, which he tested in four different studies with over 4,500 test subjects on positive and negative stimuli. Over many years of research, Hawkins used kinesiology's basic muscle test "involving millions of calibrations, on thousands of test subjects of all ages and personality types, and from all walks of life ... of all nationalities, ethnic backgrounds, and religions, ... covering a wide spectrum of physical and emotional health, ... [and] the results were identical and reproducible."[3]

Nonetheless, applied kinesiology remains relatively unknown, dismissed out of hand by traditional doctors, scientists, and institutions. Hawkins recognized that most of those professionals, along with their industry and academic associations, still cling to a Newtonian worldview, despite the upheavals of quantum physics. As a result, their ability to accept new discoveries is constricted. Of this he wrote, "Kinesiologic demonstrations often result in paradigm shock for people who have an investment in strict materialism. One such observer, a research psychiatrist, responded by first trying to prove that the demonstration was a fake. When he failed to do so, he walked away, saying, 'Even if it's true, I don't believe it.'"[4]

How sad, I thought after reading that, *mainstream science has become a kind of religion*. Like Catholicism, traditional science has its dogma and its heresies, its saints and sacred texts, and its methods of persecuting those who dare to question. That had been made clear in *The Field* and was reconfirmed as I read other research on paranormal abilities. There are many modern-day Galileos.

Applied kinesiology demonstrates the quantum principle that everything in the universe is entangled, that once something, anything, is connected, it remains connected for all time. Therefore, Hawkins concluded, we "can bypass the artificial dichotomy between subject and object, transcending the limited viewpoint that creates the illusion of duality. The subjective and objective are, in fact, one and the same."[5]

Kinesiology works, Hawkins pointed out, because the human body is a quantum instrument.

> All of us have available at all times a computer far more advanced than the most elaborate artificial intelligence machine—the human mind itself. The basic function of any measuring device is simply to give a signal indicating the detection by the instrument of a slight change. ... The reactions of the human body itself provide such a signal. ... The body can discern, to the finest degree, the difference between that which is supportive of life and that which is not.[6]

Kinesiology is a method by which anyone can access information in the zero point field. It will tell us what is destructive of life or life-supporting, and whether a statement is true or false. The muscle test is one hundred percent accurate and one hundred percent replicable, Hawkins asserted, so long as the tester and testee themselves test at an energy level at or above 10^{200}.[7]

* * *

After the kinesiology workshop, I began seeing Donna professionally and we gradually became friends. Donna was working in Athens as an apprentice acupuncturist, and I saw her monthly for an acupuncture treatment for health maintenance purposes. (Sadly, Dr. Pan had passed away.) As a bonus, Donna was also highly skilled in facelift acupuncture. She would put several needles in my legs and feet, a couple in my arms and hands, and about a hundred in my face. The needles, she explained, stimulated the body's chi, increased circulation in the face, and built collagen in the skin. I could feel the energy flowing through my body and, every now and then, when Donna put a needle in an acupressure point in my face, a charge would run through my limbs, strong enough to make my foot jump!

After inserting all the needles, Donna did ReUnion with me. ReUnion grew out of the work of Dr. George Goodheart, the discoverer of kinesiology. Another chiropractor, Dr. Alan Beardall, realized that by testing a muscle, he was able "to 'ask' the body what it 'felt,' or was willing to reveal about itself."[8] In other words, he'd found a way to make conscious that which we have tucked away in our subconscious. ReUnion is nothing less than a shortcut to the subconscious, to our own personal inner truths, without years of angst, struggle, or expensive therapy.

Beardall shared his techniques of muscle testing, hand modes, and files with an English osteopath, Dr. Solihin Thom, who further developed them into a procedure "that allowed the body to confront its own physical conditions, and also those emotional and spiritual conditions that may be at the root of those conditions."[9] In other words, our own bodies can tell us what medical intuitives can read in our energy field. ReUnion is a conversation with the Inner, a treatment modality that uses the trinity of body, mind, and spirit to heal the whole person.

Edgar Cayce's Source once revealed that a soul chooses "the time and place to reenter the earthly plane [and] specific choices are made regarding family, genetics, physical attributes, and personality." Karma, defined by the Source as "the impact that one incarnation has on another," gradually paints over our original Self with ancestral identities and current and past life decisions, emotions, and relationships.[10] ReUnion therapy allows individuals "to recover inner resources, to open to one's true power … It untangles us from our ancestral core, … [removes] those overpainted pictures on our sense of self, … and clears those forces which are altering our core frequencies and creating our mortal reality."[11] In other words, ReUnion is a way to clear karma—or to put it in more scientific terms—our epigenetics.

Donna wrote out my many ReUnion sessions for me to reflect upon. My question for the first session was "Who am I?" I was puzzled by the rejection of the name Anne for Debbie in our kinesiology workshop, and I wanted to know what was behind it. I loved the name

Anne; I felt I was Anne. She was the survivor, the warrior who had created a second life from the ashes of death and loss.

The initial answer was "Anne, fearless, open Anne. Self-recognition, play. All the possibilities rise up as living fragrances from the sacred attributes of love. Aware that all possibilities exist." Once again, infinite possibility, the itinerary of my second life's journey.

Then that answer was flipped to the negative, and took a dive into my innermost fears: limiting possibility, inner rigidity, loss of joy. Donna traced the seed of those emotions back to a female ancestor, twenty-seven generations before, to a genetic inheritance that "negates life, making one unable to receive grace. A fog of confusion created by a belief structure befuddles the clear perception of grace. I am guilty and unable to face the truth. As a result, a belief is held to make the self right and others wrong."

In subsequent sessions, she found emotional codes and implants from other incarnations. In one former life, I faced an existential choice: die emotionally, by not marrying the man I loved from outside my tribe, or die physically, by marrying him and being banished from the tribe, a death sentence in prehistoric times. I connected that revelation to how strongly influenced I was by my mother's approval of Jonathan as my husband.

The struggles of my first life and my rejection of spiritual connection came into clear focus: "Instinctive understanding is smothered by a loss of faith in self. A hidden anxiousness inflames distrust and an irritable unease arises from the inwardly tangled ancestor. One's shaping reach is altered, confused, or squeezed down. When reaching out to God and others, one feels one is stumbling blindly and is blind to one's heart's desire, unable to find true union and intimacy." Donna was reading the emotional energy trail of my first life.

At the bottom of this downward spiral Donna found a genetically encoded implant that "commands being disconnected, rejecting or being rejected by others." She led me through a meditation to remove it. Even as I followed her guidance, I doubted my ability to really heal, to find that "I am in joyous and intimate companionship with others."

Without my having to speak the doubt I felt, Donna uncovered yet one more layer, "a trance of being forsaken and without true partnership or friendship, a fear of being found out or of something being revealed. Hidden within the heart's knowing are two contrary beliefs that create anxiety: first, that the desire will happen and, second, that the desire won't happen. Due to this anxiety, the future is unable to present with one's greatest possibilities."

Donna read my soul to me, my innermost thoughts and feelings, the ones I shared with no one, the ones I barely admitted to myself. I heard echoes of my Akashic record reading, that my greatest fear was true honesty, with others and myself. I wanted to be known, truly known, but feared being abandoned if I were. "Part of you is still hiding," Jean Read had said during our session. "You're afraid that if you let others see the core of your being, you will be abandoned. Fear of abandonment is behind your fear of total honesty."

The ReUnion session peeled back layer after layer until the fundamental essence of that false belief was bared. I felt cleansed and healed. The new abilities that the session promised were "a sensitivity of the feeling self to that which nourishes, heals, and gives direction" and "feeling at home and more able to act with authority and confidence in one's universe."

Over time, the ReUnion sessions with Donna moved from my personal healing to collective healings, first with my family, then with larger, unnamed groups. Some of those, interestingly, were connected to my hopes and fears about writing. The healings, "opening your spirit to miracles and happiness," would lead to new abilities and blessings, "recognition of your true path, allowing the optimism and strength in your heart to guide you, giving you the courage to be free and powerful, and giving yourself and others the gift of healing abundance and beauty." What more could I hope for!

CHAPTER TWENTY-THREE

Mother's Day Presents

The first Mother's Day after Todd died, Jason and Dane gave me a pair of pearl-and-diamond stud earrings and signed the card "Love, Jason, Dane, and Todd." I cried. Never again would Todd be with me on that day.

One night, close to Mother's Day in 2010, I once again found myself keenly aware that I was sleeping but not dreaming. I felt Todd nestle against me, his cheek on my chest, my cheek resting on the top of his head. I felt his hair soft against my skin. Love rushed through me and we held each other close for a long time, the sensation diminishing as awe and gratitude overwhelmed the connection. "Todd wants you to know that he will always be with you," Dwanna had said. I knew it was true.

Although I found solace in the many ways Todd connected with me after his death, memories of the depression and hopelessness that poisoned his last year still preyed upon my peace. Over and over, my thoughts went back to what I'd do differently. How I wished for another chance with him! "The life has gone out of me and I can't get it back." Those words made my mind wince.

That summer, toward the end of July, my sister Edna called and left a message on my machine. Busy finalizing orientation for the incoming MBA class, I didn't listen to her message until two days later: "I've got to tell you about our weekend at Omega. Call me!"

I called her as soon as I could. She began with a blow-by-blow description of her weekend with her husband Kenny, from the bumpy start on Friday driving to the Omega Institute in Rhinebeck, New York, to their departure on Sunday.

"Did I tell you we signed up for a yoga weekend at Omega?" she said. "No? Well, Kenny has a crush on the yoga teacher Lillias Folan, and wanted to go to her workshop. I'm telling you, Anne, by the time we got in the car Friday afternoon, I was so mad at Kenny I wasn't speaking to him. By Saturday morning I'd calmed down. We got up early and walked over for breakfast." I'd been to Omega for workshops, so knew she was talking about the dining hall of the 250-acre campus, a lovely old house at the top of a small hill.

"Everyone at our table introduced themselves and said what workshop they were taking," she continued. "The guy next to me said he always thought he had psychic abilities, and that he was taking James Van Praagh's beginners workshop. I told him I'd heard of him, that my sister read his book on grief after her son died. Then we all went our separate ways.

"Sunday afternoon, Kenny and I were walking back to the parking lot and the same guy comes running up and gives me this big hug. Hands me his business card and says, 'Have your sister call me.' His name is Rich Fletcher. I told him you live in Georgia and work at UGA. He's cute. I think you should call him."

When I stopped laughing, I said, "Why would I call him? Edna, I don't even know him. What would I say? 'You met my sister at Omega and she thinks you're cute'?"

"You could at least email him. I liked him a lot. He's in global consulting. And he has a blog, called *Ozark Light*. Check it out and see what you think. He's a really nice guy." I could hear that she really wanted me to get in touch with this Rich guy, but it felt so awkward.

"I don't know, I'll think about it," I promised. Before we hung up, she urged me again to give Rich a call. Or email him. She thought we should connect.

The next day after work, I checked out the *Ozark Light* blog. No red flags there, so I figured there was no harm in emailing him, if nothing else to humor my sister. So that evening, I wrote the email and hit send.

The next morning, Rich responded.

Anne,

How nice to hear from you and, yes, I believe our paths were meant to cross as well. … I would love to talk with you. Let me know a good time to call. … Today and this evening are good and tomorrow's good as well. Monday I'm doing a reading for the father of someone I met at Omega.

In another of the exercises, I got a sixteen- or seventeen-year-old boy that seemingly didn't belong to anyone. ... Did you live near Hackensack before moving to Georgia?

I don't want to raise expectations—so let's see where we're led (if you feel ready). If you want, I'll be happy to tape-record the session and please know that I'm not doing this professionally! :) Sometimes I'm a little slow, but I know that if the intention is right, wonderful healing messages come through.

Best regards,

Rich

I could hardly believe it, that Todd would find this crazy, roundabout way to reach me. But he was sixteen and a half when he died and I had grown up in New Milford, right next door to Hackensack. I answered Rich that same afternoon.

Rich,

Tonight at seven would be great. That sixteen-year-old boy may belong to me. And yes, I lived one town over from Hackensack—grew up in New Milford, NJ.

Thank you for sharing your gift,

Anne

Rich responded, confirming the time.

Wonderful. ... Spend about ten minutes beforehand in meditation and we'll send good intentions and prayers to your son and loved ones on the other side. ... Talk to you later. ...

Rich

The remainder of my workday flew by. When I got home, I spent an hour on yoga practice. I tried to remain calm, but excitement raced through me. I followed Rich's instructions, meditated on the prayer he sent, then simply sat next to the phone on the floor of my bedroom in wonder and anticipation. Todd smiled down from his photograph on the wall.

I discovered that in Rich, Todd had chosen a sensitive, truly gifted medium. What follows is from the recording of our phone conversation.

Rich opened the session with a prayer, then said, "Okay. Feel free to just speak up and say if you want me to explain something. My initial impression of this young man was vivid, V-I-V-I-D, because he seemed just so full of the life-force, just absolutely completely vivacious and alive. I was curious. I didn't understand how he died and still don't."

Rich later wrote in greater detail on his blog about his first encounter with Todd.

> There were easily two hundred people in James's workshop. ... It was a great experience and helped me feel more comfortable doing the work, and of trusting what I get when I do readings. But in one instance, I did a reading for my group of ten or twelve people, and a young man came through— a teenager—he told me where he was from and he had a quality of being a little ADHD—he was zooming all over the place on a skateboard. No one in my group knew this young man nor of anyone that he might belong to, so I simply thanked him for his presence and acknowledged his effort at getting through to me. ...

Fast-forward two days later—the workshop has ended and I'm back in the dining hall to eat lunch before leaving. Sitting at a table is the couple I'd met earlier, so I sit down and we start talking about our experiences. ... They asked me about the workshop, and I related a few of my experiences, and then I said, "You know, sometimes though (as a medium), I don't get the complete picture. The other day I had a young man come through, a teenager—he said he was from New Jersey, and he loved his skateboard! He was in constant motion—in fact, it was hard to get him to tell me much that was specific—mostly it was my simply getting a sense of who he was, that he was hyperactive and that he experimented with drugs, that he was reckless. He died suddenly, but he didn't show me how. He didn't belong to anyone in my group."

At this, her face registered shock and disbelief; tears welled in her eyes. "I think that's my nephew," she said. We talked a bit more before she asked for my contact information—"I want to send your information to my sister, his mom."[1]

That explained Edna's insistence that I contact Rich. She said she didn't tell me the real reason because she didn't want to get my hopes up. Even more telling was Rich's description of the teenager zooming around the room on a skateboard. It was the Disney *Tarzan* movie again! Todd was zooming around the room the way Tarzan zoomed through the jungle using giant leaves like a skateboard. As Rich later wrote when I told him about the *Tarzan* connection, "The skateboard—when he first made himself known to me, he was literally surfing around the room—I mean, flying! The whole time, he's been reaching out consistently and in such a beautiful way—so much freedom and joy and love."

Rich continued the reading. "He's actually calling me Mr. Fletcher." He chuckled. "I've told him it's okay to call me Rich." That sounded so much like my Todd, the high school kid respectfully addressing the adult.

"Did Todd have any pet phrases?"

"I'm trying to remember." My mind had gone blank. I was so eager to hear from Todd, to be present in the moment, that my brain wouldn't go back to the past.

"Was he impulsive in any way?" Rich continued.

"Yes, I think that was related to his death. My question to him is, was it accidental or was it suicide?"

"Okay. Let's pause. I got very early on, before we were on the phone, that he was very impulsive and, in a way, reckless. So let's step back a minute. Were you getting divorced at that time?"

"Yes. My husband was an alcoholic, in business for himself, and I was essentially trying to support everyone. I was going back to school and had decided to get a divorce. Then Todd started falling to pieces. It was just one thing after another."

"There's no doubt that he was really, really angry with his dad," Rich said. "And Todd didn't know how to handle his anger. He just didn't have the tools yet and, combined with his personality," Rich sighed, "and an inability, really, to reach out, he internalized it.

"But when I was in meditation, and he said 'Mr. Fletcher' to me, I got a sense of someone who … he's very light, there's no heaviness here, there's no guilt or grief on his part. There's a much more complete understanding now. And from one of the things that he said to me early on, I felt he was a very, very young soul, not a lot of incarnations here. And this impulsivity and recklessness was tied to that. He said you needed a baby and he volunteered to come. Do you remember that time in your life? It sounds like if you had two others twenty-three months apart, you probably didn't need another baby."

I laughed. "I knew I wanted three children. There was something going on between Todd and his dad from the very beginning, from the instant Todd was born. He had a crossed eye. My husband lost a daughter when she was two years old, she had a brain tumor. This was before we were married. He said he went to her crib one morning to kiss her goodbye before he went to work, and her eye was turned in. And so when Todd was born with a crossed eye, I think it triggered things in Jonathan. There was always friction between them, from the first."

"That's huge. I'm thinking about your husband, his inability to process his grief, and the fact that the Universe gave him an opportunity, in Todd, to come back to that and look at it in a different way, to experience it in love, rather than fear. But he wasn't able to do that.

"Ultimately, that's okay. We all get opportunities, and we take the ones we're ready to take. So he wasn't ready. But there had to have been underlying resentment, almost as if he wanted to protect himself from loss again."

"The irony is that Todd died, too," I said. "When his daughter died, his wife had a nervous breakdown and his mother-in-law killed herself. This time there was a very different experience of death and loss, because the family came together in love to support each other. That was different for Jonathan. He didn't get sober right away. Too late to put his life back together, but he did eventually sober up."

Rich gave a great sigh. "Okay."

"I've come to understand a little bit about addiction, that it's a search for spiritual connection. Todd helped Jonathan and me both that way," I admitted.

"Okay …" Rich paused and started afresh. "So what you need to know is that you're the light of your son's life. You need to know that. *You are the light of his life.*"

Tears filled my eyes. I remembered my first encounter with Dwanna, her saying, "He's singing to you. He's singing 'You Light Up My Life.'" I told Rich, "There were moments of connection between Todd and me that will live with me forever."

"Right," Rich said. "And the intensity and the purity of that connection, at a soul level. What about his brothers? How did his brothers deal with his death? Before you answer that, there's a concern for his brothers, and maybe more for one than the other. Is one of them more like your ex-husband than the other?"

I sighed. Todd was still worried about Jason. "Yes, his brother Jason. They were always bickering. I think Jason has a lot of guilt."

"One of the things that may be emerging here is most men have so little ability to navigate their own grief. They don't know how to own their feelings. How do I go on in the face of something so difficult and over-whelming? How old are those boys now?"

"Thirty-two and thirty," I answered. "Jason just got engaged. We're pretty close. I do believe Jason buries his feelings about Todd. And I don't know how to help him."

"Well, you help him by being a witness to his life, by being his mother, offering him a place of security and love, and recognizing that he's on his own spiritual jour-ney. And trust that will be what it will be.

"I feel like Todd is kind of in the background here. He seems quiet and reserved right now. I think he un-derstands the implications, the consequences that his death had on his family."

"We miss him terribly."

"Honestly, Anne, Todd's not letting me into this place around his death, but I ... let me see if I can ..." There was a long pause, then Rich said, "He was too young, too immature, to understand consequences. He had no concept really, of how far out the consequences would extend." Rich paused again. "One of the things that happens when they go over to the other side, is that they're whole again in a way they weren't here. But that doesn't mean everything is all worked out and copasetic. Our ability to forgive on this side absolutely affects them on the other side. It lightens them, it enables them to look at their lives differently, and to even go back and reexperience their lives in a different way.

"So one of the reasons you and I are having this conversation is that, if there's any place where my work is going to be meaningful, it's with people on this side and the other side for whom forgiveness and healing are still necessary. And it's more than healing the wound of grief. It's coming to a place of understanding and acceptance that frees us from our attachment to our grief. Doing that, we also free them, and the bond grief has created. And you know whether this resonates for you."

"Five years after Todd died, I had an amazing year of healing," I said, remembering my first encounter with Todd through Melissa. "It was never a question of forgiveness, it was always a question of self-reproach: Did I do enough? I don't know if I can ever let go of that." Not only my grief, but my attachment to it, connected us. *The life has gone out of me and I can't get it back.* Understanding and acceptance eluded me still.

"There's no doubt that he's always with you and you with him," Rich said. "I can't pretend to know what losing a child must be like. I don't think we're going to get the answer to your question right now. I think the important piece of this is the connection."

"Actually, I've gotten to a place where the answer doesn't—"

Rich finished my sentence. "—doesn't matter as much anymore. Right. That's a good place for you. Because it really *doesn't* matter anymore. My feeling is that Todd knew this was going to be a short trip. He knew it. But I also think he understands now, in a much more complete way, that choices have consequences, that we always have the ability to make choices, and to make choices in our own best interest, even though it may seem like we're hemmed in and have no choice.

That's not the case. We always have the ability to make better choices for ourselves."

At this point Rich shifted his tone to match the impressions he was getting. "I seem to be going back to a time when he was twelve, and I'm just going to say what I get with regard to his father. It's *'Christ, can't he see? Can't he see who I am? Can't he acknowledge who I am?'* And that was between the two of them, that wasn't between you and Todd. So the roots of this way of thinking—around something unfair, or I don't have a choice—go back to that time."

"Todd was searching for who he was," I said, remembering Todd's frustration with Jonathan, "and didn't get any guidance from his dad."

"No," replied Rich, "because his dad was so shut down. Was he a particularly sensitive kid? Because what I feel is that his sensitivity made him a sink for all the feelings, all the unexpressed emotion—"

"—of the entire family." This time I finished his sentence. I was amazed by Rich's insight. "Yes, that's absolutely dead-on. Todd took on all the anger everyone in the family felt toward Jonathan."

Rich sighed again. "Let me sit with that for just a minute … He has a great deal of compassion for his father now that he wasn't able to have in this life."

Again I caught myself thinking, *If only we'd had more time.*

Rich and I were both silent until finally, he spoke. "I'm just going to ask him: We need to understand, Todd, why you've come here today. We need to know the reason your mom and I are having this conversation."

There was another long silence. Then Rich said, "Okay, so he just said, 'Mom, if I could undo everything, I would.' Going back to our question about his death, he understands now that there were consequences far beyond what he had the ability to imagine for himself and the people who loved him. What those consequences would be. And I really feel, Anne, that he's coming here asking for forgiveness in a way he's not been able to ask for it before.

"As I said, he's very light, he's not burdened with this. He can see it more clearly now. And that's what he's offering: *an opportunity for you to see him in a different way, because your grief has tied you to how he was in this life.* It's almost like he wants to say, 'Mom, look at me like an adult.' And with that is a sense of responsibility and accountability that he himself now owns. Okay?

"That's important. *It's not you.* It's he himself who now takes responsibility for his actions. He understands them. He wouldn't have mentioned this intricate piece with his dad if he hadn't come to a full understanding of who he was in this life. And so he wants you to see him in a different way, to be at peace with the knowledge he now has, which is expansive, huge. He understands the depths of love in a way he never understood it. And he's more whole because of that understanding.

"Your strength has been imparted to him. It wasn't only imparted in this life, it's been imparted from you, from our place of being, to his place of being. He's getting that from you, he continues to get that from you. Right now, you're sitting with viewing him differently than you've been able to. That is what he wants. In fact, I think that's the answer to our question about why you're here.

"He wants you to look at him differently. Even at sixteen, he was his own person and made his choices, well-informed or ill-informed, and none of that was your responsibility. It was completely his. And it's something he himself now takes complete responsibility for."

I remembered my reading with Jean Read, my question: "I'm trying to find closure with Todd's death. What were the lessons for me?" And Jean replied, "They're about forgiveness and the independence of each soul. There is no blame for an event that happens to someone else."

Rich said, "So it feels like what he wants from you is understanding. He knows he has your forgiveness. But there's something else here. He sees your ability to understand, at an intellectual level and at an emotional and spiritual level. There's something much greater at work in all of this. He's been a lesson in love to your entire family."

"We do cherish each other so much, because of him," I said. "That's so lovely, Rich." I was so moved. Todd was leading me to an acceptance I could never have achieved without him. My heart overflowed with gratitude. "One of the things I've come to understand is my contract with Todd. I agreed to it because he insisted. When he says he takes responsibility and understands the consequences and the terrible pain, yes, it all fits."

"Todd sees in you the strength of someone who gave so much of herself," Rich said. "In your spiritual journey you sacrificed so much, and yet you're intact, you are whole, you're more deeply connected to people around you and to this spiritual dimension. And your work isn't done. It's almost like he's saying, 'Mom, I was a rung on that ladder you're climbing. I was more than one rung— I was a lot of rungs on the ladder.' So he wants you to use this toward your own life purpose, and believes you're doing that. He sees it more holistically now. He can see that without grief, and with understanding.

"When Todd came in, I was sensing this kind of reckless, impulsive kid. I don't sense that at all now. I sense enormous peace and courage, because it takes courage to face the consequences of your actions. And he's done that completely. That's what he needs to impart to you now. See him not as he left us, but as he is now, much stronger, more whole, more able to participate in life than he ever was before.

"So he's at an entirely different level of awareness and understanding now, and his life here with you enabled him to get there. So it's a lot less now about how he died or the loss, and much more about who he is as a soul, as a divine being himself. That is what he wants to leave with you. 'Mom, I'm so much more now.' And he says, 'I was a teacher to my father.'"

The immensity of Todd's message overwhelmed me. I thought back again to that first reiki session with Melissa, when she asked me what I wanted for Todd. "If there's a way, I want him to continue to grow and develop. I want him to continue on his journey, whatever that is." I was so proud of him. How far he had come! I cried, "Thank you, Todd, for the gift that you are!"

"Absolutely, the gift that you are!" Rich echoed. "He's ... oh my goodness, I'm just feeling this so intensely right now. When I said teacher, that Todd was a teacher for his father, he sees himself as a teacher and I think he would have been a good teacher here on this earth plane. But he continues, it's more like he has fully come into his own as a teacher on the other side. And I feel like he's working with kids, using the benefit of his knowledge and experience to work with kids on this side and the other side.

"There's just peace, there's peace around him and his dad. There's understanding of his father's life and what made his father the man he was. And with that understanding, a great deal of compassion for him."

I gave a great sigh, as if my breath could release all the tenderness and love I held in my heart at that moment.

Rich heard my sigh. "How are you feeling?"

"Oh, it's a lovely ending you've given me, Rich," I said.

"We all come to this awareness of the spiritual aspects of our lives when we finally allow it to happen. We might be led to that place often, but there is a time at which we simply allow it."

"Yes, or we fight it for so long," I could laugh then at myself and the memory, "that we're totally broken and have no choice but to surrender."

"That's exactly right. At some point, you have to surrender. I'm just thinking about your other two sons. I see your future daughter-in-law as a wonderful balance to Jason. She'll be bringing an aspect to his life that's been missing. There's a lot of goodness and light around the two of them. She's very good for him."

"I think so too," I replied.

"So there's not anything for you to do there. It's more like how you stand as a witness in their lives, and that you're able to bring joy to them by being support-ive, loving her in a way that extends the love you have for your family to encompass her. I see a lot of goodness around that.

"I don't see much around Dane right now, but he seems like a happy and centered person. There seemed to be more of a connection between Todd and him that was more brotherly, in a wonderful way. And maybe you could share some of this with him. What do you think?"

"Yes. I've already shared some of my experiences with both of them, but I think it's a little woo-woo for them."

"It is for Jason in particular, but I think it's less so for Dane."

"Jason is very logical. He's an old soul, though. I would expect Jason to connect."

"Sometimes the old souls have the most resistance, and it's that resistance that needs to be overcome in this life. And that is what it is," Rich said. "I just want to tell you it's an honor and a privilege to be with you and Todd in this moment."

"Thank you very, very much, Rich. I'm so grateful. This has been amazing."

"Meant to be, meant to be. So okay, let's close. We give thanks for Todd, for Anne, for Jonathan, for the role they had in giving life in this plane. Goodness and light on each of them, and on the extended family. Blessings and peace be with us now and forever, amen."

After I hung up the phone, I looked at Todd's photograph and connected with his eyes. *He wants me to think of him as an adult now.* I tried to picture him as he would be at twenty-eight years old. I imagined Jason, Dane, Todd, and I having dinner together in Atlanta, and smiled—I'd be the envy of every woman in the room, with the three handsomest men there all to myself.

Neither Todd nor I was the same person of twelve years before. I understood how much Todd had learned from my strength. It was time for me to let him see how much I'd learned from him and how proud I was of him, knowing how much he'd learned about love and responsibility. Time for me to let go of another layer of sorrow and regret. Those emotions no longer applied. Love, joy, and gratitude took their place.

CHAPTER TWENTY-FOUR

Soul Connection

The euphoria I felt that Friday night after the reading with Rich carried over to Saturday morning. Mindless weekend rituals like vacuuming and doing the laundry sustained my contemplation of Todd's message. I put my house in order and my soul rejoiced. Around one thirty, the phone rang.

"Anne, where are you? Are you still coming?" It was Donna.

"Donna, I'm so sorry! I completely forgot!" I'd had a noon acupuncture appointment. "Can you still see me? I can be there in fifteen minutes."

"Yes, come on, come right away," Donna said. I grabbed my keys and ran.

When I entered the office, Donna met me at the door and we headed toward the treatment rooms. As we walked, I said, "Donna, you're never going to believe the experience I had with Todd last night."

"He's been after me all morning. I told him I can't make you come. That's why I called."

"Todd? Todd's been after you?" I asked, incredulous.

"Yes," she replied, "he's been pestering me to get you here. I'll be back in a minute. Undress and get up on the table."

I did as I was told, climbed up on the table and under the sheet. A cardinal fluttered up and down the casement windows, as if trying to get inside. There was a skylight above me. The sun hadn't reached it yet.

Donna came back in and began inserting needles. As she worked, I told her the story of my session with Rich, how Todd wanted me to think of him differently, how much he had grown spiritually, how I was the light of his life, and how happy he'd made me. Donna listened appreciatively, then left me for two hours to let the needles do their work.

As I lay on the table, eyes closed, the sun gradually moved into the skylight and bathed my entire face in its blindingly bright, yellow-orange radiance. Todd joined me there. We communed in the light. It felt like a graduation, a celebration of his achievement, and I had the sense that he was moving on to something new.

When Donna returned to remove the needles, I told her what I'd felt, that it was as if Todd had moved into another phase of existence.

"Yes," she said, "I get the feeling he's preparing to reincarnate."

I wasn't sure how I felt about that. I wondered where and into what family he would be born. More than anything, however, I wanted to revel in his achievement. My heart was singing.

When I got home I decided to listen to our song, and put the *Tarzan* CD into the player. *I'll listen from the very beginning*, I thought. As I did, the third song, "Son of Man," caught me. I couldn't help but play it repeatedly, because the song captured everything I was feeling, thinking, and wishing for, and might well have captured the same for Todd. From boy to man, growing in power, strength, and wisdom—yes, that was how far my son had traveled. I was so proud of him. Todd's choice of *Tarzan* proved perfect once again.

* * *

Fast-forward three years later, as I began writing this book. The first task I set for myself, a relatively easy one, was transcribing the recordings of my sessions with Dwanna and Rich. The depth of the session with Rich amazed me. There was so much I hadn't heard or appreciated during it. Transcribing that session, I felt as if I were hearing it for the first time.

Two things in particular grabbed my attention: Todd's frustrated inner cry to Jonathan, "Christ, can't he see? Can't he see who I am? Can't he acknowledge who I am?" and his compassionate soul-statement, "I was a teacher to my father." I, too, had tried to get Jonathan to see Todd differently, to see that his feelings about Todd might be a reaction to his grief for Ryder. Not only had Todd been born with a crossed eye to remind him of her, but he'd had surgery as a baby, too, just as Ryder must have. I remembered how Jonathan couldn't stay in the recovery room with Todd, but had to leave.

And then it dawned on me—Todd and Ryder might actually be connected to each other. But how? Something whispered to me that they were the same soul, but I didn't trust my intuition. So at my next ReUnion session, my question for Donna was, "Were Todd and Ryder connected?"

When I asked the question, we were seated together on the daybed in the spare bedroom of her house. Donna formed a mudra with her right hand, a hand position used in ReUnion to link individual energy with universal energy, and tapped my forehead.

"They are the same soul," she cried, "Todd and Ryder are the same soul!"

I gasped as Todd's words took on a whole new meaning: "Christ, can't he see? Can't he see who I am? Can't he acknowledge who I am?" Ryder had come back to Jonathan as Todd, to give her father another chance to heal and find spiritual connection, and Jonathan wouldn't connect, not with Todd, not with Spirit. I, too, through all my trials, had been determined to power through on my own, and failed to connect spiritually. Todd couldn't fulfill his sacred contract with either of his parents.

I thought back to the reading with Dwanna, to the part where Todd said, "I had no reason to be on this earth plane. ... Life was a drudge." He'd been stymied, defeated in his soul's purpose. "I may betray someone to be true to my own soul. Todd did this," Jean Read had said. He died to give his father another chance to make peace with loss, and to lead both his parents to discover spiritual connection. Yet again I forgave Todd for the betrayal and abandonment I felt at his death. And I marveled at the Universe and the intricate interweaving of our souls' journeys.

A long ReUnion session with Donna followed, a collective healing of Jonathan's and my ancestral lines. Our family members, living and dead, joined the session.

"Todd is here," Donna announced, "and he wants us to include your future grandchildren." The ReUnion session became a guided meditation to heal the Cooper and Capone clans of the spiritual and genetic scourge of addiction. I felt drained when we finished.

"This will take two nights to completely process," Donna said, "so get to bed early. You're going to need a lot of sleep."

"I will," I promised. "I was so touched that Todd included my grandchildren."

"He's reincarnating. He wants back into the family," Donna replied.

"My family?" Jason and Kelly had married in October 2011, but they had no immediate plans to start a family. Dane was still single.

"Yes," Donna answered. In my heart I was shouting for joy, but I stayed calm. I would not get my hopes up. But I couldn't help but wonder: would Todd know me when he returned? Would I know him? There are children who remember a past life before they reach the age of five, before the ego develops and they forget.[1] *We'll connect at the soul level*, I assured myself, *that will be enough*. I wanted Todd to make a fresh start, to live a long, full life, the life of *his* dreams, free of a commitment to save others by sacrificing himself.

Driving home, I went over everything Jonathan had ever told me about Ryder—which wasn't much. I remembered the double take he did when I told him that my birthday was October ninth, and how he said he always went to Florida in October to visit Ryder's grave. *Had she died in October,* I wondered. I decided to order a copy of her death certificate from the state of Florida. I learned from the website that it wouldn't show the cause of death, but that didn't matter to me. I knew how she died. I wanted to know when.

Two weeks later, I had my answer. Ryder had died in 1969, on May 30—the same day that Jason was born! Poor Jonathan—he never saw that the Universe was signaling to him, reminding him of the spiritual goals he'd set for himself, and of the choices open to him, choices that would set in motion certain consequences for his future. How would he choose to interpret the serendipity of his son being born on the same day of the same month that his daughter died? Would he see it symbolically, as an invitation to heal, as an inspiration for changing his life? Or would he see it as a reminder of his pain? No wonder he'd been sick and drinking the entire week after Jason was born.

I recalled Rich's words: "I'm thinking about your husband, his inability to process his grief, and the fact that the Universe gave him an opportunity, in Todd, to come back to that and look at it in a different way, to experience it in love, rather than fear. But he wasn't able to do that."

The Universe first warned Jonathan—through our firstborn, Jason—and then literally gave him a second chance when Ryder came back to him—in the same lifetime—as Todd! I looked at Ryder's death certificate again for her birthday. The date was October 10, 1966. *Of course, Jonathan visited Ryder's grave on her birthday.* And Todd had died on my birthday, October 9, the same day my first life ended and my second life began, the day before Ryder's birthday. It was almost unbelievable.

Birth, death, and rebirth. It was all there, in the dates. I couldn't help but take them as a sign, the great hand of the Universe pointing to the profound design of our lives and the contracts we make with each other. I recalled my Akashic record reading, when Jean told me that Todd had completed his life's purpose. I understood that now.

Twice, the young soul that was Todd had tried to use the death of a child as a teachable moment for Jonathan. Todd had indeed been a teacher to his father, because Jonathan ultimately did stop drinking. Perhaps Jonathan had found spiritual connection, too, as I had. But the method was so harsh. And Todd learned that there were other ways to teach.

"He has a great deal of compassion for his father now that he wasn't able to have in this life," Rich said. Todd's message to me was "Mom, if I could undo everything, I would." And Rich had explained further, "He understands now that there were consequences far beyond what he had the ability to imagine for himself and the people who loved him. And I really feel, Anne, that he's coming here asking for forgiveness in a way he's not been able to ask for it before."

Not only did I forgive him completely, heart and soul, I marveled at the miracles of love he had showered upon me after he died. I was awed by the intricate interweaving of themes, life purposes, and lessons that the Universe and we, its partners, contrived, so we might grow to become fitting companions to the Almighty.

Profoundly grateful to him, I called Rich the next day to share my discoveries and the new level of meaning I'd found in our session of three years earlier. And then I played "Son of Man" again, because I heard another level of meaning in its final verses. As a teacher to his father, Todd had learned so much himself about compassion, love, and making choices that served him as well as others. And having learned all he could from his lifetime as Todd, he was preparing for a new life, with new goals and contracts, to experience in the flesh the wisdom and power of his spiritual growth. The song echoed my prayer that, in his new life, Todd would give himself the time to grow to manhood and fulfill his soul's purpose.

CHAPTER TWENTY-FIVE

Full Circle

Losing my way had made my world so much bigger. Intuitively, I knew I was close, so close to connecting where I was lost to what I was seeking. Reading the works of Dean Radin, one of the scientists featured in *The Field* and Director of Research at the Institute of Noetic Sciences, brought me to my final destination.

Radin has authored three books, *The Conscious Universe* in 1997, *Entangled Minds* in 2006, and *Supernormal* in 2013. The subject of each is "psi phenomena"—the scientific term given to paranormal effects like telepathy, presentience, psychokinesis, and clairvoyance. In each book, despite the passage of time, Radin found it necessary to patiently explain how science has proven psi conclusively, beyond any doubt. Applying scientific and statistical methods readily accepted in other fields, he not only refuted the arguments of skeptics, but also proved that scientifically, it's no longer a question of whether psi is real, but of how it works.[1]

In *Entangled Minds: Extrasensory Experiences in a Quantum Reality*, Radin theorized that psi is the human experience of quantum entanglement.

> At a level of reality deeper than the ordinary senses can grasp, our brains and minds are in intimate communion with the universe. It's as though we lived in a gigantic bowl of clear Jell-O. Every wiggle—every movement, event, and thought—within that medium is felt throughout the entire bowl. Except that this particular form of Jell-O is a rather peculiar medium. ... It extends beyond the bounds of ordinary spacetime, and it's not even a substance. ...
>
> Because of this "nonlocal Jell-O" in which we are embedded, we can get glimpses of information about other people's minds, distant objects, or the future or past. We get this not through the ordinary senses and not because signals from those other minds and objects travel to our brain. But because at some level our mind/brain is already co-existent with other people's minds, distant objects, and everything else. ... From this perspective, psychic experiences are reframed not as mysterious "powers of the mind" but as momentary glimpses of the entangled fabric of reality. ... Within a holistic medium we are always connected.[2]

Here was a way to understand the miracles occurring in my life, as human experiences of a quantum Universe. Whether through natural ability or focused practice, the psychics that had connected me with Todd were able to tune into and exchange information with the Universe, the zero point field. However, those encounters pointed to far more: Melissa, Dwanna, Rich, and even I myself had connected to the organized energy that was Todd, and he relayed to us his emotions and thoughts *after* his death: "Mother, I'm so sorry, Mother, I'm so sorry"; his concern for Jason and how his big brother was dealing with his death; his desire that I not continue grieving. My interactions with Todd after his death were sufficient proof to me that death is not the end, but a continuation.

What happened to the energy, the life-force that was Todd? He continues—on some other plane, in some other dimension. Heart and soul, I believe it to be true. Entangled as we are, Todd has reached out to help me take that leap of faith. With him as my guide, I've found my way and, in the process, discovered a Universe. Its exquisite design humbles me. I embrace and accept it—a loving Consciousness and unfathomable Source of all order, energy, and life.

In the concluding chapter of *Entangled Minds*, Radin looked forward to the time when psi is accepted and changes our Western worldview. He saw that Western thought was scientifically proving what Eastern thought has held true for thousands of years.

> Virtually all meditative traditions take for granted that what we call psi is simply the initial stages of awareness of deeper levels of reality. If psi can be confirmed using Western scientific methods, then what shall we make of the rest of Eastern lore? Does some aspect of mind survive bodily death? Are there other forms of existence?[3]

After scientific acceptance of psi, Radin hoped that science will explore the big questions of life and death and meaning, until now considered the exclusive territory of religion and metaphysics.

> The Western scientific understanding of life and mind may have been examining only a tiny portion of our capabilities. As a famous Sufi parable teaches, it's as though we've lost our house key somewhere on the road, but we've only been looking for it near the streetlamp because that's where the light is. Perhaps we've been seduced by our tools to only look in certain places. ... Perhaps [these questions] can be probed with increasingly refined scientific methods, without invoking fear and ignorance of the unknown.[4]

I strongly suspect that kinesiology is one of the "increasingly refined scientific methods" that Radin looks to the future to provide for a more far-reaching, meaningful exploration of the Universe.

My intellectual comprehension of the connection between science and spirituality evolved ever so slowly. My miraculous interactions with Todd after his death were the impetus to explore their connection. Ultimately those miracles taught me to accept what is beyond my mind's comprehension. But still I keep trying.

We are all connected to each other through the zero point field, the Universe, a field I don't hesitate to connect to God, Source, Consciousness, whatever name you prefer to call a loving, creative, universal energy. We are one with that energy. We are here on this earth plane in a lower vibration, to learn spiritual lessons through human experience, to feel in the flesh the truth of love, compassion, and spiritual grace. It connects us beyond the grave, through however many dimensions there may be. That is why my son continues to love and learn and grow and connect with me. *Energy is neither created nor destroyed.*

I had come full circle. As a young woman, I rejected religion based on a science-driven Western worldview. As an older, wiser one, I discovered spirituality through a shower of miracles from my beloved son. They led me to learn just how far Western science has come—so far, in fact, that West is East. Western science is validating eastern metaphysics—and the existence of a universal field of energy I no longer hesitate to call God.

* * *

November 2015. It was four thirty on a Friday afternoon and I was driving back to Athens from Atlanta. I'd accompanied a team of four MBA students to a case competition, where they competed against teams from other schools to solve a strategic business problem. As I approached Athens I thought, *If I go back to the office, I'll get there just in time to leave.* I decided to go straight home.

It was a beautiful, sunny day and the weather was mild, temperatures springlike—perfect for a long walk. As soon as I got home, I changed clothes and got into comfortable shoes. I considered taking my phone and earbuds to listen to music, but opted instead for quiet. I unlocked my front door and stepped outside. It was a good-to-be-alive kind of day.

I fell naturally into a quick pace. It felt great to get my legs moving. I was fully present, entertaining no thoughts, simply enjoying the sensations of warm sun and an occasional breeze.

From my side street I headed to the main road that ran through the subdivision. I'd walked it many times after work and today, I told myself, there would be hardly any cars, because I was earlier than usual. There were no sidewalks, but each side of the street was lined with a concrete edging that varied in width from ten to fifteen inches. I walked against traffic, usually on the blacktop, always on the concrete when cars approached.

No sooner had I crossed over to the main road than a voice spoke in my head. "I came back for my father, of course I'll come back for you." And then, just as clearly, "You could get killed walking along the side of the road like this."

I knew it was Todd, just as I knew it wasn't my own mind telling me to be careful. It wasn't natural for me to think of what could go wrong, what dangers might be lurking in my day-to-day life. My mind didn't work that way, so I paid attention.

The only place I could think of where there was a risk of getting hit by a car was at the T-intersection at the far end of the subdivision, where a pretty island flower-bed divided the two sides of the street. Tall cedars and the entrance sign blocked the view of oncoming traffic. I decided I'd make ninety-degree turns there instead of cutting diagonally across the street, so I could see cars turning into the neighborhood. And I'd stay on the concrete.

Walking almost at a jog, I thought back over my interactions with Todd. He'd never spoken to me directly before, and I wondered if my mind was playing tricks on me. Was it just wishful thinking—that he would come back to me in this lifetime? I played with the thought in the serenity of the late afternoon.

Approaching the back entrance to the subdivision, I reminded myself not to cut across the street to the island. That same moment, the sound of screeching tires jerked me to attention. An old Volvo station wagon skidded into its left turn, headed straight for me. I leapt onto the grass shoulder. The driver swerved sharply and roared off.

I crossed to the opposite side of the street and kept walking. I was astonished that I could. My heart was pounding, my brain reeling as I processed what had just happened. If I'd cut across the street—as I usually did— I'd have been in the center of the road, unable to jump out of the way. The driver was going so fast he couldn't have stopped. I would have been killed.

Todd saved my life. His warning had been deadly accurate. I said a prayer of thanks to him and the Universe, my heart and soul overflowing. And then I knew—without question—that the rest of his message was equally true: *I came back for my father, of course I'll come back for you.*

Nine months later, Jason and Kelly announced they were pregnant—my first grandchild. The baby's due date, the doctor informed them, was March 27, Todd's birthday. And I knew it was no coincidence, but one more miracle from my loving son, to announce that he is coming back to find his place among the ones he loves!

My grandson wasn't born on his due date—that was an announcement—but on April 4, 2017. My experiences with Todd have taught me that birthdates—at least in my family—are signposts, so I knew the date of my grandson's birth held significance. Its meaning dawned on me just before Father's Day, a gift to share with Jason so that he might acknowledge who his son is and heal from knowing how much his brother loves him and wants to be in relationship with him.

So why April 4? Todd died on my forty-fourth birthday; April 4 is 4-4. As for 2017, in numerology it equals 2 + 0 + 1 + 7, or ten, 1 + 0, that is, 1. The number one in numerology signifies a new beginning—a new beginning for my beautiful son.

Birth, death, and rebirth, once again the pattern runs true. The poem that follows, written by Rich Fletcher as a gift for my grandson, closes the circle.

Love, Tru

For Love
So loved the world,
There was you,

Light, poured into life,
Toes and fingers,
Eyes and ears,

The intricate mystery
Made perfect,
And true,

Welcome to grace,
That has a place
Called, "You,"

And to this cobbled path
Of heart and stone,
Upon which

You have come
To walk, and we,
With you, once again,

To gaze at the moon,
Or fly a kite,
Or sail an ocean

In hemisphere
Of blue,
For Love,

That so loves the world,
And us,
There is you.[5]

ACKNOWLEDGMENTS

So rarely do we get to formally thank the people present in our lives for their love and support, so I am grateful this memoir gives me that opportunity. To my sons, Jason, Dane, and Todd Cooper, my husband Jonathan, parents, Barbara and Ed Capone, brothers, Robert, Ed, Jim, and John, sisters, Edna, Mary, and Theresa, and all their spouses and children, I could not have traveled this path without you near me, body, heart, mind, and soul. What I have come to recognize is that we are a soul group, and I delight in knowing that we travel through eternity together as we strive to become fitting companions to the Almighty.

To the many friends who supported me during the darkest times of my life, Susan and John Barrett, Lane Miller, Lacy and Tom Camp, Larry and Doris Colbert, Farris Johnson, Jr. MD, Norman and Sue Stern, Tom and Joanna Eaton, Jane and Kip Mann, Bill and Vicki Orr, Mike and Donna Ward, Marge and Jim Dyson, Tom Richards, Sue Lawrence, Don Randall, Pete McCommons, Terry Daly, Diane Morrison, Svea Bogue, Don Perry, Heidi and Al Davison, Mary Baker, Reverend

Jon Appleton, and most particularly, the mothers of Todd's friends, Madelon Dickerson, Connie Bruce, and Kitty Lay, I am indebted to you and will always remember your loving kindness. To all of Todd's many friends, especially Ryan Dickerson, Jenny Dillard, and Laura Martin, the gifted artist and photographer who took Todd's portrait, I hope this book will give you solace and reconnect you with him.

As for the miracles of my second life, there are no words that can express the depth of my love and gratitude to Shannon Schultz, Chris Neilands, Patt Farrell, Lori Benton, Melissa Moulder Dowd, Jean Read, Dwanna Paul, Donna Terrazas, and Rich Fletcher.

To my editor Arlene Robinson, thank you, thank you—your superb editorial skills, imagination, and feeling heart have guided me through to this happy ending and new beginning.

Finally, I invite my readers to take a dive into the books that led me to my new understanding. I could not have found my way without them. On the following page, I present them in the approximate order that I read them, but you must find your own way.

RECOMMENDED READING

Many Lives, Many Masters by Brian L. Weiss, MD.

"Finding Her Here" by Jayne Relaford Brown, in *My First Real Tree*, published by FootHills Press, 2004. www.foothillspublishing.com.

The Body Ecology Diet: Recovering Your Health and Rebuilding Your Immunity by Donna Gates.

Anatomy of the Spirit: The Seven Stages of Power and Healing by Caroline Myss.

Women's Bodies, Women's Wisdom: Creating Physical and Emotional Health and Healing by Christiane Northrup, MD.

Healing Grief: Reclaiming Life After Any Loss by James Van Praagh.

Nourishing Traditions: The Cookbook That Challenges Politically Correct Nutrition and the Diet Dictocrats by Sally Fallon and Mary Enig, PhD.

The Art of Possibility: Transforming Professional and Personal Life by Rosamund Stone Zander and Benjamin Zander.

Dance of the Dissident Daughter by Sue Monk Kidd.

The Invitation by Oriah Mountain Dreamer.

Crossing into Avalon by Jean Shinoda Bolen, MD.

Sacred Contracts: Awakening Your Divine Potential by Caroline Myss.

The Field: The Quest for the Secret Force of the Universe by Lynn McTaggart.

Edgar Cayce: An American Prophet by Sydney D. Kirkpatrick.

Destiny of Souls by Michael Newton, PhD.

Power vs. Force: The Hidden Determinants of Human Behavior by David R. Hawkins, MD, PhD.

Radical Forgiveness by Colin Tipping.

The Little Soul and the Sun by Neale Donald Walsch.

Awakening the Heroes Within: Twelve Archetypes to Help Us Find Ourselves and Transform Our World by Carol S. Pearson.

The Intention Experiment: Using Your Thoughts to Change Your Life and the World by Lynn McTaggart.

The Conscious Universe: The Scientific Truth of Psychic Phenomena by Dean Radin, PhD.

Entangled Minds: Extrasensory Experiences in a Quantum Reality by Dean Radin, PhD.

Supernormal: Science, Yoga, and the Evidence for Extraordinary Psychic Abilities by Dean Radin, PhD.

EQUAL PARTS And Other Poems by Richard Norrid Fletcher.

ENDNOTES

Chapter 2

1. *Baltimore Catechism*, Volume 1.
2. Hobbes, Thomas. *Leviathan* (New York: Pearson Longman, 2008), 83.

Chapter 5

1. Daugherty, Ray and O'Bryan, Terry, *Talking With Your Kids About Alcohol* (Lexington: Prevention Research Institute, 1988).
2. Daugherty, Ray and O'Bryan, Terry, *PRIME For Life* (Lexington: Prevention Research Institute, 2000).
3. Daugherty, *PRIME For Life*.

Chapter 6

1. Weiss, Brian L., *Many Lives, Many Masters* (New York: Simon & Schuster, 1988), 27–31.
2. Weiss, *Many Lives, Many Masters*, 54–59.
3. Weiss, *Many Lives, Many Masters*, 185.

Chapter 9

1. Brown, Jayne Relaford, "Finding Her Here," *My First Real Tree* (Wheeler: FootHills Publishing, 2004).

Chapter 14

1. Myss, Caroline, *Anatomy of the Spirit: The Seven Stages of Power and Healing* (New York: Three Rivers Press, Random House, 1996), 1–10.
2. Myss, *Anatomy of the Spirit*, 33–34.
3. Myss, *Anatomy of the Spirit*, 35.
4. Myss, *Anatomy of the Spirit*, 35.
5. Myss, *Anatomy of the Spirit*, 94–101.
6. Daugherty, *PRIME For Life.*

Chapter 15

1. Northrup, Christiane, *Women's Bodies, Women's Wisdom: Creating Physical and Emotional Health and Healing* (New York: Bantam Books, Random House, 2002), 85.
2. Northrup, *Women's Bodies, Women's Wisdom*, 82.
3. Brown, *My First Real Tree.*

Chapter 16

1. Van Praagh, James, *Healing Grief: Reclaiming Life After Any Loss* (New York: New American Library, Penguin Putnam, 2001), 27.
2. Van Praagh, *Healing Grief*, 278.
3. Van Praagh, *Healing Grief*, 25–28.
4. Van Praagh, *Healing Grief*, 77.
5. Van Praagh, *Healing Grief*, 255–258.

Chapter 17

1. Wiktionary contributors, "God does not play dice with the universe," *Wiktionary, The Free Dictionary*, https://en.wiktionary.org/w/index.

php?title=God_does_not_play_dice_with_the_ universe&oldid=36367635 (accessed July 27, 2017).

2. McTaggart, Lynn, *The Field: The Quest for the Secret Force of the Universe* (New York: HarperCollins, 2008), XXV.

3. McTaggart, *The Field*, XXVI.

4. McTaggart, *The Field*, XVIII.

5. McTaggart, *The Field*, XVIII.

6. McTaggart, *The Field*, 24–25.

7. McTaggart, *The Field*, 27–28.

8. McTaggart, *The Field*, 91.

9. Myss, *Anatomy of the Spirit*, 35.

10. Zander, Rosamund Stone and Benjamin, *The Art of Possibility: Transforming Professional and Personal Life* (New York: Penguin Books, Penguin Putnam, Inc. 2000), 21.

Chapter 18

1. Fallon, Sally, with Mary G. Enig, PhD, *Nourishing Traditions: The Cookbook that Challenges Politically Correct Nutrition and the Diet Dictocrats* (Washington, DC: NewTrends Publishing, 2001), xi–xii.

Chapter 19

1. Myss, Caroline, *Sacred Contracts: Awakening Your Divine Potential* (New York: Three Rivers Press, Random House, 2003), 166.

2. Myss, *Sacred Contracts*, 39.

3. Steinem, Gloria, *Women and Power* (Rhinebeck: Omega Media Works, 2004).

4. Lesser, Elizabeth, *Women and Power* (Rhinebeck: Omega Media Works, 2004).

5. Marion Woodman, *Women and Power* (Rhinebeck: Omega Media Works, 2004).

6. Ford, Deborah, *The Dark Side of the Light Chasers* (New York: Penguin Random House, LLC, 1999), 3.

Chapter 21

1. Kirkpatrick, Sydney D., *Edgar Cayce: An American Prophet* (New York: Riverhead Books, Penguin Putnam, Inc. 2000), 529–530.

2. *Edgar Cayce's A.R.E.*, http://edgarcayce.org.

3. Kirkpatrick, *Edgar Cayce*, 290.

4. Kirkpatrick, *Edgar Cayce*, 254.

5. Kirkpatrick, *Edgar Cayce*, 271.

6. Newton, Michael, *Destiny of Souls: New Case Studies of Life Between Lives* (Woodbury: Llewellyn Publications, 2000), xi.

7. Newton, *Destiny of Souls*, xii.

8. Newton, *Destiny of Souls*, 2–9.

9. Newton, *Destiny of Souls*, 1.

10. Kirkpatrick, *Edgar Cayce*, 256.

11. Newton, *Destiny of Souls*, 16–19.

12. Newton, *Destiny of Souls*, 13.

13. Tipping, Colin, *Radical Forgiveness* (Boulder: Sounds True, 2009), 14.

14. Tipping, *Radical Forgiveness*, 19.

15. McTaggart, *The Field*, 102.

16. McTaggart, *The Field*, Chapter Six, "The Creative Observer."

17. McTaggart, *The Field*, Chapter Ten, "The Healing Field."

18. McTaggart, *The Field*, Chapter Eleven, "Telegram From Gaia."

19. Kirkpatrick, *Edgar Cayce*, 411.

20. Kirkpatrick, *Edgar Cayce*, 258.

21. Tipping, *Radical Forgiveness*, 27.

22. Tipping, *Radical Forgiveness*, 29.

Chapter 22

1. Hawkins, David R., *Power vs. Force: The Hidden Determinants of Human Behavior* (Carlsbad: Hay House, 2012), 377–379.

2. Hawkins, *Power vs. Force*, 90–92.

3. Hawkins, *Power vs. Force*, 352.

4. Hawkins, *Power vs. Force*, 62.

5. Hawkins, *Power vs. Force*, 62–63.

6. Hawkins, *Power vs. Force*, 86.

7. Terrazas, Donna, *ReUnion Training Materials*.

8. Terrazas, *ReUnion*.

9. Kirkpatrick, *Edgar Cayce*, 289–290.

10. Terrazas, *ReUnion*.

11. Terrazas, *ReUnion*.

Chapter 23

1. Fletcher, Rich, www.trustallowaccept.com/2014/07/someone-love-takes-life/.

Chapter 24

1. Horn, Stacy, "The Children Who've Lived Before," *Reader's Digest*, February 2015, 116–122.

Chapter 25

1. Radin, Dean, *Entangled Minds: Extrasensory Experiences in a Quantum Reality* (New York: Simon & Schuster, 2006), Chapter 14.
2. Radin, *Entangled Minds*, 264–266.
3. Radin, *Entangled Minds*, 277.
4. Radin, *Entangled Minds*, 277.

Postscript

1. Fletcher, Richard Norrid, *EQUAL PARTS And Other Poems* (Wayfare of the Heart Press, 2016) 31–32.